FUNDAMENTALS OF LEGAL RESEARCH

Third Edition

AND LEGAL RESEARCH ILLUSTRATED

Third Edition

Roy M. Mersky
Hyder Centennial Professor of Law
and Director of Research
Tarlton Law Library
University of Texas

J. Myron Jacobstein
Professor of Law and Law Librarian
Stanford University
Law Library

ASSIGNMENTS

Joyce Saltalamachia, Co-Editor
New York Law School Library

Robert J. Nissenbaum, Co-Editor
Cleveland State University Cleveland-Marshall College of Law Library

Contributing Editors

Kathleen Carrick, Case Western Reserve University
Georgia Chadwick, Jenkens and Gilchrist
Donald J. Dunn, Western New England College
Patricia Harris, Case Western Reserve University
Gary McCann, American University Washington College of Law
John Pickron, University of Hawaii
Lynn Wishart, Yeshiva University

Mineola, New York
THE FOUNDATION PRESS, INC.
1985

COPYRIGHT © 1985

By

THE FOUNDATION PRESS, INC.

All rights reserved

ISBN 0-88277-300-3

TO THE STUDENT:

To master the numerous nuances of legal research requires exercising the skills acquired through the Fundamentals of Legal Research (3d ed.) or Legal Research Illustrated (3d ed.). That is the purpose of this assignment book.

We have provided numerous types of problems to introduce many aspects of legal research. The chapters in the assignment book correspond with the chapters in the Fundamentals and Legal Research Illustrated except for additional materials on Canadian legal research. Students in the northern tier of the United States may find the Canadian problems particularly useful.

Some problems specifically direct you to a particular source. Other problems require you to choose a specific title within a series or multi-volume work. Another group of problems is less directive as to the resource which may answer the question. This variety of assignments is provided to exercise two skills: an ability to choose among different approaches to resolving a legal problem and an ability to glean the most information when limited to a particular resource.

Keep in mind four criteria when choosing among resources. First, what is the scope of a particular title? Does this title exclusively cover the information you desire or will you have to deal with superfluous information in order to answer the problem? Secondly, how is a particular title arranged? Does the title contain only current information or must you relate to both current and retrospective historical information? Is the information arranged appropriate to your particular inquiry, e.g., chronologically as opposed to subject? Does the title provide a "How to Use" guide? Thirdly, how is the title you have chosen to answer the question indexed? Is there a combination of tables and indexes which provide a comprehensive approach to the information in the title or is access limited? Finally, how current is the information provided in the title? Do you need current information to answer the question? How is the information updated--through cumulative supplements, pocketparts, replacement volumes, looseleaf pages or new editions? Is the indexing appropriately current to the form of updating?

Although these issues appear generic, their application to a problem can aid you as you pursue the course of study as outlined in the Fundamentals or Legal Research Illustrated and this assignment book. If you are not comfortable in using certain types of legal materials following your readings in Fundamentals or Legal Research Ilustrated and classroom lectures, apply the scope, arrangement, index and update strategy. This analysis is particularly useful having the book(s) in hand. A few moments in the library using this approach can save hours of frustration.

We have provided many duplicate types of problems so your classmates will not have to share one particular book. Although you may not be doing the same problems the questions are designed to be balanced and to exercise identical or similar skills. There are no "trick questions." If you find you are laboring over a particular question longer than fifteen minutes, seek assistance from your instructor or librarian. Maintain a detailed record of your research strategy (or pathfinder). When you encounter obstacles in your research, reviewing the pathfinder with an instructor or librarian can facilitate clarifying your confusion.

Problem solving in the legal profession involves gathering the operative facts, identifying the legal issues, researching the legal issues and resolving the legal issues through effective writing by applying the law to the factual setting. Each of these steps builds upon the other. Successful lawyering requires analysis and research. Your first year of law school introduces each step. Equal attention must be given to each process component if you are to be successful as a lawyer. Many times poor analysis or confused writing is the result of ineffectual research. Diligence in using these assignments in conjunction with the <u>Fundamentals of Legal Research</u> or <u>Legal Research Illustrated</u> provides you with a sound foundation in the legal process.

A problem book of this magnitude is the result of intellectual and clerical hard work. We particularly thank our chief editor, Professor Joyce Saltalamachia, Director of the Law Library at the New York Law School. Without her steadfast commitment to this project, the assignment book would not have been written. Professor Saltalamachia was assisted in the compilation and editing of the manuscript by Professor Robert J. Nissenbaum, Director of the Law Library at Cleveland State University's Cleveland-Marshall College of Law.

Several outstanding law librarians prepared manuscripts for chapters of the assignment book or updated previous edition chapters. Professors Saltalamachia and Nissenbaum received editorial assistance from: Professor Kathleen Carrick, Director of the Law Library at Case Western Reserve University; Professor Donald J. Dunn, Director of the Law Library at Western New England College; Professor John Pickron, Director of the Law Library at the University of Hawaii; Ms. Lynn Wishart, Director of the Law Library at the Benjamin Cardozo School of Law of Yeshiva University; Ms. Patricia Harris, Associate Law Librarian and Instructor in Law at the Case Western Reserve University School of Law Library; Mr. Gary McCann, Assistant Director for Public Services, American University Washington College of Law Library; and Ms. Georgia Chadwick, Law Librarian for the Dallas, Texas law firm of Jenkins and Gilchrist.

Joyce Saltalamachia wishes to thank her colleagues at the New York Law School Library for their bibliographic assistance. Particularly, Professor Saltalamachia wishes to acknowledge the assistance Kitty MacLeod and Marie Newman for their invaluable help in the final preparation of the manuscript. In particular, thanks also goes to Margot Thomas of New York Law School Library for excellent typing services.

Robert J. Nissenbaum expresses his appreciation to Judith Kaul, Reference/Media Librarian at Cleveland State University and his research assistant Paul John Caputo '85, Cleveland State University, Cleveland-Marshall College of Law.

Donald J. Dunn gratefully acknowledges the assistance of Christine Archambault, Michele Dill, Robert LaRose, Patricia Maloney, Howard Polonsky, Renee Streese, Donna Tracy, Susan Wells, and the invaluable contributions of Bonnie White, all associated with Western New England College of Law Library.

Mr. Gary McCann expresses appreciation to Hilary Burg, Harvey Covell and Arthur Mindling of American University, Washington College of Law Library reference staff.

At the University of Texas Tarlton Law Library, invaluable word processing assistance was provided by Bach Truc Nguyen and Wendy Leiter. Manuscript coordination was provided by Wendy Leiter and Professor Mersky's research assistant, Goldie Domingue.

We close by reiterating our final thoughts in the previous edition of this problem book. Our greatest reward is in the appreciation and professional fulfillment we enjoy in knowing that many lawyers have gained from this workbook the skills necessary to solve the law's mystery.

                                    J. Myron Jacobstein
                                    Stanford University School of Law

                                    Roy M. Mersky
                                    University of Texas School of Law

Stanford
Austin
May, 1985

TABLE OF CONTENTS

	Page
TO THE STUDENT	iii

Chapter

(Conforms to chapters in Fundamentals of Legal Research and Legal Research Illustrated.)

4.	Federal Court Decisions	1
5.	State Court Decisions and the National Reporter System	26
6.	Digests for Court Reports	43
7.	Annotated Law Reports	100
8.	Constitutions	140
9.	Federal Legislation	164
10.	Federal Legislative Histories	190
11.	State and Municipal Legislation	217
12.	Court Rules and Procedure	238
13.	Administrative Law [Chapter 12 in L.R.I.]	267
14.	Looseleaf Services [Chapter 13 in L.R.I.]	273
15.	Shepard's Citations [Chapter 14 in L.R.I.]	292
16.	Legal Encyclopedias [Chapter 15 in L.R.I.]	330
17.	Legal Periodicals and Indexes [Chapter 16 in L.R.I.]	349
18.	Treatises, Restatements, Model Codes, and Uniform Laws [Chapter 17 in L.R.I.]	374
20.	Research in International Law [Chapter 19 in L.R.I.]	394
21.	English and Canadian Legal Research	418

Chapter 4

FEDERAL COURT DECISIONS

ASSIGNMENT 1
EXAMINATION OF U.S. REPORTS

Questions:

A. Using the early volumes of U.S. Reports and the latest edition of A Uniform System of Citation, find the U.S. Reports (U.S.) volume number for the following nominative reports. Put your answer in proper citation form.

1. 2 Dallas

2. 12 Howard

3. 8 Wheaton

4. 6 Cranch

5. 20 Wallace

6. 5 Peters

7. 1 Dallas

8. 15 Wallace

9. 10 Wheaton

10. 1 Black

11. 2 Cranch

12. 1 Peters

13. 24 Howard

14. 4 Wallace

15. 3 Cranch

16. 16 Peters

17. 3 Wheaton

18. 6 Howard
19. 12 Wallace
20. 9 Cranch
21. 12 Wheaton
22. 8 Peters
23. 3 Howard
24. 21 Wallace
25. 2 Peters
26. 3 Dallas
27. 4 Peters
28. 3 Wallace
29. 23 Howard
30. 9 Wheaton
31. 7 Cranch
32. 6 Peters
33. 16 Wallace
34. 11 Wheaton
35. 2 Black
36. 21 Howard
37. 4 Wallace
38. 4 Cranch
39. 15 Peters
40. 4 Wheaton
41. 7 Howard
42. 13 Wallace

43. 8 Cranch

44. 7 Wheaton

45. 9 Peters

46. 22 Wallace

47. 4 Howard

48. 3 Peters

49. 4 Dallas

50. 3 Wallace

51. 1 Howard

52. 12 Peters

53. 7 Wallace

54. 20 Howard

B. Using the latest edition of A Uniform System of Citation and U.S. Reports (U.S.), find the names of the following cases and cite them properly in your answer.

1. 340 U.S. 581

2. 293 U.S. 388

3. 283 U.S. 494

4. 288 U.S. 290

5. 300 U.S. 5

6. 306 U.S. 451

7. 315 U.S. 32

8. 397 U.S. 337

9. 399 U.S. 66

10. 378 U.S. 368

11. 358 U.S. 133

12. 367 U.S. 643

13. 402 U.S. 415

14. 401 U.S. 154

15. 399 U.S. 66

16. 397 U.S. 254

17. 396 U.S. 435

18. 395 U.S. 752

19. 394 U.S. 576

20. 372 U.S. 335

ASSIGNMENT 2
U.S. REPORTS - RELATED MATERIALS

Method:

For each of the citations to the official U.S. Reports (U.S.), locate the unofficial parallel citations in the United States Supreme Court Reporter (S. Ct.) and the United States Supreme Court Reports (L. Ed.).

Questions:

1. 358 U.S. 133
2. 367 U.S. 643
3. 402 U.S. 415
4. 401 U.S. 154
5. 399 U.S. 66
6. 397 U.S. 254
7. 396 U.S. 435
8. 395 U.S. 752
9. 394 U.S. 576
10. 372 U.S. 335
11. 340 U.S. 581
12. 293 U.S. 388
13. 283 U.S. 494
14. 288 U.S. 290
15. 300 U.S. 5
16. 306 U.S. 451
17. 315 U.S. 32
18. 397 U.S. 337
19. 399 U.S. 66
20. 378 U.S. 368

21. 376 U.S. 665
22. 378 U.S. 226
23. 380 U.S. 451
24. 381 U.S. 676
25. 383 U.S. 569
26. 384 U.S. 73
27. 386 U.S. 237
28. 389 U.S. 31
29. 390 U.S. 62
30. 393 U.S. 5
31. 394 U.S. 831
32. 395 U.S. 100
33. 405 U.S. 34
34. 406 U.S. 164
35. 411 U.S. 1

ASSIGNMENT 3
FEDERAL CASES

Questions:

A. Using the set Federal Cases (F. Cas.) and the latest edition of A Uniform System of Citation, find the name of the following cases and properly cite them.

   1. Federal Case Number 358

   2. Federal Case Number 18,210

   3. Federal Case Number 7,881

   4. Federal Case Number 9,317

   5. Federal Case Number 2,865

   6. Federal Case Number 1,424

   7. Federal Case Number 2,344

   8. Federal Case Number 3,555

   9. Federal Case Number 6,994

   10. Federal Case Number 13,753

   11. Federal Case Number 9,596

   12. Federal Case Number 11,825

   13. Federal Case Number 8,260

   14. Federal Case Number 14,249

   15. Federal Case Number 15,959

B. Using the Table of Citations in the Digest volume of Federal Cases (F. Cas.), locate the following decisions. Put your answer in proper citation form. [Instructions: Locate the digest volume to the set Federal Cases. Within it is a Table of Citations (these are on colored pages in the edition used by the editor) listing reporters alphabetically. A parallel citation is given to the Federal Case Number.]

   1. 1 Fish. Pat. Cas. 483

   2. 19 Int. Rev. Rec. 108

   3. 5 Dill. 549

4. 1 Leg. Gaz. Rep. 279
5. 12 O.G. 1026
6. 1 McLean 120
7. Abb. Adm. 529
8. 7 Biss. 426
9. 8 N.B.R. 525
10. 1 Lowell 91
11. 2 Sumn. 108
12. 2 McLean 464
13. 1 Bond 1
14. 4 Brewst. 250
15. Spear, Extrad. (2d ed.) 451

ASSIGNMENT 4
FEDEERAL RULES DECISIONS

Method:

　　　Use the cumulative index to articles in the Federal Rules Decisions (F.R.D) (v. 1-50 or v. 51-80) to locate an article in F.R.D. concerning the topics below. Give the author, title and the cite to F.R.D. (volume and page) where the article appears.

Questions:

1. The business of judicial administration.

2. Can the courts find improvement through science?

3. Discovery in criminal cases.

4. Techniques for shortening trials.

5. Part-time clerkships for law students.

6. The judicial panel on multi-district litigation.

7. Pre-trial procedure in rural districts.

8. Jury instructions and forms for federal civil cases.

9. Damages allowable under rent control laws.

10. Business administration of the United States Courts.

11. Immigration and Nationality System of the United States.

12. Postconviction applications viewed by a federal judge -- revisited.

13. Problems of statutory interpretation.

14. Techniques for proof of complicated scientific and economic facts.

15. Ancillary jurisdiction and the joinder of claims in the federal courts.

16. Alternatives to the present hearsay rules.

17. Use of special verdicts in federal court.

18. Courtroom decorum.

19. Procedural changes in Michigan.
20. Observations on anti-trust procedures.
21. Originality in the law of intellectual property.
22. Removal of defendants in federal criminal procedure.
23. Selected jury instruction forms in SEC criminal cases.
24. The veto power of the president.
25. Sentencing in federal tax fraud cases.
26. Liberty under the Bill of Rights.
27. Objectivity in predicting criminal behavior.
28. Bail as a rich man's privilege.

ASSIGNMENT 5
DRILL PROBLEMS

Drill Problem I:

A. Nominative Reports

1. Using the early volumes of the U.S. Reports give the official U.S. volume number citation for each of the following:
   (a) 1 Cranch
   (b) 7 Wheaton
   (c) 4 Dallas

2. Compare the volume designated 6 Cranch with 420 U.S. and answer the following questions:
   (a) Contrast the features of the two volumes.
   (b) Provide the full citation for the case which is printed in part on page 100 of each volume.

B. Using the parallel citations tables in the Supreme Court Reporter and the United States Supreme Court Reports, Lawyers Edition, find the parallel citations for each of the following cases:

1. Fuller v. Oregon, 417 U.S. 40 (1974)

2. Hanson v. Denckla, 357 U.S. 235 (1958)

3. Ring v. U.S., 419 U.S. 18 (1974)

4. Piascik v. U.S., 434 U.S. 1062 (1978)

C. Lower Federal Court Cases

1. Using volume 425 of Federal Reporter, Second Series, answer the following:
   (a) Who was the Circuit Justice for the Fifth Circuit?
   (b) Give the correct cite for the case of Boyk v. Mitchell.
   (c) Cite the case that defines "blatantly lawless."
   (d) Cite any cases that construe 25 U.S.C. 357.
   (e) How many headnotes in Rhodes v. Craven?

2. Using volume 300 of Federal Supplement, answer the following:
   (a) Who is the Chief Justice of the U.S. Customs Court?
   (b) Give the correct citation for Bjarsch v. DiFalco.
   (c) What case defines the term "motorboat"?
   (d) What article and section of the Tennessee Constitution are construed in this volume?
   (e) What is the docket number of Arrow Transportation Co.

3. Using volume 200 of Federal Reporter answer the following:
   (a) What courts are covered by this volume?
   (b) Who was the Chief Justice of the First Circuit Court of Appeals?
   (c) On what page does the case of Bernardini v. Tocci appear?
   (d) Are any California statutes construed? Which one?
   (e) What case begins at p. 859?

4. Using Federal Cases, answer the following:
   (a) Give the full citation of the following cases:
       (1) F. Cas. No. 5
       (2) F. Cas. No. 25
   (b) Give the Federal Case Number of the following cases:
       (1) Wood v. Wells
       (2) Reid v. Rochereau

5. General Questions - answer concisely.
   (a) Why is Federal Rules Decisions unique among case reporters?
   (b) Can one find all Federal District Court cases in Federal Supplement?

Drill Problem II:

A. Nominative Reports

1. Using the early volumes of the U.S. Reports give the official U.S. volume number citation for each of the following:
   (a) 2 Wallace
   (b) 8 Peters
   (c) 1 Black

2. Compare the volume designated 17 Howard with 406 U.S.
   (1) Contrast the features of the two volumes.
   (2) Give the full citation for the case which is printed in part on page 100 of each volume.

B. U.S. Reports - Parallel Citations

1. Using the parallel citations tables in the Supreme Court Reporter and the United States Supreme Court Reports, Lawyers Edition, find the parallel citations for each of the following cases:
   (a) Travis v. U.S., 364 U.S. 631 (1961)
   (b) Amell v. U.S., 384 U.S. 158 (1966)
   (c) Rust v. Nebraska, 434 U.S. 912 (1978)
   (d) U.S. v. Sweet, 399 U.S. 517 (1970)

C. Lower Federal Court Cases

1. Using volume 542 of Federal Reporter, Second Series, answer the following:
   (a) Who was the Circuit Justice for the District of Columbia Circuit?
   (b) Give the correct citation for the case of In re Bianchi.
   (c) Give citation for the case that defines "innocent spouse."
   (d) Cite any cases that construe 11 U.S.C. 35(a).

2. Using volume 405 of Federal Supplement, answer the following:
   (a) Who is the Chief Justice of the Tenth Circuit?
   (b) Give the correct citation for Porter v. Bainbridge.
   (c) What case defines the meaning of "nolo contendere?"
   (d) What section of the Ohio code is construed in this volume?
   (e) What is the docket number for U.S. v. Ockel?

3. Using volume 130 of Federal Reporter answer the following:
   (a) What courts are covered by this volume?
   (b) Who is the Chief Justice of the Sixth Circuit Court of Appeals?
   (c) On what page does the case of American Soda Fountain Co. v. Sample appear?
   (d) Are there any California statutes construed? Which one?
   (e) What case begins at page 670?

4. Using Federal Cases, answer the following:
   (a) Give the full citation of the following cases:
       (1) F. Case No. 124.
       (2) F. Case No. 625.
   (b) Give the Federal Case number of the following cases:
       (1) Gillet v. Pierce.
       (2) Allen v. Magruder.

5. General questions - answer concisely.
   (a) Why is Federal Rules Decisions unique among case reporters?
   (b) Can one find all Federal District Court cases in Federal Supplement?

Drill Problem III:

1. Using the early volumes of the U.S. Reports give the official U.S. volume number citation for each of the following:
   (a) 10 Wheaton
   (b) 6 Cranch
   (c) 3 Peters

2. Compare the volume designated 16 Wallace with 416 U.S. and contrast the features of the two volumes.

Drill Problem IV:

A. Nominative Reports

1. Give the full citation for the following cases. Using the latest edition of A Uniform System of Citation put your answer in proper citation form.
   (a) The case in volume 4 of the reports of John William Wallace at page 189.
   (b) The case located in volume 16 of the reports of Richard Peters at page one.
   (c) Using volume 2 of the reports of Henry Wheaton, state when Bushrod Washington became Associate Justice of the Supreme Court.

2. Making your answer complete and concise, compare volume 6 of Benjamin C. Howard's reports with volume 380 of the United States Reports in the follcwing respects:
   (a) Contrast the features of the two.
   (b) Provide the full citation forthe case appearing on page 163 of each volume.

B. Find the following cases in the Supreme Court Reporter and the United States Supreme Court Reports, Lawyers Edition by using their parallel citation tables. State volume and page.

1. Briscoe v. Bell, 432 U.S. 404 (1977).

2. Zwicker v. Boll, 391 U.S. 353 (1968).

3. Miami Herald Publishing Co. v. Tornillo, 418 U.S. 241 (1974).

C. Lower Federal Court Cases

1. Using volume 617 of the Federal Reporter, Second Series, answer the following:
   (a) Who was the Chief Judge of the Second Circuit?
   (b) Using the latest edition of A Uniform System of Citation, give the correct citation for Narenji v. Civiletti.
   (c) Cite the case defining "arbitrary."
   (d) How many cases in this volume came from the Third Circuit?
   (e) What case construed the American Bar Association's Code of Professional Responsibility? Properly cite it.

2. Using volume 483 of the Federal Supplement, answer the following:
   (a) On what court did George H. Barlow sit prior to his death?
   (b) Using the latest edition of A Uniform System of Citation, give the citation for the case defining "controversial."
   (c) What case interpreted the Wisconsin Constitution?
   (d) Who represented the plaintiff in Hawkins-El v. Williams?

3. Using Federal Cases, answer the following:
   (a) Give the full citation of Federal Case Number 3,914.
   (b) Find the federal case number of Ross v. Peaslee. Properly cite the case in your answer.

4. What does Federal Rules Decisions contain that you can find in no other case reporter?

Drill Problem V:

A. Nominative Reports

1. Give the full citation for the following cases. Using the latest edition of A Uniform System of Citation, put your answer in proper cite form.
   (a) The case located in volume 20 of the reports of Benjamin C. Howard at page 486.
   (b) The case located in volume 2 of the reports of Henry Wheaton at page 248.
   (c) A case located in volume 4 of the reports of John William Wallace which deals with prisoners of war.

2. Making your answer complete and concise compare volume 16 of Richard Peters' reports with volume 418 of the United States Reports in the following respects:
   (a) Contrast the features of the two.
   (b) Provide the full citation for the case appearing on page 153 or each volume.

B. Find the following cases in the Supreme Court Reporter and the United States Supreme Court Reports, Lawyers Edition by using their parallel citation tables. State volume and page.

   1. Blount v. Rizzi, 400 U.S. 410 (1971).

   2. Reading Co. v. Brown, 391 U.S. 471 (1968).

   3. Mandel v. Bradley, 432 U.S. 173 (1977).

C. Lower Federal Court Cases

   1. Using volume 637 of the Federal Reporter, Second Series answer the following:
      (a) Each of the Justices of the Supreme Court serves as a Circuit Justice for one of the federal circuits. As of the time of volume 637, who sat as the Circuit Justice for the Fourth Circuit?
      (b) Using the latest edition of A Uniform System of Citation, give the correct citation for the case interpreting Fed. R. Civ. P. 24(a).
      (c) Give the correct citation for the case defining "carry."
      (d) What states or political subdivisions are in the Third Circuit?
      (e) Who dissented in a case involving Roadway Express, Inc.?

   2. Using volume 497 of the Federal Supplement, answer the following:
      (a) How many cases were decided by the District Court of Puerto Rico?
      (b) Cite the case which defines "citizen."
      (c) Cite the case interpreting the Alabama Code.
      (d) What judge decided United States v. Wenzel?

   3. Using Federal Cases, answer the following:
      (a) Give the full citation of Federal Case Number 1,408.
      (b) Find the Federal Case Number of Clark v. Bininger. Is there an opinion printed in Federal Cases?

   4. What does Federal Rules Decisions contain that you can find in no other case reporter?

Drill Problem VI:

A. <u>Nominative Reports</u>

1. Give the full citations for the following cases:
   (a) The case located in volume 2 of the Reports of Henry Wheaton at page 178.
   (b) The case located in volume 6 of the Reports of Benjamin C. Howard at page 190.
   (c) The case dealing with costs located in volume 16 of the Reports of Richard Peters.

2. Making your answer concise and complete, compare volume 16 of John William Wallace's Reports with volume 391 of the United States Reports in the following respects:
   (a) Contrast the features of the two.
   (b) Provide the full citation for the case appearing on page 244 of each volume.

B. Find the following cases in the <u>Supreme Court Reporter</u> and the <u>United States Supreme Court Reports, Lawyers Edition</u> by using their parallel citations tables. State volume and page.

1. <u>Jones v. Hildebrant</u>, 432 U.S. 183 (1977).

2. <u>Preiser v. Rodriguez</u>, 411 U.S. 475 (1973).

3. <u>United States v. Ventresca</u>, 380 U.S. 102 (1965).

C. <u>Lower Federal Court Cases</u>

1. Using volume 587 of the <u>Federal Reporter, Second Series</u>, answer the following:
   (a) Who was the judge most recently appointed to the United States Court of Appeals for the Ninth Circuit?
   (b) Properly cite the case construing the Tennessee Rules of the Supreme Court.
   (c) Cite the case defining "open court."
   (d) What was the docket number of <u>Rumme v. Estelle</u>?
   (e) How many cases originated in North Carolina?

2. Using volume 505 of the <u>Federal Supplement</u>, answer the following:
   (a) Where did Judge Charles B. Fulton earn his law degree?
   (b) Cite the case defining "target area."
   (c) Cite the case construing the Alaska Statutes.
   (d) Who was Mickey Clenny's attorney?

3. Using Federal Cases, answer the following:
   (a) Give the full citation of Federal Case Number 7,810.
   (b) Find the Federal Case Number of Clarke v. Druet, and properly cite the case in your answer.

4. What does Federal Rules Decisions contain that you can find in no other case reporter?

ASSIGNMENT 6
THEME PROBLEMS

Theme Problem I:

Plessy v. Ferguson is one of the best known decisions of the United States Supreme Court. It can be found at 63 U.S. 537. Locate that volume and answer the following questions:

1. Does the case have headnotes?

2. Who wrote the majority opinion?

3. Was there a concurring opinion?

4. Was there a dissenting opinion? By whom?

5. What was the date of decision

6. What act does the case concern?

7. At 163 U.S. 546 the Court cites Railroad Company v. Brown, 17 Wall. 445. What other designation does 17 Wall. have? Locate the case.
   (a) Does the case have headnotes?
   (b) Who wrote the majority opinion?
   (c) Was there a concurring opinion?
   (d) Was there a dissenting opinion?

8. Other reports of Plessy v. Ferguson may be found at 16 S. Ct. 1138, 41 L. Ed. 256. Locate those cases.
   (a) How many headnotes in each?
   (b) Are there any other differences between the materials found in each of these sets?
   (c) Decide for yourself which set you prefer.

9. At 163 U.S. 548 the Court cites McGuinn v. Forbes, 37 F. 639 (D.C.D. Md. 1889). Locate that case.
   (a) In what court does it arise?
   (b) Does it have headnotes? How many?
   (c) Who wrote the opinion?
   (d) Does this volume have a case table?

10. The Supreme Court reversed Plessy in the landmark decision in Brown v. Board of Education, 347 U.S. 483 (1954). Locate this case.
    (a) Does this case have headnotes?
    (b) Who wrote the majority decision?
    (c) Does the majority opinion cite any secondary authority?

11. <u>Brown v. Board of Education</u> can also be found in two unofficial reporters at 74 S. Ct. 686, 98 L. Ed. 873. Locate these cases.
    (a) Do they have the same number of headnotes? Skim them. Which seems more useful to you?
    (b) Do the Opinions differ?
    (c) Compare the "extras" in each volume: front matter, tables, indexes, etc. List what's available in each.
    (d) Are there any annotations in the <u>Lawyer's Edition</u> volume?

12. In footnote 9, <u>Brown</u> cites 98 F. Supp. 797. Locate this case.
    (a) Give the complete citation.
    (b) In what court does it originate?
    (c) How many headnotes does it have?
    (d) Who wrote the opinion?
    (e) What courts are reported in this volume of the <u>Federal Supplement</u>?
    (f) What kind of tables and indexes does it offer?

13. How could one determine if the Supreme Court has decided any cases on school segregation in its current term? Has it?

Theme Problem II:

<u>Roe v. Wade</u> was one of the most talked about decisions of the past decade. It can be found at 410 U.S. 113 (1973). Locate the case and answer the following questions:

1. Who wrote the majority opinion?

2. Is there a concurring opinion or opinions? If so, who wrote it, or them?

3. Is there a dissenting opinion or opinions? If so, who wrote it, or them?

4. What is the date of decision?

5. How many headnotes precede the case?

6. Who is Wade?

7. Who reargued the case for appellants?

8. Roe v. Wade can also be found at 93 S. Ct. 705 and 35 L. Ed. 2d 147. Look up each of these and answer the following:
    (a) How many headnotes in each?
    (b) What else is different about the opinions?
    (c) Examine the "extras" in each volume: front matter, tables, and indexes, etc. List what's available in each.
    (d) Are there any annotations in the Lawyer's Edition? If so, examine one.

9. At 410 U.S. 155, the Court cites Shapiro v. Thompson, 394 U.S. 618 (1969). Locate that case.
    (a) Answer questions 1-5 above for it.
    (b) Locate the same (Shapiro) case in Supreme Court Reporter and Lawyer's Edition, 2d. Give the citations and answer questions 8(a) - 8(d) for this case.

10. Also at 410 U.S. 155, the Court cites Sherbert v. Verner, 374 U.S. 398 (1963). Locate that case.
    (a) Answer questions 1-5 for it.
    (b) Locate the same case in Supreme Court Reporter and Lawyer's Edition, 2d. Give the citations and answer the questions 8(a) - 8(d) for that case.

11. At 410 U.S 155 the Court cites Crossen v. Attorney General, 344 F. Supp. 587(E.D. Ky. 1970). Locate that case.
    (a) In what court does it arise?
    (b) Does it have headnotes? How many?
    (c) Who wrote this opinion?
    (d) Does this volume have a case table? Key Number Digest section?

12. At 410 U.S. 158 the Court cites Montana v. Rogers, 278 F.2d 68 (CA7, 1960).
    (a) What does (CA7, 1960) mean?
    (b) Answer the questions posed in 11(a) - 11(d) for the case.

13. How could one determine if the Supreme Court has decided any cases on abortion in its current term? Has it?

Theme Problem III:

Gideon v. Wainright was a case of importance in setting our standards for criminal justice. It can be found at 372 U.S. 335 (1963). Locate the case and answer the following questions:

1. What is the date of decision?

2. Who wrote the majority opinions?

3. Is there a concurring opinion or opinions? Who wrote it, or them?

4. Is there a dissenting opinion or opinions? Who wrote it, or them?

5. Where did the case originate?

6. Who argued the case for Gideon?

7. Are there any headnotes?

8. What is the result?

9. Gideon v. Wainwright can also be found in the Supreme Court Reporter and Lawyer's Edition, 2d.
    (a) Locate it, give the citations to the unofficial reporters.
    (b) How many headnotes in each?
    (c) Is there any difference in the opinions?
    (d) Examine the "extras" available in each volume: front matter, tables and indexes, etc. List what is available in each.
    (e) Are there any annotations in the Lawyer's Edition? If so, examine one.

10. At 372 U.S. 338 the Court cites Betts v. Brady. What is the official citation for Betts? Locate that case and answer questions 1-5 for that case.

11. At 372 U.S. page 346, Justice Douglas cites The Slaughter House Cases, 16 Wall. 36. What other designation does 16 Wall. have? Locate that case and answer questions 1-5 for it.

12. What case does Gideon v. Wainwright overrule? Find the Supreme Court Reporter and Lawyer's Edition citation for that case.

13. At 372 U.S. 351 in footnote 5, Justice Harlan cites Henderson v. Bannan, 256 F.2d 363 (C.A. 6th Cir. 1958). Locate that case:
    (a) What does C.A. 6th Cir. mean?
    (b) How many headnotes does the decision have?
    (c) Who wrote the opinion?
    (d) In what court did it originate?
    (e) Could this decision be found anywhere else?

14. How would one determine if the Supreme Court dealt with any cases concerning a criminal defendant's right to counsel this term? Has it?

Theme Problem IV:

Among the more controversial opinions you will read this year is that of Justice Cardozo in Palsgraf v. Long Island R.R. Co., 248 N.Y. 339, 162 N.E. 99 (1928). There, in determining whether a woman on the platform of a train station could recover for injuries she received due to an explosion, Cardozo dealt at length with the topics of duty and foreseeability.

A. Martinez v. California, 444 U.S. 277 (1980) cites to Palsgraf. Answer the following with reference to Martinez.

   1. Who wrote the opinion?

   2. Who represented the Martinez family at oral argument?

   3. Did any justice write a separate opinion?

   4. What was the date of the decision?

   5. Was Palsgraf necessary to the decision of the court?

B. Martinez can also be found at 62 L. Ed. 2d 481 and 100 S. Ct. 553. Compare and contrast the treatment given the case in these reports and in the official version.

C. Palsgraf is cited in 452 F.2d at page 178.

   1. Give the full citation for the case citing Palsgraf.

   2. Which headnote(s) are supported by Palsgraf?

   3. Who was the Chief Judge of the Seventh Circuit where the case was decided?

   4. What states are served by the Seventh Circuit?

   5. How many cases in 452 F.2d came to the Seventh Circuit from Wisconsin?

   6. What case in 452 F.2d defines the term "transmission?" Properly cite it.

   7. Who wrote the opinion in the case cited in Question C.6?

   8. What case in 452 F.2d cites to 21 U.S.C.A. sec. 355(h)? Properly cite it.

Theme Problem V:

Sherwood v. Walker, 66 Mich.568, 33 N.W. 919 (1887) represents one of the fundamental cases dealing with mutual mistake in the making of contracts. In his dissenting opinion, Justice Sherwood of the Michigan Supreme Court attempts to distinguish Allen v. Hammond, 11 Pet. 63, on which the majority relies.

A. Locate Allen and answer the following questions which relate to it:

1. Give its full citation.

2. Who wrote the majority opinion?

3. Did any justices write separate opinions?

4. Who was Chief Justice at the time of the decision?

5. Who argued for the appellee?

B. The same case can be found at 9 L. Ed. 633.

1. Compare and contrast the two reports.

2. Why does the case not appear in West's Supreme Court Reporter?

C. Sherwood is discussed in 621 F.2d at 1349.

1. Give the full citation of the case which cites Sherwood.

2. For which headnote is Sherwood cited?

3. Who wrote the opinion?

4. Who dissented?

5. Who was Chief Judge of the Fifth Circuit at the time?

6. At the time, what states were located in the Fifth Circuit?

7. How many cases arose in West Virginia that were reported in 621 F.2d?

8. What case in 621 F.2d cites the Rules of the Supreme Court of the United States?

Theme Problem VI:

One of the most significant cases you will study in Civil Procedure this year is that of Erie R.R. Co. v. Tompkins, 304 U.S. 64 (1938). This case requires federal courts sitting in diversity cases to ascertain and apply the substantive law of the state in which they sit to the case they are hearing. Locate Erie and answer the following questions which relate to it.

A. The opinion itself.

    1. Which headnote in the official reports most closely approximates the holding of the case as outlined above?

    2. Who wrote the majority opinion?

    3. Who concurred by writing separate opinions?

    4. Did any justice dissent?

    5. What was the date of decision?

B. The case expressly overrules Swift v. Tyson, 16 Pet. 1. Answer the following regarding that case.

    1. What is its proper citation?

    2. Who delivered the opinion of the court?

    3. Did Mr. Justice Catron concur or dissent?

    4. Who was the Chief Justice at the time of Swift v. Tyson?

C. Erie is also reported at 58 S. Ct. 817 and 82 L. Ed. 1188. Compare and contrast the treatment given the case in these reports and in the official version.

D. Erie is cited in 527 F.2d at 527.

    1. Give the correct citation for the case.

    2. Who argued the case for the plaintiff?

    3. Who was the Chief Judge for the Sixth Circuit at the time the case was decided?

    4. What states are located in the Sixth Circuit?

    5. What headnote covers the area of law for which the court cited Erie?

Chapter 5

STATE COURT DECISIONS AND THE NATIONAL REPORTER SYSTEM

ASSIGNMENT 1
COURT REPORTS

Questions:

1. The opinions of what courts in your state are published in any form--official or unofficial?

2. List the current official and unofficial reports for your state.

3. In what form do the official decisions in your state first appear, i.e., slip opinion, advance sheet, bound volume?

4. List all units of the National Reporter System reporting state cases.

5. Examine the first volume of the National Reporter System regional unit which includes your state. In what year did the unit begin?

6. Examine the latest bound issue of the National Reporter System regional unit which includes your state. Which states are included in this volume?

7. Compare a current volume of the California Reporter and a current volume of the Pacific Reporter. The opinions of which California court are duplicated?

8. Compare a current volume of the New York Supplement and a current volume of the North Eastern Reporter. The opinions of what New York court are duplicated in both reporters?

9. Examine a current volume of the National Reporter System regional unit which includes your state. Find the "Table of Contents" and list the material contained in this volume.

10. Examine volume 444 F.2d. Who is listed as the chief judge of the circuit judges of the 3rd Circuit?

11. Examine volume 484 P.2d Cite the pages of the two tables of cases which cite Riddell v. Rhay.

12. Give the complete citation to a case in 189 N.W.2d which construes the following statute:
    North Dakota Century Code 1-02-10

13. Give the citation to a case and the page number of the case in 183 S.E.2d which defines the word "war."

14. Examine the Key Number digest section of volume 470 S.W.2d. Give the subject, key number, and citation to the first case digested.

15. Examine the case in volume 273 N.E.2d at page 252. Answer the following:
    (a) What is the name of the case?
    (b) What is the docket number?
    (c) What is the name of the court?

16. Examine the case of E. & E. Newman v. Hallock at 281 A.2d 544. Answer the following:
    (a) What is the official state report citation for this case, if any?
    (b) How many different key numbers are listed in the headnotes of this case?

17. Examine the case of De Palma v. State, 185 S.E.2d 53. Answer the following:
    (a) Headnotes 3, 4, and 5 are discussed on which page of the opinion?
    (b) Syllabus 4(b) of the court is discussed on which page of the opinion?

18. Examine the case of United States ex rel. Catena v. Elias, 449 F.2d 40. Answer the following:
    (a) In what court was the appeal heard?
    (b) What was the name of the appellee's lawyer?
    (c) What was the full name of the judge who wrote the opinion of the court?
    (d) What was the full name of the judge who wrote the dissenting opinion?

19. Cases in the National Reporter System units appear first in advance sheet form.
    (a) Is the pagination in the advance sheets the same as that in the bound volume?
    (b) Will the text of the cases found in the advance sheets always be the same as that in the bound volumes which replace them?

20. The Key Number Digest section is located at the end of each bound volume of the National Reporter system. Where is the Key Number Digest section located in the National Reporter System advance sheets?

21. Examine volume 328 F.Supp. Who is listed as the Chief Judge of the circuit judges of the Third Circuit?

22. Examine volume 113 A.2d. Cite the pages of the two tables of cases which cite Bata v. Hill.

23. Give the complete citation to a case in volume 97 N.E.2d which construes Article 8, sec. 4 of the Ohio Constitution.

24. Give the citation to a case in 106 Cal.Rptr. which defines the word "revolver," and the page number on which the definition is found.

25. Examine the Key Number digest section of volume 201 N.Y.S.2d. Give the subject, Key Number, and citation to the first case digested.

26. Examine the case in volume 89 So.2d at page 459. Answer the following:
    (a) What is the name of the case?
    (b) What is the docket number?
    (c) What is the name of the court?

27. Examine the case of State v. Waid at 67 P.2d 647. Answer the following:
    (a) Is the official state report citation given for this case?
    (b) How many different Key Numbers are listed in the headnotes of this case?

28. Examine the case of United States Cold Storage Corp. v. Stolinski, 96 N.W.2d 408. Answer the following:
    (a) Headnotes 8, 9 are discussed on what page?
    (b) Sylabus 2 of the court is found on what page?

29. Examine the case of Green v. State, 209 S.W.2d 195. Answer the following:
    (a) In what court was the appeal heard?
    (b) What were the names of the attorneys for the appellant?
    (c) What was the name of the judge who wrote the opinion of the court?
    (d) What was the name of the judge who wrote the opinion on the appellant's motion for rehearing?

30. Judicial highlights are occasionally found in advance sheets of the National Reporter System. They are printed on colored pages. Find and examine such asection in an advance sheet. What do these judicial Highlights contain?

ASSIGNMENT 2
PARALLEL CITATIONS

Method:

Using the National Reporter System Blue Books and Supplements, provide the parallel citation for each citation given below.

Questions:

1. 159 Ala. 410

2. 70 Ark. 166

3. 20 Cal. App. 252

4. 91 Ga. 840

5. 110 Ind. 294

6. 62 Or. 299

7. 97 S.C. 261

8. 86 Tex. Cr. 620

9. 112 Ga. App. 427

10. 340 Mass. 334

11. 75 N.J. Super. 192

12. 171 Ohio St. 309

13. 198 Pa. Super. 169

14. 69 Wash. 2d 144

15. 83 Nev. 1

ASSIGNMENT 3
USE OF THE TABLE OF CASES

Method:

   Using the table of cases in the reporter volumes shown, provide the proper pagination.

Questions:

1. Adler v. Bush Terminal Co., 291 N.Y.S.

2. Hensel v. Cahill, 116 A.2d

3. Thompson v. Mellon, 107 Cal. Rptr.

4. State ex rel. Harbage v. Ferguson, 36 N.E.2d

5. Burt v. Munger, 23 N.W.2d

6. Handley v. Jackson, 51 P.

7. Strickland v. Johnson, 197 S.E.

8. Savage v. Olson, 9 So.2d

9. Dabbs v. Dabbs, 71 So.

10. Gray v. Jones, 296 S.W.

11. Owens v. Daniel, 16 S.W.2d

12. Bodrey v. Bodrey, 161 S.E.2d

13. Weddle v. Cox, 394 P.2d

14. Adams v. Schneider, 124 N.E.

15. Bradway v. Netzorg, 298 N.W.

ASSIGNMENT 4
USE OF VOLUME DIGEST

Method:

Using the digest to the reporter volumes shown, provide the citation to the appropriate case.

Questions:

1. A case in 110 A.2d concerning the liability of warehousemen to the owners of goods which are lost, destroyed, or damaged.

2. A case in 71 Cal. Rptr. concerning certainty and definiteness as requisites of a statute.

3. A case in 218 N.Y.S.2d concerning the effect of old age on the testamentary capacity to make a will.

4. A case in 18 N.E.2d concerning acts or conduct constituting contempt of court.

5. A case in 538 S.W.2d concerning limiting the time or scope of argument of counsel.

6. A case in 290 S.W. concerning breach of the peace.

7. A case in 223 So.2d concerning the care required and liability in general of inn keepers.

8. A case in 472 P.2d concerning the nature and theory of the right of subrogation.

9. A case in 308 A.2d concerning injury to or destruction of fish.

10. A case in 154 N.W.2d concerning discretion of the court relating to new trial.

11. A case in 186 N.W. concerning enforcement of mechanics' liens.

12. A case in 59 N.E.2d concerning nature of a constructive trust.

13. A case in 245 N.Y.S.2d concerning the inheritance of property from or through bastards.

14. A case in 7 A.2d concerning the power to control and regulate highways.

ASSIGNMENT 5
USE OF THE TABLE OF STATUTES CONSTRUED

Method:

Using the table of statutes construed for the reporter volumes shown, provide the citation to the appropriate case.

Questions:

1. Uniform Fraudulent Conveyance Act, sec. 4 (112 A.2d)

2. 26 U.S.C.A. §1033 (72 Cal. Rptr.)

3. U.S. CONST., amend. I (203 N.Y.S.2d)

4. Ohio General Codes, sec. 26 (65 N.E.2d)

5. Uniform Commercial Code, 2-201 (2) (536 S.W.2d)

6. Louisiana Code of Criminal Procedure, art. 920 (308 So.2d)

7. Alabama Code tit. 14, §213 (267 So.2d)

8. Wyoming Revised Statutes of 1931, sec. 22-353 (103 P.2d)

9. U.S. CONST. art. IV, §1 (535 P.2d)

10. North Dakota Century Code, 1-01-06 (150 N.W.2d)

11. New York Partnership Law §10 (69 N.E. 2d)

12. South Dakota Compiled Laws, 1-26-36 (195 N.W.2d)

13. N.Y. TOWN LAW §268 (2) (229 N.Y.S.2d)

14. Pa. RULES CRIM. P. 150 (340 A.2d)

ASSIGNMENT 6
USE OF WORDS AND PHRASES

Method:

　　Using the Words and Phrases section of the reporter volumes shown, provide the citation to the appropriate case.

Questions:

1. "Can," 111 A.2d.

2. "Totten Trusts," 212 N.Y.S.2d.

3. "Employer," 85 Cal. Rptr.

4. "Direct Evidence," 83 N.E.2d.

5. "Enclosed Structure," 534 S.W.2d

6. "Fall," 306 So.2d.

7. "Cloud on Title," 317 So.2d.

8. "Child," 108 P.2d.

9. "Mutual," 152 N.W.2d.

10. "Duress," 49 N.E.2d.

11. "Unfitness," 128 N.W.2d.

12. "Domicile," 85 N.E.2d.

13. "Reasonable," 204 N.W.2d.

14. "Tender Years Doctrine," 296 A.2d.

15. "Lapsed Legacy," 173 N.Y.S.2d.

ASSIGNMENT 7
THEME PROBLEMS

Theme Problem I:

A. Brown v. Board of Education is cited at 358 A.2d 835. Locate this decision and answer the following questions about the case that contains it.

1. What is the name and citation of the case which cites Brown?
    Rybeck 358, A 2d 828
2. Which is the official citation?

3. Who represented defendant Evans?

4. If you wanted to find other cases in this volume dealing with the same point for which Brown is cited, how would you do it? Are there any?

5. What states does this reporter cover?

6. Give the name and citation of any case in this volume that mentions the Constitution of New Hampshire.

7. Give the name and citation of a case in this volume that defines "startling event."

8. Who was the chief justice of the Maine Supreme Judicial Court when Rybeck was rendered?

B. Brown v. Board of Education is also cited at 223 S.E.2d 617 in a dissent. Locate this citation and answer the following questions concerning the case in which the citation is found:

1. What is the name and citation of the case?

2. Is there an official citation given? If so, what is it?

3. Who wrote the dissent that cited Brown?

4. Why does no headnote cover the part of the opinion in which the citation of Brown occurs?

5. What states does this reporter cover?

6. Give the name and citation of any case in this volume that cites the North Carolina Code of Judicial Conduct.

7. Who was the Chief judge of the Georgia court of Appeals at the time this case was decided?

34

Theme Problem II:

A. Roe v. Wade cites the case found at 354 S.W.2d 161. Locate this case and answer the following questions concerning it:

   1. Give the correct name and citation of the case.

   2. Note there is no official citation. List two reasons why this may be.

   3. Who represented the state?

   4. What is the result?

   5. If you wanted to find other cases in this volume on the topic covered under headnote seven, how could you do it? Are there any?

   6. Give the names and citations of any cases in this volume that interpret the Kentucky Constitution.

   7. Give the name and citation of a case in this volume that defines the term "gondola."

   8. Who was the presiding judge of the Kansas City (Missouri) court of appeals when this case was decided?

B. Roe v. Wade also cites to 250 So.2d 857. Locate that case and answer the following questions concerning it:

   1. Give the correct name and citation of this case.

   2. List the counsel who participated.

   3. List any concurring opinions.

   4. What is the result?

   5. If one wanted to locate other cases in this volume that deal with the point covered in headnote 1, how could one do it? Are there any?

   6. What other states are covered by this reporter?

   7. Give the names and citations of any cases in this volume that mention the Florida Code of Ethics.

   8. Where in this volume could one find the opinion in Rachal v. Rachal?

   9. Give the name and citation of a case in this volume that defines the term "religious."

35

10. Name the person who was presiding judge of the Louisiana 3rd Circuit Court of Appeals as of the decision in Walsingham.

Theme Problem III:

A. In footnote 2 at p. 338 of its opinion in Gideon the Court cites the case of Artrip v. State, 136 So.2d 574 (Ct. App. Ala. 1962). Locate that case and answer the following:

1. Who wrote the opinion? Were there any concurrences or dissents?

2. Which headnote covers the issue on right to counsel in capital offenses cases discussed in Gideon? How could one find other cases in this volume on that point?

3. What other states are covered by this reporter?

4. What case in this volume defines the term "pimp?"

5. Are any parts of the Mississippi constitution dealt with by cases in this volume? Give the names of the cases and the citations.

6. Who was the chief justice of the Alabama Supreme Court at the time Artrip was decided?

B. Also in footnote 2 the court cites Shaffer v. Warden 211 Md. 635, 126 A.2d 573 (1956). Using 126 A.2d, answer the following:

1. Who wrote the opinion? Were there any concurrences or dissents?

2. Which headnote applies more directly to the issues of the Gideon case?

3. What was the court's determination?

4. Are there any other cases in this volume that deal with the issues raised in Gideon? How could you tell?

5. Cases for what other states are reported in this volume?

6. Who was the vice chancellor of the Delaware Court of Chancery when this case was decided?

7. What is the name and citation of a case in this volume that defines the word "fish?"

8. Give the names and citations of any cases in this volume that interpret Art.I. of the Pennsylvania Constitution.

9. What is the correct citation for Hatalowich v. Nagy?

Theme Problem IV:

Palsgraf v. Long Island R. Co. is located at 162 N.E. 99.

A. Answer the following with regard to Palsgraf:

1. What is the citation in the official reporter?

2. Give the full names of the three dissenting judges.

3. Who represented the railroad?

4. What other jurisdictions are reported in this volume?

B. Palsgraf is referred to at 350 N.Y.S.2d 651. Answer the following with regard to that case:

1. Give its full citation, indicating on what page the court cites to Palsgraf.

2. For what reason does it refer to Cardozo?

3. Cite another case in the volume which defines "motorcycle."

4. What case in the volume deals with the first amendment to the United States Constitution?

Theme Problem V:

A. In interpreting Pennsylvania law, the Erie court relies on Falchetti v. Pennsylvania R. Co., 160 A. 859. Answer the following relative to Falchetti:

1. What is the citation in the official reporter?

2. Give the full name of the judge who wrote the opinion.

3. Who represented the plaintiff?

4. Which headnote most closely assists the Erie opinion?

B. Falchetti was later discussed at 225 A.2d 528. Answer the following relative to that case:

1. What is the citation in the official reporter?

2. What effect did it have on Falchetti?

3. Cite a case in the same volume referring to the sixth amendment to the U.S. Constitution.

4. What jurisdictions are reported in this volume?

Theme Problem VI:

A. Sherwood v. Walker can be found at 33 N.W. 919. Look at the case and answer the following questions:

1. What is the citation in the official reporter?

2. What other jurisdictions are represented in the same volume?

B. Sherwood is referred to at 294 N.W. 708. Answer the following questions relating to that case:

1. What is the full citation?

2. How does the organization of its headnotes differ from Sherwood?

3. What is the full name of the justice who wrote the opinion?

C. A later Michigan case extends the concept of mistake from a settlement agreement to vacating a consent judgement at 185 N.W.2d 64.

1. Who represented the City of Warren in that case?

2. What case in the same volume defines "abuse of discretion?"

3. How many cases in the volume come from South Dakota?

ASSIGNMENT 8
DRILL PROBLEMS

Drill Problem I:

National Reporter System. Answer as concisely as possible.

1. Parallel citations. Give the National Reporter Citation for the following cases. Use the National Reporter Blue Books.
   (a) 363 Mo. 442
   (b) 264 Ind. 313
   (c) 280 Md. 332

2. Features of the National Reporter System volumes
   (a) Table of Cases. Using the volume shown, provide the page citation for the listed cases.
       (i) In 477 S.W.2d, Travelers Ins. Co. v. Speer.
       (ii) In 520 P.2d, State v. Clark.
       (iii) In 290 N.E.2d, Slocum v. Fire and Police Comm. of City of East Peoria.
   (b) Statutes Construed. Using the volume shown, provide the page citation to the case that cites the following statute.
       (i) In 344 A.2d, Rule 803(6) of the U.S. Federal Rules of Evidence.
       (ii) In 568 S.W.2d, Art. 6, §9 of the Tennessee Constitution.
   (c) Words and Phrases. Using the volume shown, provide the page citation for the case that defines the following terms:
       (i) In 241 S.E.2d, "Suit at Law"
       (ii) In 349 So.2d, "As the Case May Be"

Drill Problem II:

National Reporter System. Answer as concisely as possible.

1. Parallel Citations. Give the National Reporter Citation for the following cases. Use the National Reporter Blue Books.
   (a) 69 Ill. 2d 488
   (b) 50 Del. 28
   (c) 242 Ark. 292

2. Features of the National Reporter System Volumes
   (a) <u>Table of Cases</u>. Using the volume shown, provide the page citation for the listed cases.
       (i) In 281 So.2d, Tyrrell v. Tyrrell.
       (ii) In 183 N.W.2d, Swartz v. Bly.
       (iii) In 235 A.2d, Thomas v. State.
   (b) <u>Statutes Construed</u>. Using the volume shown, provide the page citation to the page that cites the following statute.
       (i) In 243 S.E.2d, Ga. Code, §3-601.
       (ii) In 362 So.2d, Fla. Const., art. 2, §3.
   (c) <u>Words and Phrases</u>. Using the volume shown, provide the page citation for the case that defines the following terms:
       (i) In 578 P.2d, "Nor"
       (ii) In 270 N.W.2d, "Hit and Run"

<u>Drill Problem III</u>:

National Reporter System. Answer as concisely as possible.

1. Parallel Citations. Give the National Reporter Citation for the following cases. Use the National Reporter Blue Books.
   (a) 76 Cal. App. 3d 302
   (b) 240 Ga. 479
   (c) 85 Idaho 226

2. Features of the National Reporter System Volumes
   (a) <u>Table of Cases</u>. Using the volume shown, provide the page citation for the listed cases.
       (i) In 167 S.E.2d, <u>Young v. State</u>.
       (ii) In 232 N.E.2d, <u>Zoppo Co. v. Com</u>.
       (iii) In 539 P.2d, <u>Zylstra v. Piva</u>.
   (b) <u>Statutes Construed</u>. Using the volume shown, provide the page citation of the case that cites the following statute.
       (i) In 583 P.2d, Kansas Statutes Annotated 21-3302.
       (ii) In 269 N.W.2d, A.B.A. Code of Professional Responsibility, D-R 5-104(A).
   (c) <u>Words and Phrases</u>. Using the volume shown, provide the page citation for the case that defines the following terms:
       (i) In 565 S.W.2d, "Liberty"
       (ii) In 380 N.E.2d, "Or"

Drill Problem IV:

A. Parallel Citations. Using the National Reporter Blue Books, give the National Reporter citation for the following cases:

1. 126 Colo. 11

2. 399 Mich. 515

3. 201 Tenn. 444

B. Using the volume indicated, provide the full citation for the following cases:

1. In 355 A.2d, a case in which International Business Machines Corporation was the plaintiff.

2. In 605 P.2d, a case in which Robert Teresinski was the defendant.

3. In 413 N.E.2d, a case construing the Indiana Small Claims Rules.

4. In 266 N.W.2d, a case construing the North Dakota Rules of Civil Procedure.

5. In 594 S.W.2d, a case defining "exigent circumstance."

6. In 256 S.E.2d, a case dealing with Weapons.

Drill Problem V:

A. Parallel Citations. Using the National Reporter Blue Books, give the National Reporter citation for the following cases:

1. 187 Kan. 458

2. 10 N.Y.2d 859

3. 4 N.C. App. 652

B. Using the volume indicated, provide the full citation for the following cases:

1. In 364 S.2d, a case in which the Shell Oil Company was the defendant.

2. In 213 S.E.2d, a case in which George Vick was the defendant.

3. In 564 S.W.2d, a case construing the Texas Election Code.

4. In 237 N.W.2d, a case defining "Criminal Assault."

5. In 399 N.E.2d, a case dealing with Fines.

6. In 582 P.2d, a case from Utah involving a sugar company.

Drill Problem VI:

A. Parallel Citations. Using the National Reporter Blue Books, give the National Reporter citation for the following cases:

1. 141 Ga. App. 678

2. 265 Ind. 616

3. 115 R.I. 303

B. Using the volume indicated, provide the full citation for the following cases:

1. A case in 424 A.2d, in which Barry Brann sued the tate of Maine.

2. A case in 415 N.E.2d, in which John Green was the defendant.

3. A case in 283 N.W.2d, construing Mich. Comp. Laws §430.53.

4. A case in 614 P.2d, defining "Arms."

5. A case in 273 S.E.2d, dealing with Products Liability.

6. A case in 621 P.2d, dealing with a taxicab company, decided by the Nevada Supreme Court.

Chapter 6

DIGESTS FOR COURT REPORTS

ASSIGNMENT 1
USE OF THE AMERICAN DIGEST SYSTEM

Method:

Using the indexes of the Decennial Digest specified at the beginning of each problem, carry out the following six steps in accord with the example given at the beginning of the problems:

(1) Answer the question with a "yes" or "no," basing your answer on information found in the specified digest.

(2) List the Topic and Key Numbers(s) under which the digest paragraph was found.

(3) Using the Topic Outline, what is the specific subject of the Topic and Key Number(s)?

(4) Using the latest edition of A Uniform System of Citation for proper form, give the case name and full citation to which the digest paragraph you located applies.

(5) Are there any cases in the first ten volumes of the General Digest Sixth Series under the same Topic and Key Number(s) as found in (2) supra? Answer with either the specific volume number(s) or the word "none."

(6) Give the corresponding or most nearly similar Century Digest (1658-1896) Topic and Section Number for the Topic and Key Number in (2) supra.

Example:

QUESTION: Use Fifth Decennial. Mr. Ned Lee of Webster County, Mississippi, sued the Memphis, Tennessee Publishing Company, a Delaware corporation, for damages arising out of an allegedly defamatory and libelous article published by the defendant. Service of process was effected against, among others, the Secretary of State of the State of Mississippi. Defendant moved for dismissal based on lack of jurisdiction, stating it was not "present" within the state, that it was not doing business within the State of Mississippi, and that (by implication) it would violate due process of law contrary to Section 1 of Article XIV of the U.S. Constitution to subject defendant to local jurisdiction. Should the defendant prevail?

ANSWER:
(1) Yes.
(2) Constitutional Law 309(3).
(3) Constitutional Law - Due Process of Law - Civil Remedies and Proceedings - Parties and Process or Notice - Service on Agent of Nonresident.
(4) <u>Lee v. Memphis Publ. Co.</u>, 195 Miss. 264, 14 So. 2d 351 (1943).
(5) None.
(6) Constitutional Law - §§ 929-30.

Questions:

1. Use First Decennial. In a civil case, the postmark on a letter was introduced into evidence. Is the postmark admissible into evidence without proof?

2. Use Second Decennial. Eddie Norton was adjudged an incompetent by reason of habitual drunkenness. Are Eddie's subsequent contracts which affect his property rendered void by this adjudication?

3. Use Third Decennial. A petition was filed with the Minnesota Board of Law Examiners seeking the disbarment of an attorney for alleged misconduct in signing a will as a witness after the testatrix had died. Was the evidence of this alleged misconduct sufficient to sustain the charge?

4. Use Third Decennial. A city in Arkansas sued to recover possession of a block of land which the city alleged had been dedicated to public use. A plot of the land had been filed in the office of the Recorder of Deeds. The block in question was designated "Franklin Square," but was not put to public use nor ever accepted by the City Council as a public place. Did the marking of the block as a "square" constitute an implied dedication of the land to the city?

5. Use Third Decennial. A physician and a sanitarium company in Georgia were sued for injuries sustained because of the physician's alleged negligence. The physician was the president and a principal stockholder of the sanitarium company. Was this sufficient to hold the sanitarium liable for negligence?

6. Use Third Decennial. Mrs. Gardener planted a tree on her property about three feet from her east property line. The tree flourished. Jones, who was her adjoining property owner on the east, decided one day that he was no longer going to duck his head to avoid bumping into the branches of this tree, so he sawed the limbs off at the property line. May Mrs. Gardener recover damages?

7. Use Third Decennial. Green sold a tract of land to Redman. This tract was surrounded by land owned by Green and other people. There was no way to get to the Redman tract except over the land of Green and the others. Redman claims he is entitled to an implied easement over Green's land for a way to and from Redman's tract. Is this correct?

8. Use Third Decennial. Jeff had a wife and three children. At the time he made his will his wife was pregnant. The will devised that this unborn child would receive a stated share of Jeff's property on Jeff's death. A few days after making the will and before the child was born Jeff died at his home in Anycity, Louisiana. Subsequently, the child was born and appears to be normal. The will is contested on the ground that the unborn child could not take anything under the will. Is this correct?

9. Use Fourth Decennial. Plaintiff sued for rent under a written lease. After a finding for the defendant, plaintiff contended that the court lacked jurisdiction since the order had been entered before return to proof of service had been filed. In New Hampshire does failure to file the return deny the court jurisdiction?

10. Use Fourth Decennial. At the time John Petty was placed in the county jail, he requested the jailer not to place him with the other prisoners because he knew that it was the custom of the prisoners to organize a Kangaroo Court and try new prisoners on some fictitious charge. The jailer refused his request and placed him with the prisoners. The prisoners gave him a trial and, because he could not pay the fine, severely injured him. Petty has sued the Board of County Commissioners for the damages resulting from these injuries, alleging that the Board had statutory authority to make rules and regulations governing the conduct of prisoners confined in county jail and that the Board had neglected to do so. Will Petty recover?

11. Use Fourth Decennial. Joe Andrews, a Franklin County, Montana, rancher, took his sheep to Lawrence County for grazing during the winter months. Are the sheep taxable in Lawrence County where they were taken for the purpose of winter feeding?

12. Use Fourth Decennial. The State University at Franklin instituted a condemnation action in order to obtain land for use as grounds for a new library building. The owner of the land questions the right of the University to exercise the power of eminent domain. Is the University entitled to take the land?

13. Use Fifth Decennial. Relying on the Mississippi statute which provided that one was presumed dead if absent for seven years without having been heard from, Freda, whose first husband had been absent and not heard from for more than seven years, married Bill. Subsequent to Freda's marriage to Bill it was discovered that Freda's first husband was alive. Was the marriage of Freda and Bill void?

14. Use Fifth Decennial. Patrolman Harry Bigfoot had stopped a motorist in Anycity, Michigan. As the officer was talking to him, the motorist told Harry to get out of the way and drove off in a burst of speed. In doing this the automobile ran over Harry's right foot. May the motorist be convicted for the felony of assault with a dangerous weapon?

15. Use Fifth Decennial. The Maryland physician who testified as to the condition of three year old child injured in an automobile collision received the history of the case from the patient's mother and not from the child herself. Was the attending physician's opinion evidence, which was partially based on the mother's statements, admissible?

16. Use Fifth Decennial. The mortgage made by Smith to Bank provided that Bank could sell the property mortgaged after default by publishing notice of sale in the newspaper. Smith defaulted. The Bank bought the property at the foreclosure sale. Smith sues Bank for the purpose of vacating the sale. Should the sale be vacated?

17. Use Fifth Decennial. A jury convicted Frank Pasco of murder. He was sentenced to life imprisonment. He appealed on the ground, <u>inter alia</u>, that the trial court erred in excusing ten jurors because of illness and then failing to state, in open court, that such excuses had been made. Is it within the discretion of the trial judge to determine if jury members may be excused before and during the trial?

18. Use Fifth Decennial. The Circuit Court of Wayne County, Michigan, refused to confirm a mortgage foreclosure sale, basing its decision on allegedly inadequate bids. Presuming the tentative purchaser can show that its bid is about as high as can be reasonably expected, should the Circuit Court be ordered to confirm the sale on foreclosure?

19. Use Sixth Decennial. A San Francisco attorney entered into a contingent fee contract with a client. The contract had the effect of providing additional compensation if a cross-complaint was filed and successfully defended. Does this make the contract illegal, unfair or inequitable?

20. Use Sixth Decennial. A women filed a complaint against an attorney with the Monmouth County, New Jersey, Ethics and Grievance Committee. He retaliated by starting a malicious prosecution action against her. May an attorney predicate a malicious prosecution action on the filing of such a complaint?

21. Use Sixth Decennial. A bankrupt fishing company had from time to time over a two and one-half year period delivered to a Massachusetts fish-freezing plant and public warehouse various lots of fish for freezing and storage. At the time of the fishing company's bankruptcy, the warehouse still had in its possession eleven such lots. The fishing company owed (1) $258.11 on account of unpaid charges on the eleven lots and (2) $1,126.84 as unpaid charges on other lots previously stored but withdrawn before bankruptcy. Seeking to secure the receipts due it, the warehouse claimed a lien on the eleven lots as security for the total account: $1,384.95. The trustee in bankruptcy maintained that the lien was only for $258.11, because under Massachusetts law the warehouse lost its lien on the other lots by surrendering possession of them. Was the trustee correct?

22. Use Sixth Decennial. The will of Mrs. Smith gave to her husband "any home belonging to me in which we are residing at the time of my death." At the time of her death, Mr. and Mrs. Smith were living in a dwelling owned by her in Georgia and occupied by her and her husband seven or eight months of each year. Also, Mrs. Smith owned a summer cottage in Michigan occupied by her each summer but visited by her husband only for short periods of time. Is he entitled to both houses?

23. Use Sixth Decennial. Johnson was a member of the bar of state X and also a member of the bar of U.S. Supreme Court. Johnson was disbarred in state X. Does this disbarment in state X automatically disbar Johnson from membership in the bar of U.S. Supreme Court?

24. Use Sixth Decennial. A maid in a hotel found a brooch as she was cleaning a room. She assumed that X, who occupied this room, had lost the brooch, so she placed the brooch on the dresser. X saw the brooch and since it was not his, turned it over to the manager of the hotel with the understanding that the manager would hold it until claimed by the rightful owner but that if it was unclaimed the manager would return it to X. It was not claimed. The manager refused to return the brooch to X. May X recover the mislaid brooch?

25. Use Sixth Decennial. X obtained a room at a hotel in Anycity, Oklahoma. The hotel provided automobile parking space without extra charge to guests and the automobile was placed in this garage by a hotel attendant. During the night the automobile and its contents were stolen. Is the hotel contributorily negligent and thus liable for the loss?

26. Use Sixth Decennial. X and his wife, Y, were without children. With X's consent, Y was artificially inseminated. As a result a child was born. Is the child a bastard?

27. Use Sixth Decennial. After the funeral of Joesph Jackson's grandfather, all of the flowers which had been donated by friends and relatives were left at the grave site. During the evening on the day of the funeral, Jackson returned to the grave site. He was shocked to find that all of the flowers had been removed. On investigating, he discovered that the florist shop had taken the flowers in order to use the forms and stands again. Jackson maintains that he, as an heir of the deceased person, accepted the flowers as gifts from the friends and that title to the flowers had vested in him. Jackson is seeking damages from the florist shop. Did title to the flowers vest in Jackson?

28. Use Sixth Decennial. A Richmond County, New York jury convicted Louise Sorge of performing an abortion. During the trial, she had been extensively cross-examined about other abortions. On appeal, she alleged that prejudice resulted from the vigorous cross examination. On appeal of this criminal conviction would the court overturn the trial court's findings as to this question of fact?

29. Use Sixth Decennial. Fred Messerly, leaving a bar in Zortman, Montana, struck the decedent, one Peter Dorey, several times, apparently without provocation. Mr. Messerly introduced evidence to show that his blows were not the primary cause of Mr. Dorey's death, that Dorey had fainted several hours earlier. Messerly was convicted of manslaughter. On appeal, he assigns as error the trial court's refusal to give him a directed verdict for lack of evidence. In this homicide, did Messerly's admissible evidence as to passion and provocation deserve a directed verdict?

30. Use Sixth Decennial. William A. (Wilmar) Norman and James W. McIver entered into a joint venture. They had a falling out, but did not abandon the enterprise. McIver demanded an accounting, and Norman's motion to dismiss the suit was granted by the Multomah County, Oregon Court. Did the contract of the joint venture remain in force for purpose of winding up rather than canceling it immediately?

31. Use Sixth Decennial. Trico Products Corporation sued the Delman Corporation for patent infringement. It appeared that the patents related to an apparatus for discharging liquid onto automobile windshields for cleaning purposes, and were merely the application of mechanical means other than "inventions." The federal trial court rendered judgment for defendant Delman. Under the Federal Rules of Civil Procedure did the review by the appellate court of the district court's findings and conclusions as to questions of fact result in an affirmance?

32. Use Sixth Decennial. Mr. Lawrence Hawthorne borrowed two sums ($45,000 and $18,000) in 1954 from his partners, Mr. and Mrs. J. M. Walton, and was charged an illegally high interest rate. Mr. Hawthorne repaid the sums and interest, and then sued to recover the excess interest. Has Mr. Hawthorne waived or released his claim of usury by payment?

33. Use Sixth Decennial. Mr. Kinzer was indicted for housebreaking and larceny. The trial ended with a hung jury. During the second trial, Kinzer's counsel moved to subpoena the court reporter from the first trial, for use in cross-examination of government witnesses, after the court denied defendant's request for a free transcript. Disregarding the trial court's denials of defendant's motions, as a general rule will stenographers or reporters notes, taken at a former trial, be dismissed to impeach testimony of witnesses?

34. Use Seventh Decennial. The treasurer of a union local entered into a scheme with the other members of the union's executive board whereby he sold union property and pocketed part of the proceeds. In California does pocketing part of proceeds from sale of realty belonging to union constitute embezzlement?

35. Use Seventh Decennial. An actress entered into a contract with an agency to be her exclusive representative for a period of five years. Under the contract she was to pay the agency 10% of her earnings. Simultaneously the agency allegedly made an oral agreement to pay 5% of her earnings to another agent to whom she was already under contract. In New York, does the statute of frauds bar enforcement of such an oral agreement made in conjunction with an artist's exclusive agency contract?

36. Use Seventh Decennial. Twice daily a farmer drove his herd of cattle along the main road through a village in Maryland from his barn on one edge of the village to his pasture on the opposite edge. Residents of the village complained that the dropping of manure on the roadway was a nuisance and sought to enjoin the farmer from driving his cattle through the village. In Maryland, does the driving of cattle along a public highway to pasture constitute a nuisance per se?

37. Use Seventh Decennial. Walter J. Borowicz, five years old, was injured in Maplewood, New Jersey, when he was struck by William J. Hood's car. Walter's parents sued Mr. Hood. A policeman, Officer Schuler, testified that he had measured Mr. Hood's skid marks as 63 feet in length. As instructions regarding speed and control of the automobile where injuries resulted from the negligent operation of the vehicle, should the court have instructed the jury as to the skidding?

38. Use Seventh Decennial. Mrs. Geneva Rose and Lawrence Rose, the widow and son, respectively, of the decedent, were sentenced to 10 years for slaying John Rose. Only circumstantial evidence was introduced and that evidence was conflicting. Was this sufficient proof of guilt as to a homicide under criminal law?

39. Use Seventh Decennial. Mr. Gary Mullendore was rear-ended while he was stopped in a line of Kansas City traffic. He sued and won. The defendant appealed, claiming the trial court erred in giving an instruction allowing the jury to assess damages for mental suffering even though there had been no testimony to that effect. Was defendant's appeal successful?

40. Use Seventh Decennial. At the close of a rather lengthy trial, a jury determined that the decedent's gift three years prior to death had been a valid inter vivos gift, and judgment was rendered in favor of the defendant recipient of the gift. Plaintiff appealed, challenging the jury's finding of fact with respect to intent, delivery, and acceptance. Was the jury's determination allowed to stand on appeal?

41. Use Seventh Decennial. A mechanical speciality contractors' bid depository provided that the depository would forward member contractors' bids only to general contractors which requested same and agreed to use only bids received from a depository as implemented by a required agreement on the part of the general contractors' bidding through the depository. Was this arrangement a restraint of trade under a contract not to engage in competing business?

42. Use Seventh Decennial. Alice Papierre, wearing high heels, visited Mr. Ralph F. Greenwood's store and tripped while descending the stairs from the second to the first floor. She sued Mr. Greenwood, testifying, inter alia, that the stair covering was "old and worn," and won a jury verdict. Mr. Greenwood appealed, alleging trial court error in denying his motion for a directed verdict. Was there negligence on the part of the defendant in omitting to correct the condition of the building?

43. Use Seventh Decennial. Mr. Harry S. Foster was fired from his tenured teaching position with the Carson School District number 301, Skamania County, Washington. He appealed to the superior court and lost. He next appealed to the State Supreme Court. Did his contract of employment in this case demand automatic renewal?

44. Use Seventh Decennial. When Bill Poor died, his widow, Mary, was financially unable to purchase a cemetery lot. Her sister-in-law, the widow of his brother, suggested that he be interred in her lot alongside his brother. This offer was accepted by Mary. Mary's finances have now improved and she has purchased another cemetery lot for herself and her husband. It is her desire to transfer the remains of her husband to this cemetery lot. The sister-in-law objects. May Mary remove the body?

45. Use Seventh Decennial. On his way home from a New Year's Party at the Ritzy Hotel in Anycity, California, Tipsy was stopped by a patrolman. Mrs. Tipsy, while not agreeing with the patrolman that her husband was too drunk to drive, agreed to drive her husband home. The patrolman noted all the necessary information and the next day a charge against Tipsy was filed in municipal court for drunk driving. The warrant for the arrest of Tipsy was served on him at his home in Anycity on the following July 1. Tipsy filed a motion to dismiss on the grounds that he had at all times been available for arrest and that because of this factor he had been deprived of his right to a speedy trial, as guaranteed by the Constitution. Should the case be dismissed?

46. Use Seventh Decennial. Mr. Clark finally found a parking space in the city of X. After parking he discovered that he did not have any change for the parking meter. He went for change. Upon returning he discovered a ticket for illegal parking tucked under his windshield wiper. Clark was tried and convicted in municipal court. The ordinance of X makes it unlawful to have a vehicle in a parking space when parking meter signal indicates the space is illegally in use "other than such time as is necessary to operate the meter to show legal parking." Clark appeals on the ground his actions fall within this exception. Will Mr. Clark lose?

47. Use Seventh Decennial. The board of education of a county in Kentucky had hired an attorney to represent the school board in cases which were defended by them for protection of the board's corporate action and decisions. No statute specifically gave the board the authority to hire an attorney. However, the board claimed they had implied authority under statute which read that the board could "do all things necessary to accomplish the purposes for which it is created." Did the board have the right to employ an attorney in these cases?

48. Use Seventh Decennial. Jerry, a 13 year old orphan, had been living in Albenkin, New Mexico, with his unmarried aunt who was his guardian. Jerry wanted to live with his uncle who lived on a nearby farm so Jerry filed an application with the court appointing his uncle as guardian. Assuming that the uncle was competent, suitable, and proper person and not one of bad reputation, should the court grant the application?

49. Use Eighth Decennial. Mr. Louis discovered some heretofore unpublished letters and intended to include those letters in a book. These letters were written by a husband and wife to their children. The children's parents were convicted of treason and ultimately executed. The children attempt to enjoin publication of these letters claiming they are copyrighted. Does the "fair use" doctrine permit use of these materials if it is done in a reasonable manner?

50. Use Eighth Decennial. Sandra and Harry Henry were on a trip across Massachusetts when their car was struck by defendant's vehicle. Sandra was pregnant with viable twin fetuses which were subsequently stillborn. Sandra filed a wrongful death action on behalf of the estates of the two children. Is a stillborn child, a "person" under the Massachusetts Wrongful Death statute?

51. Use Eighth Decennial. A prison inmate was burned over thirty percent of his body when another inmate hurled a "Molotov Cocktail" into his cell. As a result, the inmate was hospitalized for four months, underwent painful skin grafts, and suffered severe nightmares. He was awarded $25,000 for past and future suffering. Were these damages excessive?

52. Use Eighth Decennial. Mary responded to a beauty parlor advertisement for a permanent and wave for only $12.50. The beautician suggested a more expensive and different treatment. Mary agreed. Within a few days her hair became dry and brittle and broke when ever she brushed it. To hide her embarrassment she bought several hair pieces and later took air treatments to stop her hair from breaking off at the scalp. A jury awarded damages of over $2000 for her suffering and out of pocket expenses. Was this award reasonable?

53. Use Eighth Decennial. A New York pharmacist advertised through local newspapers discounts on all drug needs and offered free $2.00 certificates for use with all drug purchases. The State Board of Pharmacy charged that this advertising practice was unethical and a violation of a state regulation prohibiting the advertising of discount prescriptions. Was this regulation found to be unconstitutionally vague?

54. Use Eighth Decennial. As Joe was proceeding down the highway he was passed by a large tractor trailer truck. Almost immediately the tires of the truck began to smoke and shroud the view of the occupants of the cars following behind. The truck driver, noticing the smoke, slowly began to reduce his speed and then stopped in the center lane of the highway. Joe crashed into the rear of the truck. Does Joe's action of continuing to drive into the cloud of smoke constitute negligence?

ASSIGNMENT 2
USE OF TABLES TO CONVERT FROM CENTURY DIGEST SECTION NUMBERS TO DECENNIAL DIGEST KEY NUMBERS

Method:

Refer either to Volume 21 of the First Decennial Digest or to Volume 24 of the Second Decennial Digest. Using the table in either location (they're identical), convert the below-listed Century Digest Section Numbers to appropriate Decennial Digest Key Numbers.

Example:

    QUESTION: Licenses sec. 41
    ANSWER: Animals - 4

Questions:

1. Accord and Satisfaction sec. 15

2. Admiralty sec. 33

3. Adultery sec. 5

4. Animals sec. 96

5. Appeal and Error sec. 1772

6. Appeal and Error sec. 2883

7. Appeal and Error sec. 3676

8. Arrest sec. 17

9. Arson sec. 61

10. Associations sec. 11

11. Attorney and Client sec. 1

12. Attorney and Client sec. 199

13. Bail sec. 363

14. Bailment sec. 77

15. Banks and Banking sec. 331

16. Bankruptcy sec. 735

17. Bastards sec. 51

18. Bastards sec. 158
19. Bastards sec. 211
20. Bills and Notes sec. 1916
21. Bonds sec. 137
22. Burglary sec. 35
23. Carriers sec. 1137
24. Chattel Mortgages sec. 16
25. Chattel Mortgages sec. 215
26. Constitutional Law sec. 778
27. Constitutional Law sec. 884
28. Contracts sec. 517
29. Convicts sec. 19
30. Corporations sec. 163
31. Costs sec. 760
32. Counties sec. 153
33. Courts sec. 804
34. Criminal Law sec. 198
35. Criminal Law sec. 1247
36. Damages sec. 371
37. Death sec. 150
38. Deeds sec. 344
39. Depositions sec. 166
40. Depositions sec. 339
41. Descent and Distribution sec. 197
42. Discovery sec. 55
43. Dismissal and Nonsuit sec. 119

44. Eminent Domain sec. 223
45. Extradition sec. 26
46. Fish sec. 12
47. Guaranty sec. 38
48. Homicide sec. 549
49. Infants sec. 177
50. Insurance sec. 1116
51. Landlord and Tenant sec. 567
52. Mechanics Liens sec. 256
53. Mines and Minerals sec. 135
54. Mortgages sec. 1608
55. Navigable Waters sec. 107
56. Obscenity sec. 16
57. Parent and Child sec. 76
58. Paupers sec. 184
59. Railroads sec. 358
60. Statutes sec. 56
61. Taxation sec. 104
62. Time sec. 19
63. Trusts sec. 379
64. Usury sec. 219
65. Wills sec. 1630

ASSIGNMENT 3
USE OF U.S. SUPREME COURT DIGESTS

Method:

Using either the Lawyers Cooperative Publishing Company, <u>U.S. Supreme Court Digest</u>, <u>Lawyer's Edition</u> or West's <u>U.S. Supreme Court Digest</u>, answer the problems listed below and provide:

- (1) A "Yes" or "No" answer to the question, basing your reply on a relevant digest paragraph.
- (2) The "Lawyers' Edition Digest" Topic and Section Number <u>or</u> the "West's U.S. Digest" Topic and Key Number which covers the digest paragraph which answers the question.
- (3) The complete citation to the case in point using the latest edition of <u>A Uniform System of Citation</u> for proper form.

Example:

QUESTION: Has the United States Supreme Court spoken about the justification for punishing libels according to Illinois law?

ANSWER:
- (1) Yes.
- (2) (a) Lawyers' Edition Digest: Libel and Slander §22
  - (b) West's U.S. Digest: Libel 6 Slander - 141
- (3) <u>Beauharnais v. Illinois</u>, 343 U.S. 250(1952).

Questions:

1. Is the admission of attorneys to practice an "exercise of judicial power?"

2. Does the existence of a statutory right imply the existence of all necessary and appropriate remedies?

3. Does the Elkins Act Forbid solicitation of rebates from carriers by any person, no matter for whose benefit the rebates are sought?

4. Is loss of freight a proper element of damage in a case involving collision of vessels?

5. Can the jurisdiction of federal courts be expanded by judicial interpretation?

6. Is it a valid exercise of a District Court's discretionary authority to decline to hear a declaratory judgment action as a matter of whim or disinclination?

7. Is a bailee who fails to pay a tax on admission fees guilty of embezzlement?

8. Does a father have a constitutionally protected right to the custody, care, and management of his children?

9. Is the sale of home-made liquors, within a state, subject to state control?

10. Is the Federal Kidnapping Act limited to kidnappings for either pecuniary gain or an ultimately illegal purpose?

11. Are lotteries mala in se?

12. Can a person other than a citizen take an oath to support the Constitution of the United States?

13. Is a week a definite period of time, commencing on Sunday and ending on Saturday?

14. Can hearsay be the basis for the issuance of a search warrant?

15. Does the accidental destruction of a house by fire relieve the lessee of liability for rent?

16. X was charged with adultery with Y, a married woman. X claimed as a defense the fact that he was unmarried. Can X be convicted? (Use West's U.S. Digest only).

17. A city in Mississippi closed its public swimming pools rather than attempting to operate them on a desegregated basis. One of five formerly segregated pools was subsequently leased to a private organization and subsequently appeared to be open only to whites. Was this a denial to Negroes of equal protection?

18. An oral confession was used which was made to a doctor at a hospital one hour after the arrest of the defendant who had been shot and had been given two large injections of morphine. Is this in violation of due process?

19. Defendant was convicted in a state prosecution for violation of a public drunkenness statute after the court ruled as a matter of law that chronic alcoholism was not a defense. Was he acquitted on appeal? (Use West's U.S. Digest only).

20. The debt of X to his creditor was discharged in bankruptcy. Is a subsequent promise by X to pay sufficient to revive the debt?

21. Is evidence by comparison of handwritings admissible when the witness had had no previous knowledge of the writings, but is called on to testify merely from a comparison?

22. A contract was signed by one of the parties on Sunday, and delivered to an agent of the other party. The assent and signature of the other party were not given until a weekday. Was the contract void, being in violation of a statute making it penal to do any manner of business on Sunday?

23. A testator gave certain real and personal property to a city in trust, forever, for the purpose of building and supporting two colleges. None of the property purchased therefore was to be sold, ever. Is this void as creating a perpetuity?

24. Is a Texas law constitutional in that it requires osteopaths professing to heal human ailments (by scientific manipulation affecting the nerve centers) to have scientific training?

25. On trial for polygamy, evidence was offered by the defendant to show that polygamous marriage was a part of his religion. Is such evidence admissible?

26. Are punitive damages authorized by Alabama law when there is a willful and malicious wrong?

27. May a witness in federal criminal prosecution be asked leading questions if the inference which will be drawn from the question is factually true?

28. Is the enactment of Workmen's Compensation laws (which do away with the fellow servant and assumption of risk doctrines) a valid exercise of legislative power?

29. May a state arbitrarily deny admission to practice law?

30. X, a guest in the office of a hotel was advanced upon by an assailant with a deadly weapon. X claims he had a right to remain where he was and to resist the attack and do whatever was necessary to save his life or protect himself from great bodily harm, and that there was no duty to retreat. Was this valid even to the point of committing homicide himself?

31. In federal court, can a defendant be tried on charges that are not made in the indictment against him?

32. Does a state have power to require a license and to regulate the business of an employment agent?

33. Will the federal courts grant relief in the form of a declaratory judgment where the record does not disclose an actual controversy?

34. Would a zoning ordinance which is clearly arbitrary and unreasonable and without substantial relation to public health, safety, or general welfare be declared unconstitutional?

35. Can a judgment be collaterally attacked? (Use L. Ed. only.)

36. May the government, by mandamus, lawfully proceed against a corporation it has chartered, to compel the performance of any duty imposed by the charter or statute?

37. A contract exists between a wharf and a city by which the city becomes part owner of the wharf, which ownership is inalienable except by a four-fifths vote of the qualified voters. Does this preclude the exercise by the city of the right of eminent domain to acquire title to the property?

38. Is a particular form of words essential to create a trust, provided there is reasonable certainty as to the property, the objects, and the beneficiaries?

39. May a grantor in deed conveying real property, signed and acknowledged, with a blank for the name of the grantee, authorize another party to fill in the blank?

40. A statute of state A required all marriages to be entered into in the presence of a magistrate or clergyman and required that the marriage be preceded by a license. The statute was silent as to whether a marriage not complying with its provisions was void. X and Y did not follow this formal procedure but lived together as husband and wife. They claim a common law marriage and that, therefore, their marriage is valid. Are they correct?

41. X had $1,000.00 cash and owned a home with a $500.00 mortgage on it. The mortgage was due Oct. 1, 1971. Y desperately needed $1,000.00 and persuaded X to lend $1,000.00 to him. It was agreed that the $1,000.00 with interest would be repaid on Sept. 1, 1971 in plenty of time for X to pay the $500.00 due on the mortgage. Y failed to pay. As a result the mortgage on X's home was foreclosed and X forced to move out of it. X sues Y for the $1,000.00 together with interest and the additional damages caused, including the moving expenses and rent X was required to pay as a result of being forced from his home. Is Y's claim correct that X can only recover interest for his delay as damages?

42. Does the fact that an alien plaintiff resides in the same state as defendant deprive the federal courts from having jurisdiction of the case?

43. Green was convicted of a crime and he appeals. He had been tried previously for the same offense but the jury had been unable to agree. One of his contentions on appeal of his conviction was that the second trial violated the constitutional provision against double jeopardy. Is Green correct?

44. The legislature of state A passed a special act granting X a divorce from Y. Is this divorce valid even though not given by a court of competent jurisdiction?

45. If an attorney had been appointed by the court to represent an accused, must the attorney do so?

46. X, a nonresident of Massachusetts, had an automobile accident while driving in Massachusetts. In this accident the automobile of Y was damaged. Y, a resident of Massachusetts, desires to sue X in the Massachusetts courts. A Massachusetts statute authorizes service on a nonresident motorist by delivery of process to the registrar and mailing a copy to nonresident. Is this statute constitutional?

47. Defendant applied for a writ of habeas corpus on the ground that the judge failed to ask the defendant represented by attorney whether defendant had anything to say before sentence was imposed. Is this sufficient error for the court to grant the writ?

48. John White and Bill Smith were members of a religious sect that believed in polygamy. John moved to Ogden, Utah, from Arizona with several of his wives. Later Mary White, another of John's wives, who remained for a while in Arizona, was brought to Ogden by Bill Smith. Can Smith be convicted under the federal statute making interstate transportation of a woman for an immoral purpose an offense?

49. The public health law of state X provides that any doctor practicing medicine after being convicted of a felony shall be guilty of a misdemeanor. Is this provision valid?

50. The federal government has authority over navigable waters. In order to be classed as a navigable water, must the waterway be in fact navigable rather than susceptible to navigation in ordinary conditions?

51. May the positive testimony of a witness to a particular fact, uncontradicted by anyone, be disregarded if his manner creates doubts of his sincerity? (Use L.Ed. only)

52. Did the Constitution of South Carolina, which was adopted in 1868, permit a married woman to make a will? (Use L.Ed. only)

53. X was convicted in federal court for stealing mail while it was in custody of the Post Office. X appeals on the grounds that the evidence shows that the mail alleged to have been stolen had been deposited in addressee's box and therefore was not in the custody of the government. Will the case be reversed on appeal?

54. One J. H. Chisholm conveyed certain real property belonging to J. H. Chism to X by means of a written instrument to which he signed his own name, that is, J. H. Chisholm. Is this forgery?

55. X had for many years occupied certain public lands of the U.S. Government. Subsequently, the federal government granted a plot of land to Y. This plot included that land occupied by X. X claims to have obtained the government's land by adverse possession and that the grant of the land by the government to Y is therefore void. Is this contention correct?

56. Defendant was charged in federal district court under its admiralty jurisdiction with the commission of a crime. As a defense he alleged that by treaty between the United States and Great Britain the boundary line between this country and Canada runs through the center of the Great Lakes and consequently the Great Lakes cannot be considered "high seas." Is defendant correct?

57. Must courts take judicial notice that late in 1929 there was a great decline in values of securities and other properties and that a depression commenced, without the necessity of offering evidence in court to prove this contention?

58. A took from B a mortgage on certain real estate containing sandstone quarries which, however, had not been sufficiently worked to determine their extent or value. B, C, and D certified that they had resided in the neighborhood for 20 years and that in their best opinion and judgment the value of the quarry was 150 per cent more than the loan. Upon foreclosure the land brought less than one-sixth the amount of the loan. A sued B, C, and D for damages caused him by their fraud and misrepresentation. Can A recover?

59. Does the miscegenation statute adopted by Virginia to prevent marriages between persons solely on basis of racial classification violate the equal protection and due process clauses of the Fourteenth Amendment?

60. Defendant was convicted in state court in New Mexico for involuntary manslaughter. At the trial evidence was admitted concerning results of a blood test made by using blood withdrawn from defendant by physician while defendant was unconscious after the accident. Defendant attacks the conviction on the constitutional ground that a defendant may not be compelled to be a witness against himself and that as a result he was deprived of his liberty without due process of law. Will defendant win a reversal of the case on this ground?

61. The Georgia House of Representatives refused to seat a duly elected representative because of his statements attacking the policy of the Federal Government in Vietnam and the Selective Service laws. Was this refusal unconstitutional based on denial of freedom of speech.

62. A Pennsylvania statute prohibits the operation over Pennsylvania highways of any motor vehicle carrying any other vehicle over the head of the operator of the carrier vehicle. Is this statute unconstitutional under the Commerce Clause of the U.S. Constitution insofar as it applies to vehicles engaged in interstate commerce?

63. Bill, a citizen of Florida, was convicted of using diving equipment to take sponges from the Gulf of Mexico off the coast of Florida in violation of a Florida statute. The acts occurred on the high seas outside the territorial limits of the United States. Bill appeals to the U.S. Supreme Court on grounds that this criminal state statute cannot have extraterritorial operation outside the State of Florida. Will Bill win on appeal?

64. Susan was born in New York of naturalized Swedish parents. While still a child Susan and her parents returned to Sweden and resumed their Swedish citizenship. After reaching the age of majority Susan returned to the U.S. and claimed U.S. citizenship. Is Susan a citizen of U.S.?

ASSIGNMENT 4
USE OF THE MODERN FEDERAL PRACTICE DIGEST
AND WEST'S FEDERAL PRACTICE DIGEST, 2d

Method:

Refer to the Modern Federal Practice Digest or to West's Federal Practice Digest, 2d. The date the case was decided is given in parenthesis at the end of each problem. In relation to each problem, provide:

(1) A "Yes" or "No" answer to the question contained in the problem.

(2) The Topic and Key Number under which you found the digest paragraph that answered (1), supra.

(3) The complete citation to the case in point using the latest edition of A Uniform System of Citation for proper form.

Example:

QUESTION: Presume that a federal taxpayer has no office, no telephone, no furniture, no seal, and does not hold any meetings. Do these facts establish that the taxpayer is not an association taxable as a corporation?
ANSWER:
(1) No
(2) Internal Revenue - 815
(3) Keating-Snyder Trust v. Commissioner, 126 F.2d 860 (5th Cir. 1942).

Questions:

1. According to the United States Court of Appeals for the Seventh Circuit, are the standards employed in reviewing a police officer's assessment of probable cause for arrest without a warrant for a criminal charge the same as those employed in reviewing a magistrate's assessment prior to issuing a warrant? (1973)

2. Presume that a trustee in bankruptcy institutes actions against two parties to recover pre-bankruptcy accounts receivable. Presume, too, that even after notice, neither party appears in any hearings before the referee in bankruptcy and does not comply with the bankruptcy court's orders. Will such parties be deemed to have consented to or waived objection to the jurisdiction of the bankruptcy court and to be subject to a default judgment? (1973)

3. May the trier of fact consider custom and usage of similar banks as evidence in determining the duties of bank directors, according to the Oklahoma federal trial court? (1972)

4. According to a Washington federal court, was the Federal Food, Drug and Cosmetic Act of 1938 intended to be liberally construed so as to carry out its beneficient purpose? (1948)

5. Under Pennsylvania law, may a court of equity, once it has properly assumed jurisdiction, grant legal relief in the form of money damages? (1973)

6. According to the federal appellate court in the District of Columbia, can the Federal Rules of Civil Procedure have the effect, as rules of court, of repealing prior inconsistent statutory provisions? (1973)

7. Under Georgia law, is the enforcement for the forfeiture of gambling devices a proceeding in personam? (1952)

8. According to Michigan law, is the wife obligated to contribute her services to her husband and follow him in his choice of domicile? (1940)

9. Does the federal trial court have jurisdiction to determine controversies between Indian tribes and their members in actions by, against, or involving Indians? (1971)

10. According to the New York federal trial court, may a plaintiff be allowed to ignore an essentially alternative decision on the merits from a judgment of the state court and in the United States court seek a de novo determination of the merits of his constitutional claim? (1973)

11. Has a federal court in Illinois declared the federal kidnapping statute unconstitutional? (1940)

12. Under Mississippi law, is it essential in a suit for malicious prosecution that either the prosecution has been terminated in favor of the accused or that the prosecution has been abandoned? (1973)

13. Has a federal court in Minnesota ever spoken under their power to make or authorize improvements of navigable waters, regarding the necessity, the character and extent of a given improvement? (1941)

14. According to the Nebraska federal trial court, may a public officer charge the person benefited by a service, for additional compensation, absent express statutory authorization? (1946)

15. May the doctrine of res ipsa loquitur be applied under Idaho law in a malpractice action against a physician? (1973)

16. According to federal courts in Delaware, do the IRS records made during an audit of an individual's income tax liability constitute an "investigatory file compiled for law enforcement purposes" within the meaning of the Freedom of Information Act? (1973)

17. Has any Texas federal court spoken about the exhaustion of administrative remedies as a condition precedent to exercising one's right of action in a suit to quiet title of a leasehold interest? (1961)

18. Under Minnesota law, where a contract case is submitted to a jury on the theory of negligence alone, does the Minnesota 6-year limitation on contract actions apply? (1973)

19. Has the United States Court of Claims determined that the Uniform Commercial Code did alter pre-existing law as to a surety's rights of subrogation? (1970)

20. Has any federal court ever passed on the effect to First Amendment rights of free speech concerning the White House restrictions on demonstrations which put a damper on the use of streets and public places for demonstration purposes? (1973)

21. Between vendors and purchasers of real property, if the title is not marketable, must the purchaser accept the conveyance even though she may have to defend it in subsequent litigation, according to the Michigan federal district court? (1962)

22. According to the Second Circuit's interpretation of 18 U.S.C. § 922(a)(3), is scienter an element of the statute making it unlawful to transport into one's state of residence a firearm or other weapons purchased outside the state? (1973)

23. Has a United States District Court for the Virgin Islands ever passed on whether a zoning regulation modification permitting the construction of a shopping center is "spot zoning" when it is in furtherance of the convenience of the community and in accordance with the comprehensive plan? (1968)

24. In an action for deportation, does the Fifth Circuit hold that improper entry into the United States will not be made retroactively legal by a subsequent lawful entry? (1973)

25. Is ignorance of an available remedy an excuse for delay in bringing an action? (1969)

26. Is the collection and arbitration of claims "the practice of law?" (1940)

27. Does a bank have the right to countermand a traveler's check which it has issued?

28. Does a purchaser of a cemetery lot acquire a property right which the law recognizes? (1950)

29. Does the doctrine of confusion of goods apply when the quantity and value of each owner's portion can be identified? (1956)

30. Is a lawyer an "officer of the court" within the meaning of the statute empowering courts to punish as contempt misbehavior of its officers in their official transactions? (1956)

31. Is a published imputation or charge of adultery libelous per se? (1951)

32. Does the designation of a tract of land on a plat as "beach" show an intention of the platter to dedicate the "beach" area to the general public as a beach? (1941)

33. In a prosecution for keeping a house of ill fame resorted to for the purpose of prostitution or lewdness, is evidence of the general reputation of the establishment admissible? (1956)

34. Under Tennessee law, is a hospital strictly liable for administering a transfusion of blood which is infected with serum hepatitis? (1975)

35. Do members of the public in general have a common law right of access to public records or files? (1951)

36. Is a sheriff an "officer of the court," even though in some of his duties he is commonly known as a public official? (1950)

37. Does the use of force to obtain a legitimate union demand for higher wages evidence the requisite intent for a conviction of extortion? (1973)

38. Is loss of prospective profits a proper measure of damages for failure to perform a publishing contract? (1972)

39. In the event of death at sea, does the master of the ship have absolute discretion to determine the place of burial? (1941)

40. Contractor agreed with X to complete a building by a certain date. The agreement also provided for liquidated damages of $50 per day for each day of delay beyond completion date. There was a delay of 94 days. Contractor claimed the delay was not his fault. X sent contractor a letter saying he intended to deduct $50 per day from contract price for each day's delay for which contractor was at fault. Later X sent check to contractor for the contract balance less $50 for 40 days with notation to that effect. Contractor cashed the check and sues X for $2,000.00. X claims there has been an accord and satisfaction. Will contractor win his case? (1958)

41. Is there a common law right of arbitration? (1955)

42. Brown who was a patient in a hospital in Minnesota planned to have an operation on his left leg. The surgeon, without Brown's consent, operated on the patient's right leg instead. Did this constitute assault and battery? (1955)

43. Smith came to the parking lot of defendant and became abusive. Defendant ordered Smith to leave. Smith advanced toward defendant as if to harm him. Defendant shot Smith. Smith has sued defendant for damages. May Smith recover? (1967)

44. Is it ethical for a member of the bar to represent the accused even if he knows the accused is guilty? (1959)

45. A village passed an ordinance prohibiting the flight of aircraft over the village at an altitude of less than 1,000 feet. Is the ordinance constitutional? (1952)

46. Sarah and Spencer were born in the United States at the time their father was a duly accredited diplomatic representative of the French Republic to the United States. Were they citizens of the United States as a result of being born in the United States? (1942)

47. An interstate pipeline carrier received its entire supply of natural gas from outside of state X. It made direct sales within state X to industrial and domestic users. It claimed that since it was engaged in interstate commerce it was not subject to the rate regulations of the state X. Is the carrier's contention correct? (1951)

48. The Hooters, a well-known fraternal organization, had been in existence for many years. Another fraternal organization known as The Hooters of Slippery Elm was recently organized. The Hooters seek an injunction restraining The Hooters of Slippery Elm from using this name. Will the injunction be granted? (1951)

49. Where it is necessary to determine what the common law is, American courts will, under certain circumstances, look at the decisions of English courts. Does it make any difference whether the pertinent English decisions were rendered before or after the American Revolution? (1951)

50. The city had an ordinance which declared an automobile with two or more traffic summonses unpaid and outstanding against it to be a public nuisance and provided for the impounding of the automobile by the police department. Under this ordinance the automobile of X had been impounded because of two unpaid summonses for overtime parking violation. X sues the city for damages alleging a conspiracy of the city to violate his civil rights. Will X prevail? (1959)

51. The Federal Firearms Act made it an offense for one who has previously been convicted of a crime of violence to transport a pistol in interstate commerce. X, who had been convicted of a crime of violence prior to the passage of the Federal Firearms Act, did, after the passage of the act, transport a pistol in interstate commerce. X was charged and convicted in the trial court for violating the act and he appeals contending that as applied to him the act is unconstitutional under the <u>ex post facto</u> provision of the U.S. Constitution as he had been convicted of the crime of violence prior to the passage of the Federal Firearms Act. Will X prevail? (1963)

52. X, on the advice of his attorney, pled guilty to a charge of burglary for which he was sentenced to prison. X now claims he was denied the effective assistance of counsel in violation of his constitutional rights on the grounds that his attorney at the same time represented the victims of the burglary in an unrelated civil matter and that the attorney never informed X about these clients. Will X's contention be sustained? (1966)

53. Do courts have the power to punish one for contempt for an act committed in the presence of the court without further proof of these facts before a jury? (1949)

54. Will the fact that a work lacks artistic merit prevent it from being copyrighted? (1970)

55. X conveyed to Y a one-half acre tract which was being cut off from a thirty acre tract. Y covenanted not to, without X's permission, erect any buildings other than a filling station on the tract. X sold the balance of the thirty acre tract to B. Without B's permission Y built a grocery store on the one-half acre tract despite the covenant. May B recover damages from Y? (1944)

56. In a voluntary manslaughter prosecution based on circumstantial evidence would it be proper for the jury to consider the evidence offered by the defendant that the criminal defendant's conduct was such that he did not flee or resist arrest? (1947)

57. X owned a home in state A in which his wife and family lived. His work required him to be in state B so he purchased a house there and lived in it. Is X's domicile presumed to be in state A? (1945)

58. Can one have an easement in his own property? (1956)

59. Brown's house was damaged by a shock caused by an explosion set off in the course of construction of a dam by an agency of the federal government. Was this particular act of taking of private property for public use an exercise of power of eminent domain so that the federal government should pay Brown for the damages? (1950)

60. X had a life insurance policy. The policy provided that change of beneficiaries would take effect only on the endorsement of the change on the policy by the insurance company. X executed the papers provided by the company for change of beneficiary from A to B. X sent the papers and insurance policy to the insurance company's agent who in turn forwarded them to the company. These papers were received by the company after the insurance company received notice of X's death. B claims that he is entitled to the proceeds of the policy under the equitable doctrine that equity regards that as done which ought to be done. Is B's contention correct? (1940)

61. X was a clerk in a hotel. As a part of his wages he received free use of a room. After a time his duties were changed so that he was also an auditor. When X discovered that this change did not result in higher compensation he resigned. The management then locked him out of his room. X sues the hotel for the value of his personal property in the room, the unpaid wages claimed to be due, and for damages resulting from the false imprisonment he suffered as a result of his being locked out of his room. May X recover damages for false imprisonment? (1955)

62. Widow Brown was confined to bed in her home as a result of an automobile accident. She was attended by a practical nurse and a medical doctor. This was during very cold winter months. She was notified that the gas bill was delinquent. The gas company was notified of her condition, that she lacked funds, and that her son would pay the bill. The gas company agreed to continue service up until a certain date, provided the delinquent gas bill was paid by that time. The bill was not paid. The gas company discontinued service. As a result of the cold condition of the house, Widow Brown contracted pneumonia. Subsequently Widow Brown sued the gas company for damages resulting from their act of turning off the gas which caused her to contract pneumonia. May Widow Brown recover? (1940)

63. D received a suspended sentence for carrying a concealed weapon and was placed in prison for another crime. D applied for writ of habeas corpus on the ground that the conviction for carrying a concealed weapon was invalid. Will the writ be granted? (1963)

64. X located and held a mining claim. X was not a citizen of the United States nor had he declared his intention to become one. X conveyed his claim to Y who also was not a citizen nor had he declared his intention to become one. Z filed a location on the same mining claim. Subsequently Y became a citizen of the United States. X never became a citizen of U.S. Z brings an action against Y contending that Z's claim is good and that Y's claim is void because the statute provides that mining claims can be made only "by citizens of United States and those who have declared their intentions to become such." Is Y's mining claim valid? (1942)

ASSIGNMENT 5
USE OF POPULAR (CASE) NAME TABLES

Method:

    For the popular case names listed, and using the sources specified below, provide:

(1) The case name, if possible, volume, reporter and page number of the highest court. Parallel cites are not necessary.

(2) The sources wherein found, by underlining the productive sources and "slashing through" the unproductive sources, in accord with the example below. Use the following abbreviations in the order here given:
S =   Shepard's Acts and Cases by Popular Names: Federal and State.
A =   Popular Name Table in the Sixth Decennial Digest of the American Digest System.
F =   Popular Name Table in the Federal Digest.

Example:

    QUESTION: Sick Chicken Case
    ANSWER: (1) A.L.A Schechter Poultry Corp. v. United States, 295 U.S. 495
                    (2) S A F

Questions:

1. Ambrose Light Case

2. Atlanta School Case

3. Bad Egg Case

4. Baltimore Club Whiskey Case

5. Beef Refund Suit

6. Bell-Ringer Case

7. Betty Boop Case

8. Captive Audience Case

9. Corned Beef Sandwich Case

10. Dairy Queen Case (Maine)

11. Dance Hall Nuisance Case
12. Detectaphone Case
13. Elevator Leg Case
14. Exhaust Fumes Case
15. Fish Net Case
16. Gambler's Telephone Case
17. Heifer-Milch-Cow Case
18. Horse Shoe Case
19. Hound Dog Case
20. Indian Canoe Case
21. Influence Sale Case
22. Jack O'Lantern Case
23. Jane Froman Case
24. Japanese Curfew Case
25. Jig Saw Puzzle Case
26. Jim-Jam-Jems Case
27. John Deere Case
28. John L's Case
29. Junk Business Regulation Case
30. Kickback Tax Case
31. Kicked Can Case
32. Kirk Soap Case
33. Lead Pencil Case
34. Macaroni Case
35. Marchie Tiger Case
36. Mrs. Alexander's Cotton Case

37. Mule Case (Missouri)
38. Murder by Fright Case
39. Narrow Bridge Case
40. Oklahoma State Capitol Removal Case
41. Original Package Case
42. Ouija Board Cases
43. Paper Hangers' Case
44. Peg O'My Heart Case
45. Police Pension Case
46. Quadra Case
47. Quicksilver Mine Case
48. Retired Judges Pay Case
49. Sani-Flush Case
50. Save the Baby Case
51. Selma March Case
52. Side-End Line Case
53. Sixty Pipes of Brandy Case
54. Snoozing Case
55. Snuff Case
56. Spiked Shoe Cases
57. Tar Kettle Case
58. Upper Berth Case
59. Vinegar Case
60. Whiskey Case
61. Wild Goose Case
62. X-Ray Injury Case
63. Zoo Case

ASSIGNMENT 6
USE OF THE TABLES OF CASES OF THE AMERICAN DIGEST SYSTEM

Method:

Check the Table of Cases of the appropriate portion of the American Digest System. Locate the following cases and provide:

    (1)   The West citation only. Do not provide parallel, memo, cert. or rehearing citations.

    (2)   The first-listed Topic and its Key Number(s), if any, after the case citation.

Example:

    QUESTION: Heinbach v. Heinbach (1918)
    ANSWER: (1) 202 S.W. 1123
                  (2) Acknowledgement - 54

Questions:

1. Adoptive Parents v. Superior Court in and For Maricopa County (1970)

2. Apter v. Richardson (1973)

3. Bee-Hive Lodge No. 105 v. Durham (1952)

4. Bickell v. Moraio (1933)

5. Boies v. Dovico (1965)

6. Buffi v. Ferri (1970)

7. Cain v. Meade County (1929)

8. Capuano v. Jacobs (1969)

9. Carse v. Marsh (1922)

10. City of Hazard v. Eversole (1939)

11. Coleman v. Peyton (1965)

12. Craven v. Atkins (1949)

13. Daugherty v. Feland (1916)

14. Dobson v. Apex Coal Co. (1939)

15. Dorsey v. Petrott (1940)
16. The Eagle (1934)
17. Efstathion v. Saucer (1947)
18. Escobar v. State (1965)
19. Eustace v. Speckhart (1973)
20. Ex Parte Overturff (1953)
21. Faulk v. Soberanes (1961)
22. Feyerchak v. Hiatt (1948)
23. Gish v. Scott (1961)
24. Grasse v. Snyder (1951)
25. Gray v. Love (1935)
26. Groover v. Terrell (1919)
27. Hagerty v. Clement (1940)
28. Heil v. Rule (1931)
29. Holman v. Oriental Refinery (1965)
30. Hurst v. Davis (1963)
31. Hustmyre v. Waters (1937)
32. Idol v. Street (1951)
33. In re Ratkowsky's Will (1964)
34. Inos v. Winspear (1861)
35. Ivanhoe Grand Lodge A T & A M of Colo. v. Most Worshipful Grand Lodge of Ancient Free and Accepted Masons of Colo. (1952)
36. James River Bank v. Hansen (1927)
37. Julian v. Harris (1973)
38. King v. Flemming (1961)
39. Korf v. Itten (1917)
40. Krupp v. Taylor (1959)

41. Lee County v. James (1937)
42. Levin v. Sohn (1948)
43. Locigno v. City of Chicago (1961)
44. Merryman v. Sears (1937)
45. Mile High Poultry Farms v. Frazier (1945)
46. Monji Uyemura v. Carr (1938)
47. Nimmo v. Fitzgerald (1927)
48. Osborne v. Cox (1925)
49. Pickering v. Richardson (1910)
50. Quinlan v. Bussiere (1965)
51. Ramsel v. Dreier (1933)
52. Roskom v. Bodart (1951)
53. Sewell v. Thrailkill (1945)
54. Southern Seating & Cabinet Co. v. Gladish (1916)
55. State ex rel Quigg v. Liquidator of Sewer Districts of St. Louis County (1943)
56. Suhomlin v. United States (1972)
57. Taylor v. O'Barr (1942)
58. Tener v. Hill (1965)
59. United States v. Varlack (1955)
60. Velez v. Christian (1973)
61. Wingard v. Randall (1959)
62. Xidis v. City of Gulfport (1954)
63. Young v. Davis (1935)
64. Younghusband v. Kurlash Co. (1938)
65. Zywiec v. City of South St. Paul (1951)

ASSIGNMENT 7
USE OF THE TABLE OF CASES OF THE UNITED STATES SUPREME COURT DIGEST (West Pub. Co.)

Method:

Refer to the Table of Cases of the United States Supreme Court Digest (West Pub. Co.) and locate the following cases. For each, provide:

(1) The official (U.S.) citation to the full opinion. Do not provide parallel, memo, cert. or rehearing citations.

(2) The first-listed Topic and Key Number, if any, immediately following the case citation.

Example:

QUESTION: Mills v. Duryee
ANSWER: (1) U.S. (7 Cranch) 481
(2) Debt, Action of - 12

Questions:

1. Adler v. Fenton
2. Aquilino v. United States
3. Archawski v. Hanioti
4. Barnett v. Kinney
5. Bond v. Floyd
6. Buchanan v. City of Litchfield
7. The Charles A. Owen
8. Chemgas v. Tynan
9. Ciucci v. Illinois
10. Collier v. Stanbrough
11. Cowperthwaite v. Jones
12. De Bary v. Arthur
13. Dill v. Ebey

14. _Erskine v. Hohnbach_
15. _Ex parte Dainard_
16. _Ex parte Huey_
17. _Ex parte Zellner_
18. _Fisher v. Shropshire_
19. _Foster v. Pryor_
20. _Frank v. Maryland_
21. _Ghio v. Moore_
22. _Gomillion v. Lightfoot_
23. _Hanna v. Maas_
24. _Huff v. Ford_
25. _Hull v. Burr_
26. _Iasigi v. Van De Carr_
27. _In Re Loving_
28. _International Bank v. Sherman_
29. _Jaquith v. Rowley_
30. _Jeter v. Hewitt_
31. _Johnston v. Laflin_
32. _The Keokuk_
33. _Kilgarlin v. Hill_
34. _Kinsella v. Krueger_
35. _Leib v. Bolton_
36. _Lyon v. Singer_
37. _McBee v. United States_
38. _McKimm v. Riddle_
39. _Moelle v. Sherwood_
40. _Neil v. Biggers_

41. Nutt v. Minor
42. Omaha Hotel Co. v. Wade
43. Owen v. Dudley
44. Potts v. Chumasero
45. Procunier v. Atchley
46. Quicksall v. Michigan
47. Read v. City of Plattsmouth
48. Reaves v. Ainsworth
49. Rice v. Sanger
50. Sarlls v. United States
51. Sansom v. Ball
52. Scott v. Paisley
53. Tenney v. Brandhove
54. Town of Mineral Point v. Lee
55. Trbovich v. United Mine Workers of America
56. Urquhart v. Brown
57. United States v. Mosely
58. Vachon v. New Hampshire
59. Villalobos v. United States
60. Violett v. Patton
61. Willing v. Rinenstock
62. Wilwording v. Swenson
63. Yee Hem v. United States
64. Zahn v. Board of Public Works of City of Los Angeles
65. Zartarian v. Billings

ASSIGNMENT 8
USE OF THE TABLE OF CASES OF THE DIGESTS OF
UNITED STATES SUPREME COURT REPORTS, LAWYERS' EDITION

Method:

Refer to the Table of Cases of the Digest of United States Supreme Court Reports, Lawyers' Edition (Lawyers' Co-op Publ. Co.). Locate the below-listed cases and provide:

(1) The official (U.S.) citation to the full opinion, if any. Do not provide parallel, memo, cert. or rehearing citations.

(2) The first-listed Topic and Section Number, if any, immediately following the case citation.

Example:

QUESTION: Mitchum v. Foster
ANSWER: (1) 407 U.S. 225
(2) Civil Rights §12.5

Questions:

1. The Adeline

2. Alcorcha v. California

3. The Anastasiadis v. Little John

4. Bourjois v. Chapman

5. Calder v. Bull

6. Chemgas v. Tynan

7. Deitch v. Wiggins

8. Di Piero v. Pennsylvania

9. Duncan v. Louisiana

10. Erskine v. Hohnback

11. Ex parte Dainard

12. FHA v. Burr

13. Ferguson v. Dent

14. Fisher v. Shropshire
15. Ghio v. Moore
16. Goldsborough v. Orr
17. The Great Republic
18. Groppi v. Wisconsin
19. Hanna v. Maas
20. Hornsby v. United States
21. Illinois v. Allen
22. Jenkins v. McKeithen
23. Kaiser v. New York
24. The Keokuk
25. Kowalski v. Chandler
26. Lehnbeuter v. Holthaus
27. Loving v. Virginia
28. McDonald v. Magruder
29. MacDougall v. Green
30. Moelle v. Sherwood
31. NLRB v. C & C Plywood Corp.
32. Natarelli v. United States
33. Neil v. Biggers
34. Ohio ex rel. Lloyd v. Dollison
35. Olberding v. Illinois Cent. R. Co.
36. Orenstein & K. Aktiengesellschaft v. Koppel Industrial Car & Equipment Co.
37. Parsons v. Armor
38. Pierce v. Society of the Sisters
39. Potts v. Chumasero

40. Quinlan v. Green County
41. Reaves v. Ainsworth
42. Roberts v. Cay
43. Rohde v. O'Donnell
44. Rosenbloom v. Metromedia Inc.
45. Sampeyreac v. United States
46. Scott v. Ellery
47. Scott v. Paisley
48. Ship v. Toledo
49. Stinson Canning Co. v. United States
50. Taglianetti v. United States
51. Texas & P.R. Co. v. American Tie & Timber Co.
52. Trbovich v. United Mine Workers of America
53. Twin Falls Salmon River Land & Water Co. v. Caldwell
54. The Umbria
55. Urquhart v. Brown
56. Vachon v. New Hampshire
57. Vitoratos v. Yacobucci
58. Vose v. Bronson
59. Whittington v. Pegelow
60. Winton v. Amos
61. Wisconsin v. Yoder
62. Yazoo & M. V. R. Co. v. Mullins
63. Yeaton v. Fry
64. Zartarian v. Billings
65. Zuber v. Allen

ASSIGNMENT 9
USE OF THE TABLE OF CASES OF
WEST'S MODERN FEDERAL PRACTICE DIGEST
AND FEDERAL PRACTICE DIGEST 2d

Method:

Refer to the Table of Cases of the Modern Federal Practice Digest and the Federal Practice Digest 2d. Locate the below-listed cases and provide:

(1) The latest edition of the Uniform System of Citation for proper form. Do not cite reversing, affirming, memo, or cert. cases.

(2) The first-listed Topic and Key Number, if any, immediately following the case citation.

Example:

QUESTION: McGraw-Edition Co. v. Central Transformer Core.
ANSWER: (1) 308F.2d 70 (8th Cir. 1962)
         (2) Appeal and Error 198

Questions:

1. The A. H. Quinby
2. Aalund v. Marshall
3. Alexander v. Silverman
4. Audivox, Inc. v. F.T.C.
5. Baldwin Rubber Co. v. Paine & Williams Co.
6. Behaney v. Travelers Ins. Co.
7. Berglann v. The Winona
8. Carey v. Settle
9. Cassell v. Taylor
10. In re Chagra
11. Colvin v. Woods
12. Delesdernier v. O'Rourke & Warren Co.
13. Denison v. Udall

14. Doble v. Buck
15. In Re Doty, Inc.
16. In re Entler
17. Eyman v. Alford
18. Faubus v. United States
19. Ferguson v. Cardwell
20. Fianza Cia Nav S A v. Benz
21. G & W Towing Co. v. Barges CB-1
22. Gliptis v. United States
23. Gray v. City of Santa Fe
24. Harried v. United States
25. Hurst v. Looney
26. Iannelli v. Long
27. Johnson v. Bockman
28. Junso Fujii v. Dulles
29. Justh v. Holtman
30. Kec v. Ribicoff
31. Knoshaug v. Pollman
32. Lester v. Isbrandtsen Co.
33. Mack v. 48 Vesey Street Corporation
34. Marx v. Shiya
35. Mauran v. Mary Fletcher Hospital
36. Memphis Memorial Park v. McCann
37. Mississippi Power Co. v. City of Aberdeen
38. Morgan v. Richardson
39. NLRB v. Colten

40. NLRB v. Evans Packing Co.
41. Neggo v. United States
42. Orrie v. United States
43. Oy v. Haff
44. Patskan v. Buchkoe
45. Pence v. Tobriner
46. Perkins v. Remillard
47. Petition of Gogate
48. Quibell v. United States
49. In re Robertson
50. Robinson v. McCorkie
51. Rochford v. Volatile
52. S.S. Audrey J. Luckenbach
53. Safeway Stores v. Fannan
54. Snitkin v. United States
55. Southall v. Union Steel Co.
56. Thoms v. Heffernan
57. Turzillo v. CIR
58. U.S. v. Puchi
59. Uhlhorn Const. Co. v. Owens
60. United States v. Swank
61. Updike v. West
62. Vanhook v. Craven
63. Weil Clothing Co. v. Glasser
64. Xerox Corp. v. Nashau Corp.
65. Yearwood v. United States

ASSIGNMENT 10
JUDICIAL DEFINITIONS OF VARIOUS WORDS AND PHRASES

Method:

Using the four indicated sources, locate a judicial definition of the word or phrase stated in the problem. Give only the name of the first case cited, if any, in each source. If none, state "Not Listed."

	Sources:	(1)	Words and Phrases (W&P)
		(2)	Federal Digest (FD)
		(3)	Modern Federal Practice Digest (MFPD)
		(4)	U.S. Supreme Court Digest (West) (WD)

Example:

QUESTION:	Fence		
ANSWER:	(1)	(W&P)	Bollenback v. United States
	(2)	(FD)	Page Steel & Wire Co. v. Smith Bros. Hardware Co.
	(3)	(MFPD)	Bollenback v. United States
	(4)	(WD)	Bollenback v. United States

Questions:

1. Abnormal

2. Acre

3. Affecting

4. Alien

5. Babied Cut

6. Behavior

7. Carrying on Business

8. Clear and Present Danger

9. Contemporaneous

10. De Novo

11. Death

12. Debauchery

13. Discrimination

14. Distribution of Assets
15. Easement
16. Employee
17. Enlisted Man
18. Entrapment
19. Fief
20. First-in-first-out (Rule)
21. Garnishee
22. Gift *Inter Vivos*
23. Gratuitous
24. Greenbacks
25. Halogen
26. Highest
27. Husband
28. Incorporating
29. Inter Vivos Gift
30. Invidiousness per se
31. Jekyll and Hyde
32. Joint
33. Just Damages for Delay
34. Kick-back
35. Kid
36. Lascivious
37. Left
38. Magic Words Doctrine
39. Member
40. Mens Rea

41. Merchantable Abstract of Record
42. Merger
43. Need
44. Next of Kin
45. Ordinary Care
46. Outlaw
47. Oyer
48. Poppycock
49. Poverty
50. Quorum
51. Refuses to Answer
52. Rely
53. Restraint on Interstate Commerce
54. Salt Lick
55. Signature
56. Subrogation
57. Sunstroke
58. Thalweg Rule
59. Ultra Vires
60. Unusual
61. Venditioni Exponas
62. Vicinage
63. Waiver
64. X-Rays
65. Yield

ASSIGNMENT 11
THEME AND DRILL PROBLEMS FOR DIGESTS FOR COURT DECISIONS

The problems that follow are designed to acquaint you with the many features and impressive scope of digests. To answer these problems requires analytical thinking on your part. It also often requires you to think like an editor as you try to determine how various words and phrases in an index might provide references to the sources you are researching.

Some hints to help you along the way should make use of the digests almost enjoyable. When the directions ask you to use the most specific digest available, be sure to do so. For example, if the question says it is a U.S. Supreme Court case, use a Supreme Court digest. If it is a federal court case, use a federal digest. If it is a state case, use that state's digest, if available in your library. If the appropriate state digest is unavailable, you must use the decennials.

Note also that the problems instruct you to search under a specific Topic and Key number. Remember that Topics and Key Numbers expand or they are placed under a new Topic in subsequent digests.

Working with the digests provides you with a good opportunity to work on developing proper citation technique through use of A Uniform System of Citation ("Blue Book"). Read about the proper order for citations, parallel citations, and spacing. Place the cases you cite as answers in "Blue Book" form.

THEME PROBLEMS FOR DIGESTS

Theme Problem I:

A. In the West publication of the Brown decision, 74 S.Ct. 686, two Key Numbers under the topic Constitutional Law are assigned in the headnotes. What two numbers are they?

B. Using the Key Numbers in Brown assigned to headnote number four and its subsections as a guide, answer the following questions using the most specific digest your library has available:

1. Locate a 1968 U.S. Supreme Court decision which holds that no official student transfer plan of which racial segregation is the inevitable result can stand under the 14th Amendment.

2. Find a 1970 Federal District Court decision that holds that while no student has a constitutional right to play football, no student can be prohibited from doing so solely on the basis of race.

3. Locate a Federal Court of Appeals decision in 1972 that holds that where it is possible to determine whether a school is for whites or blacks simply by reference to the racial composition of its faculty and staff, a prima facie case of violation of Equal Protection is made out.

4. Find a 1936 Maryland case that held that a Negro student was entitled to admission to the law school of the state university where the state could furnish "separate but equal" facilities no other way.

C. Using the Topic and Key Number assigned to headnote number one of Brown as a start, answer the following questions by referring to the most specific digest available in your library.

1. Find a 1977 Georgia case that holds that a county ordinance seeking to regulate "x-rated" movies through special fees, although justified as being merely a business regulation, will be subject to judicial scrutiny.

2. Find a 1974 U.S. Court of Appeals case where a statute forbidding the acceptance of an unlawful gratuity is being invoked against a former U.S. Senator, hypothetical cases showing possible effects on First Amendment should be ignored.

3. Find a 1975 U.S. Court of Appeals decision that holds that where complaining Library of Congress employees have not pointed out certain rules as due process violations, the Court does not have to scrutinize them.

4. Locate a 1942 South Carolina case which holds that where a law condemns a business for protection of public health, the Court will inquire into the law's necessity.

5. Cite a 1977 North Dakota case where a putative father challenging an illegitimacy law who did not assert policies that show the law's unconstitutional application to others will have the Court's inquiry limited to his case.

D. Using the Table of Cases for the most appropriate digest, provide citations for the following cases:

1. Vaughn v. Califano - Federal case.

2. Zorick v. Jones - Miss.

3. Aaltio v. Chicago - 1936.

4. Alford v. Butler -Tenn.

5. Caldwell v. Sturdivant - pre-1930 case.

Theme Problem II:

A. <u>Roe v. Wade</u>, 93 S.Ct. 705 has one Key Number assigned to headnote 11 and two to headnote 16. List these three Key Numbers.

B. Using the Key Number for headnote 11 and its subsections as a starting place, answer the following questions by referring to the most specific digest available in your library.

1. Find a 1973 Federal District Court case in Connecticut that holds that a statute compelling an unwed mother to appear before a judge, name the putative father and institute a paternity action does not violate the mother's right of privacy.

2. Cite a 1978 N.J. case that affirms that states may impose stricter standards for the protection of individual rights than the Federal Constitution.

3. Find a 1978 Federal case from Texas that holds that the family of an extraordinarily talented high school basketball player had the right to assist the player in developing his talents to the fullest.

4. Cite a 1945 Oklahoma case holding that prohibiting the sale of 3.2 beer in establishments that permit dancing is not violative of state constitutions guarantee of individual rights.

5. Cite a 1967 New Hampshire case that held that a statute forbidding parades on streets and public ways without first obtaining a license did not violate First Amendment guarantees.

C. Using whichever of the Key Numbers attached to headnote 16 (and/or its subdivisions) that seems relevant as a starting place, answer the following:

1. Locate a 1977 case that held invalid a Florida statute that authorized abortions only in certified centers and required doctors to sign a stipulation before each operation.

2. Cite a 1977 Nebraska case that upholds a statute making the possession of one pound or less of marijuana a misdemeanor as not violative of equal protection.

3. Cite a 1975 Federal District Court case in Pennsylvania striking down a Pennsylvania statute that requires a woman to get signed permission from her spouse prior to an abortion.

4. Find a Federal Court of Appeals decision coming from Arizona that holds that failure to make intent a part of the crime of possession of an unregistered firearm does not violate due process.

5. Locate a 1978 Iowa case that finds the undefined term "indecent" as a standard of behavior in a statute to be violative of due process.

D. Using the Table of Cases for the most appropriate digest, provide citations for the following cases:

1. Denneny v. Siegel - Federal case.

2. Quirici v. Freeman - California case.

3. Hoffman v. Victory Rubber Co. - 1922.

4. Climax Dairy Co. v. Mulder - Colorado.

5. Tresher v. McElroy - pre-1930 case.

Theme Problem III:

A. In Gideon v. Wainwright, 83 S.Ct. 792, two Key Numbers are assigned to the headnotes. What are they?

B. Using the Key Number assigned to headnote 3 as a starting point in your search, answer the following questions using the most specific digest your library has available:

1. Locate the 1945 California decision that held that the presence of decedent's widower, "a sickly, legless old man" at X's trial for forging a will to defraud said widower of his share of decedent's estate was not violation of due process.

2. Find a 1977 Illinois decision that holds that forcing X to appear in the courtroom and stand trial while manacled is a denial of due process.

3. Locate a 1978 Washington opinion that holds that defendant's due process rights in a prosecution for cocaine possession were not violated by the state's failure to return the trench coat in which contraband was found.

4. Locate a 1906 U.S. S.Ct. case that finds that the failure of the trial court in a criminal case to see that the testimony is read or repeated to an almost totally deaf defendant is no violation of defendant's rights.

5. Cite a 1974 U.S. S.Ct. case that holds that executive privilege as to subpoenaed materials sought for use in a criminal trial based only on a generalized interest in confidentiality cannot prevail over fundamental demands of due process.

C. Using the topic and Key Number (Courts 397 1/2) assigned to headnote 1 in Gideon, answer the following:

1. Why are there no entries under this key number in the Eighth Decennial Digest? Hint! Check Subjects Excluded and Covered by Other Topics at the beginning of the topic: Courts.

2. Under what Key Numbers can related cases now be found?

3. What 1969 U.S. S.Ct. case held that where an agreement was not submitted in evidence at state trial, but where California S.Ct. treated the agreement as an important part of the record, the Supreme Court on certiorari was free to refer to the agreement.

D. Using the Table of Cases for the most appropriate digest, provide citations for the following cases:

1. Coode v. McCune - Federal case.

2. Wood v. White - Oregon.

3. Zugar v. State - 1940.

4. NLRB v. Elias Brothers Big Boy, Inc. - Federal case.

5. Zuhn v. Horst - pre-1930 case.

DRILL PROBLEMS FOR DIGESTS

Instructions:

A. For each of the hypotheticals in Section A of each Drill Problem Section, use the indicated Decennial Digest and provide:

(1) A "yes" or "no" answer to the question.

(2) The Topic and Key Number under which your answer was found.

(3) The Uniform System of Citation cite form for the case that provides the answer.

NOTE: If you are unable to locate a specific case that yields the "yes" or "no" answer, locate other Topic and Key Numbers that offer cases of interest.

B. In subsection B of each Drill Problem Section, use the case table in the appropriate set of Decennial Digests to complete the citations.

Drill Problem I:

A. <u>Questions</u>:

1. Use Third Decennial. A petition was filed with the Minnesota Board of Law Examiners seeking the disbarment of an attorney for alleged misconduct in signing a will as a witness after the testatrix had died. Was the evidence of this alleged misconduct sufficient to sustain the charge?

2. Use Fourth Decennial. Plaintiff sued for rent under a written lease. After a finding for the defendant, plaintiff contended that the court lacked jurisdiction since the order had been entered before return of proof of service had been filed. In New Hampshire does failure to file the return deny the court jurisdiction?

3. Use Fifth Decennial. Relying on the Mississippi statute which provided that one was presumed dead if absent for seven years without having been heard from, Freda, whose first husband had been absent and not heard from for more than seven years, married Bill. Subsequent to Freda's marriage to Bill it was discovered that Freda's first husband was alive. Was the marriage of Freda and Bill void?

4. Use Sixth Decennial. A San Francisco attorney entered into a contingent fee contract with a client. The contract had the effect of providing additional compensation if a cross- complaint was filed and sucessfully defended. Does this make the contract illegal, unfair or inequitable?

5. Use Seventh Decennial. The treasurer of a union local entered into a scheme with the other members of the union's executive board whereby he sold union property and pocketed part of the proceeds. In California does pocketing part of proceeds from sale of realty belonging to union constitute embezzlement?

B. Table Cases:

    1. (a)   Cain v. Meade County (1929)

        (b)   Escobar v. State (1965)

        (c)   Groover v. Terrell (1919)

        (d)   Idol v. Street (1951)

        (e)   Lee County v. James (1937)

    2. U.S. Supreme Court Citations

        (a)   Chemgas v. Tuyna

        (b)   Ghio v. Moore

        (c)   Moelle v. Sherwood

        (d)   Reaves v. Ainsworth

        (e)   Urquhart v. Brown

Drill Problem II:

A. Questions:

    1. Use Third Decennial. A city in Arkansas sued to recover possession of a block of land which the city alleged had been dedicated to public use. A plat of the land had been filed in the office of the Recorder of Deeds. The block in question was designated "Franklin Square," but was not put to public use nor ever accepted by the City Council as a public place. Did the marking of the block as a "square" constitute an implied dedication of the land to the city?

    2. Use Fourth Decennial. In a suit for specific performance of a contract to sell certain real estate in California, evidence showed that in 1921, the contract was entered into at a purchase price of $3,000, of which $2,853.32 was to be paid in installments. On July 28, 1927, plaintiff tendered $1400 to defendant and demanded that she execute and deliver a conveyance to him. She refused. In an action for specific performance in the State of California, is tender of money by purchaser, without payment, sufficient to show good faith and diligence?

3. Use Fifth Decennial. A tenant sued his landlord for injuries sustained when he injured his hand on the procelain handle of a faucet over the kitchen sink in his Chicago apartment. He rented the apartment under a month to month tenancy. The janitor of the building had allegedly promised to repair the faucet, but there was no evidence to show any promise by the landlord to make repairs prior to commencement of the tenancy. Was the landlord liable?

4. Use Sixth Decennial. A woman filed a complaint against an attorney with the Monmouth County, New Jersey, Ethics and Grievance Committee. He retaliated by starting a malicious prosecution action against her. May an attorney predicate a malicious prosecution action on the filing of such a complaint?

5. Use Seventh Decennial. An actress entered into a contract with an agency to be her exclusive representative for a period of five years. Under the contract she was to pay the agency 10% of her earnings. Simultaneously the agency allegedly made an oral agreement to pay 5% of her earnings to another agent to whom she was already under contract. In New York, does the statute of frauds bar enforcement of such an oral agreement made in conjunction with an artist's exclusive agency contract?

B. Table Cases:

1. (a)   Carse v. Marsh (1922)

    (b)   Feyerchak v. Hiatt (1948)

    (c)   Haggerty v. Clement (1940)

    (d)   James River Bank v. Hansen (1927)

    (e)   Locigno v. City of Chicago (1961)

2. U.S. Supreme Court citations

    (a)   Ex parte Dainard

    (b)   Hanna v. Maas

    (c)   Neil v. Biggers

    (d)   Scott v. Paisley

    (e)   Vachon v. New Hampshire

Drill Problem III:

A. Questions:

1. Use Third Decennial. A physician and a sanitarium company in Georgia were sued for injuries sustained because of the physician's alleged negligence. The physician was the president and a principal stockholder of the sanitarium company. Was this sufficient to hold the sanitarium liable for negligence?

2. Use Fourth Decennial. The State University at Franklin instituted a condemnation action in order to obtain land for use as grounds for a new library building. The owner of the land questions the right of the University to exercise the power of eminent domain. Is the University entitled to take the land?

3. Use Sixth Decennial. Mr. Lawrence Hawthorne borrowed two sums ($45,000 and $18,000) in 1954 from his partners, Mr. and Mrs. J.M. Walton, and was charged an illegally high interest rate. Mr. Hawthorne repaid the sums and interest, and then sued to recover the excess interest. Has Mr. Hawthorn waived or released his claim of usury by payment?

4. Use Sixth Decennial. A bankrupt fishing company had from time to time over a two and one-half year period delivered to a Massachusetts fish freezing plant and public warehouse various lots of fish for freezing and storage. At the time of the fishing company's bankruptcy, the warehouse still had in its possession eleven such lots. The fishing company owed (1) $258.11 on account of unpaid charges on the eleven lots and (2) $1,126.84 as unpaid charges on other lots previously stored but withdrawn before bankruptcy. Seeking to secure the receipts due it, the warehouse claimed a lien on the eleven lots as security for the total account: $1,384.95. The trustee in bankruptcy maintained that the lien was only for $258.11, because under Massachusetts law the warehouse lost its lien on the other lots by surrendering possession of them. Was the trustee correct?

5. Use Seventh Decennial. Twice daily a farmer drove his herd of cattle along the main road through a village in Maryland from his barn on one edge of the village to his pasture on the opposite edge. Residents of the village complained that the dropping of manure on the roadway was a nuisance and sought to enjoin the farmer from driving his cattle through the village. In Maryland, does the driving of cattle along a public highway to pasture constitute a nuisance per se?

B. Table Cases:

   1. (a) Dorsey v. Petrott (1940)

      (b) Gray v. Love (1935)

      (c) Hurst v. Davis (1963)

      (d) Korf v. Itten (1917)

      (e) Mile High Poultry Farms v. Frazier (1945)

   2. U.S Supreme Court citations:

      (a) Fisher v. Shropshire

      (b) The Keokuk

      (c) Potts v. Chumasero

      (d) Trbovich v. United Mine Workers of America

      (e) Zartarian v. Billings

Chapter 7

ANNOTATED LAW REPORTS

ASSIGNMENT 1
QUICK INDEXES:
USE OF THE QUICK INDEXES FOR A.L.R. 1ST, 2D, 3D, 4TH,
AND A.L.R. FED. TO LOCATE ANNOTATIONS ON POINTS OF LAW

Method:

Using the quick index designated in the following problem sub-sets, locate and cite, using the latest edition of A Uniform System of Citation, annotations on point for each fact situation provided. You may have to refer to the actual annotation in order to provide the year in your citation.

Example:

QUESTION: A cat as the subject of a larceny.
ANSWER: Annot., 42 A.L.R.3d 1032 (1972).

Questions:

A. Use the A.L.R. First Series Quick Index to locate the following points of law appearing in A.L.R. 1-175.

1. Right of exclusion from or discrimination against patrons of library.

2. Legality of, and injunction against, peaceful picketing by labor union of plant whose employees are represented by another union as statutory bargaining agent.

3. Coaching law students as ground for disbarment of attorneys.

4. When is an individual deemed an inhabitant of the state within taxing law?

5. The pollution of a stream by mining operations.

6. The liability of a notary public or his bond.

7. Liability of insane person for tort.

8. Irresistible impulse as excuse for crime.

9. Conviction or acquittal of larceny as bar to prosecution for burglary.

10. What constitutes a boarding house.

11. Use of mails for sales of articles having superstitious associations.

12. Correct name of married woman.

13. Civil liability for defamation of the dead.

14. Epilepsy as affecting testamentary capacity.

15. Concealment of pregnancy as ground for annulment of marriage.

16. Assault as ground for disbarment of an attorney.

17. Writings in family bible as documentary evidence.

18. Validity of bequest or trust for care of specified animal.

19. Presence of noxious weeds as ground for rescission of contract for purchase of land.

20. Immoral relations between insured and beneficiary as affecting liability of insurer or interest in proceeds of the policy.

21. Validity of will as affected by fact that testatrix and beneficiaries are inmates of house of prostitution.

22. Constitutional provision against imprisonment for debt as applicable to nonpayment of tax, fee, or other obligation to government.

23. Meaning of the term "duration" or "end of war" employed in contract.

24. Abusive words as slander or libel.

25. Liability of one starting bonfire for burning of child.

26. The burning of soft coal as a "nuisance."

27. Electrical energy as subject of larceny.

28. Footprint evidence as violating rule against self-incrimination.

29. Opprobrious words addressed to policeman as breach of peace.

30. Power of bar examiners as to approval or disapproval of law school.

31. Liability of water company to private owner for breach of its contract with municipality to supply pressure for fire purposes.

32. Measure and elements of damage for loss or delay in delivering baggage of traveling salesman.

33. What money is legal tender?

34. Inequality of population or lack of compactness of territory as invalidating apportionment of representatives.

35. Pollution of oyster beds.

36. Liability of officer for exemplary or punitive damages in action for false imprisonment.

37. False statement made under fear as perjury.

38. Unloaded gun as dangerous weapon.

39. Forcing another to transport one as constituting offense of kidnapping.

40. Unfamiliarity with English as affecting competency of juror.

41. Deportation of alien because of political views.

42. Acts of others upon which charges of bribery or improper influencing of voters are predicated as chargeable to candidate for purpose of disqualifying him for the office to which he is elected.

43. Flight as evidence of guilt.

44. Recovery of punitive or exemplary damages in an action for alienation of affection.

45. The right of railroads to discriminate in respect to switching charges.

46. Unloaded firearm as dangerous weapon.

47. What constitutes riot within criminal law?

48. Homicide as affected by humanitarian motives.

B. Use the A.L.R. Second Series Quick Index to locate the following points of law appearing in A.L.R.2d 1-100.

1. Juror's inattention from sleepiness as ground for reversal or new trial.

2. Presumption of deliberation or premeditation from the fact of killing.

3. Manifestations of grief by victim or family of victim during criminal trial as ground for reversal, new trial or mistrial.

4. Homicide by fright or shock.

5. Criminal responsibility of husband for rape or assault to commit rape on wife.

6. Public payment of tuition to a sectarian school.

7. Statement of belief as perjury.

8. Discharge for absenteeism as affecting right to unemployment compensation.

9. Identification of accused by his voice.

10. Civil liability of sheriff charged with keeping jail for death or injury to prisoner.

11. Carrier's liability to passenger for injury due to pushing or crowding of passengers therein.

12. Liability of hospital for injury or death in obstetrical cases.

13. Attorney's failure to attend court, or tardiness, as contempt.

14. Malpractice liability with respect to diagnosis and treatment of mental disease.

15. Right of the accused to have defense witnesses free from manacles.

16. Rights in cargoes of wrecked or derelict ships not cast upon the shore.

17. Rights of fraternal society to protection against the use of its name, insignia, or ritual by another organization.

18. Adoption as affecting the right of inheritance through or from natural parent or natural kin.

19. Liability of dentist using force to restrain or discipline patient.

20. Keeping of gasoline on premises as increase of hazard voiding fire insurance policy.

21. Validity of marriage as affected by intention of the parties that it should be a jest.

22. Kidnapping by fraud or false pretenses.

23. Master's liability to servant injured by farm machinery.

24. Liability of attorney for negligence in preparing or conducting litigation.

25. Right to interest on unpaid alimony.

26. Rights of Indians to fish in streams notwithstanding objections by riparian owners.

27. Landlord's liability to tenant for injury by insect.

28. Corporation's criminal liability for homicide.

C. Use Quick Index to A.L.R.3d & 4th to locate the following points of law appearing in A.L.R.3d 1-100. Note to users: At the time these problems were drafted the answers were in the main volume of the Quick Index. At some point, there is likely to be a separate Quick Index for A.L.R.3d and for A.L.R.4th. If that division occurs, use the appropriate index.

1. Claustrophobia as disqualifying juror.

2. Effect of testamentary direction as to disposition of testator's body.

3. Negligence and contributory negligence in suit by rescuer against rescued person.

4. Common-law copyright in the spoken word.

5. Penal offense of sniffing glue or similar volatile intoxicants.

6. Tenants' rights where landlord fails to make repairs, to have them made and set off cost against rent.

7. Free exercise of religion as a defense to prosecution for narcotic offense.

8. Symbols: erection, maintenance, or display of religious structures or symbols on public property as violation of religious freedom.

9. When is a will signed at the "end" or the "foot" as required by statute?

10. Sales of liquor to homosexuals or permitting their congregation at licensed premises as ground for suspension or revocation of liquor license.

11. Attack on judiciary as a whole as indirect contempt.

12. Public disclosure of person's indebtedness as invasion of privacy.

13. Infant's liability for services rendered by attorney under contract with him.

14. Activities of law clerks as illegal practice of law.

15. Prospective or retroactive application of overruling decision.

16. Educational expenses as a deduction for income tax purposes.

17. Literary property in lectures.

18. Hunter's civil liability for unintentionally shooting another person.

19. Validity of statutes making parents liable for torts committed by their minor children.

20. Right of heirs assignee to contest will.

21. Liability for pre-natal injury.

22. Possession of a bomb or Molotov cocktail as a criminal offense.

D. Use the Quick Index to A.L.R.3d & 4th to locate points of law in A.L.R.4th. Note to users: At the time these problems were drafted the answers were in the pocket supplement to the Quick Index. At some point, there is likely to be a separate Quick Index for A.L.R.3d and for A.L.R.4th. If that division occurs, use the appropriate index.

1. Privileged communications between accountant and client.

2. Products liability: animal feed or medicines.

3. Homicide as precluding taking under will or intestacy.

4. Sufficiency of access to legal research facilities afforded defendant confined in the state prison or local jail.

5. Civil liability for insulting or abusive language - modern status.

6. Regulation of the practice of acupuncture.

7. Right of jailed or imprisoned parent to visit from minor child.

8. Attorney's failure to attend court, or tardiness, as contempt.

9. Admissibility of hearsay evidence in probation revocation hearings.

10. Liability for negligent operation of dune buggy.

11. Odor of narcotics as providing probable cause for warrantless search.

12. Fact that witness undergoes hypnotic examination as affecting admissibility of testimony in civil case.

13. Modern trends as to tort liability of child of tender years.

14. Recovery by bank of money paid out to customer by mistake.

15. Disclosure or use of computer application software as misappropriation of trade secret.

E. Use the A.L.R. Federal Quick Index to locate the following points of law appearing in A.L.R. Fed.

1. Inability of employer to pay wages and damages as defense to wage order under Fair Labor Standards Act.

2. Authority of Secretary of Army to deny dredging and filling permit for ecological reasons under Sec. 10 of Rivers and Harbors Act of 1899.

3. Making, selling or distributing counterfeit tape recordings as violation of federal law.

4. Liability of the United States under Federal Tort Claims Act for damages caused by ingestion or administration of drugs and vaccines approved as safe for use by government agency.

5. Right of accused to bill of particulars in criminal prosecution for evasion of federal income taxes.

6. Acquittal or conviction In state court as bar to federal prosecution based on same fact.

7. Right of accused to inspect the minutes of federal grand jury.

8. Application in federal civil action of governmental privilege of nondisclosure of identity of informer.

9. Construction and application of Food Stamp Act of 1964 establishing food stamp program.

10. Discharge from Armed Forces on ground of conscientious objection.

11. Validity and construction of federal statute requiring registration on crossing border of narcotics user.

12. Unauthorized photocopying by library as infringement of copyright.

13. What acts amount to violation of Hatch Political Activities Act provisions against political activities of certain state and local employees?

14. Construction and application of provision of Freedom of Information Act exempting from disclosure personnel and medical files.

15. Sex discrimination in athletics, validity under federal law.

ASSIGNMENT 2
QUICK INDEXES AND DIGESTS:
USE OF TABLE OF CASES OF A.L.R. QUICK INDEXES AND DIGESTS
TO LOCATE CASE CITATIONS AND ANNOTATIONS.

Method:

   For the following problem sub-sets, refer to the Table of Cases of the Permanent A.L.R. Digest, the A.L.R.2d Digest, or the Quick Index for A.L.R.3d & 4th and locate the following case names. Provide the case citation and the cite to the A.L.R. annotation, omitting dates.

Example:

   QUESTION: Dunn v. White
   ANSWER: 206 Kan. 278, 479 P.2d 215, 47 A.L.R.3d 1289

Questions:

A. Use the Permanent A.L.R. Digest (covering A.L.R. vols 1-175) Table of Cases.

   1. Henson v. Henson

   2. Keith v. Kilmer

   3. Markovitz v. Markovitz

   4. Shulkin v. Shulkin

   5. Ziehm v. Vale

   6. Crabtree v. Crabtree

   7. Brown v. Brown

B. Use the A.L.R.2d 1-100 Digest, Table of Cases Volume.

   8. Johnson v. Johnson

   9. Kennedy v. Parrott

   10. Agnew v. American Ice Co.

   11. Coolidge & Sickler Inc. v. Regn

   12. Wilson v. Anderson

13. Cleveland v. Detroit

14. McKinley v. Long

15. Jackson v. Jackson

C. Use the Quick Index for A.L.R.3d & 4th, Table of Cases Reported.

16. Washington Post Co. v. Keogh

17. Madison v. Wirtz

18. Lincoln Casualty Co. v. Vic & Mario's Inc.

19. Shady Grove, Inc. v. Jefferson Parish

20. Marshall v. Adams

21. Grant v. Yok

22. Warren v. Allstate Ins. Co.

23. Burger v. Burger

24. Black & White, Inc. v. Love

ASSIGNMENT 3
A.L.R. QUICK INDEX FOR A.L.R.3d & 4th:
USE OF ANNOTATION HISTORY TABLE TO LOCATE ANNOTATIONS FROM AMERICAN LAW REPORTS (1st. 2d, or 3d Series) SUPPLEMENTED OR SUPERSEDED IN A.L.R.2d, A.L.R.3d, OR A.L.R. FED.

Method:

Refer to the A.L.R. Quick Index for A.L.R.3d & 4th. Find the Annotation History Table. For each of the following annotations cite any supplementing or superseding annotation. Do not consult the pocket part.

Example:

    QUESTION: 2 A.L.R. 1376
    ANSWER: Superseded 45 A.L.R.2d 1296

Questions:

1. 3 A.L.R. 1130

2. 20 A.L.R. 407

3. 29 A.L.R. 140

4. 18 A.L.R. 197

5. 17 A.L.R. 760

6. 92 A.L.R.2d 421

7. 42 A.L.R.3d 560

8. 75 A.L.R.3d 1000

9. 132 A.L.R. 191

10. 129 A.L.R. 751

11. 90 A.L.R. 1377

12. 22 A.L.R.2d 427

13. 132 A.L.R. 679

14. 118 A.L.R. 1357

15. 97 A.L.R. 1197

ASSIGNMENT 4
USE OF THE A.L.R.2d DIGEST TO
LOCATE CASES THAT HAVE BEEN
ADDED TO ANNOTATIONS

Method:

Refer to the A.L.R.2d Digest for each of the following fact situations and cite the case name and the A.L.R.2d Annotation reference that follows the case name.

Example:

QUESTION: Bobby Nissan is present when Jay Myron threatens and strikes Roy Martin. Nissan shouts encouragement to Myron to strike Martin again, which Myron does. Martin sues Nissan for the tort of assault and battery.
ANSWER: Hargis v. Horrine, 72 A.L.R.2d 1223

Questions:

1. Pedro Montez holds commercial "cockfights" or contests between two roosters armed with artificial spurs. Pedro is arrested and charged with cruelty to animals. He contends that cockfighting is a lawful sport.

2. Charlie Speedo fails to stop after the car he is driving strikes a dog. As a matter of law does his action constitute breach of the peace?

3. Donald Durham, a property owner, shoots and kills a trespassing dog. Does he incur civil liability to the owner of the dog?

4. The proprietor of a golf course offers a prize of $5,000 to any member of the public who shoots a hole in one on his golf course and pays $1 for the opportunity. Fred Fortune pays his dollar and shoots a hole in one. The golf course proprietor refuses to pay the $5,000 contending that the contract was invalid as a "gambling" contract.

5. Rosie Reed promises to give her unborn illegitimate child the given name of the putative father in return for his promise to support the child. Is Rosie's promise adequate consideration for a binding contract?

6. Police Officer Robert Rood arrests and imprisons Larry Lane under a mistaken belief that he is the man named in the warrant. Lane sues Rood for false arrest and unlawful imprisonment. Rood alleges as his defense, the lack of malice or improper motive in making the arrest.

7. Charlie Low beats and pursues his wife to a river bank. He tells her to jump or he will push her. Charlie knows she cannot swim and the river is deep. She jumps and drowns. Charlie makes no effort to help her or summon assistance. He is charged with homicide.

8. Alice and Roger, although living apart because of Roger's heavy drinking, were still married at the time of Alice's death. Eric Eager, a mortician, furnishes Alice with the usual funeral. He seeks payment from Roger, who refuses to pay, contending that his liability for the necessaries of his wife ended upon her death.

9. Adolph Sparks seeks to pay his hospitalization insurance premium on the Monday immediately following the last day of his grace period (Sunday). The insurance company cancels his policy and he sues to reinstate the policy.

10. Noe Nardi, a member of an unincorporated labor union, requests to inspect its financial records. The union refuses his request and Nardi seeks a court order.

11. Elsie Dinsmore is the beneficiary of a testamentary trust which stipulates that the entire corpus will be turned over to her at the age of 32 providing that she has not married a Catholic. She challenges this provision in court as contrary to public policy and therefore void.

12. Paul Pope, a pedestrian, is severly injured by the breaking of a plate glass window in the Arista Department Store during a windstorm. Arista denies that its negligence was the proximate cause of the injury, citing the gusty wind as a superseding cause.

13. Willie Hinkle, a burglar, was hurrying home with his loot of cash and jewels when Salty Macha waved a revolver in front of him and said, "This is a stick-up. Give me your money and jewelry." Willie handed over everything he had stolen to Salty. Salty was later apprehended and at his trial for robbery contends that the proceeds of a burglary cannot be the subject of a robbery.

14. Nuns of a Roman Catholic order teach in a public school wearing distinctive religious garb. A local organization seeks a court order to compel them to wear normal lay clothing while engaged in teaching.

15. Herman Yellin is a school teacher who is in arrears in the payment of debt to the Friendly Finance Company. Friendly Finance writes to Yellin's school superintendent stating that Yellin owes them money, that normal collection efforts have failed, and seeks advice as to whether Yellin is able to pay, before taking further action. Yellin sues for libel. Friendly Finance alleges Yellin states no cause of action without a plea of special damage.

16. Susan Bee is severly injured by the negligent driving of Allen Alfa. Susan's minor son Daniel sues Alfa for loss of his mother's care and attention. Alfa denies Daniel Bee has a cause of action.

17. Robert and Marcia marry. Shortly thereafter Robert learns that Marcia had sexual intercourse with other men prior to their marriage. Robert seeks an annulment of their marriage alleging fraud on the part of Marcia in not divulging her previous incontinence to him.

18. Dr. Hall, in the act of removing sutures from the toe of Jane Fern, a 4 year old patient, strikes her to make her lie still. A bruise remains sore for some weeks. Her father brings an action for assault and battery against Dr. Hall on her behalf.

19. John Brown, a farmer, seeing some boys in the act of stealing watermelons from his fields, fires his rifle to frighten them off. He fires toward a wooded area where unknown to him another boy is hiding. The other boy is severely injured and an action is brought against Brown for assault and battery. Brown claims he is not civilly liable as he acted in defense of his property and he did not intend to injure the boy.

20. Peter Glass, an attorney, is convicted of wilful evasion of federal income taxes, a felony. He is disbarred for conviction of an offense involving fraud or moral turpitude. He contends that income tax evasion is not an offense involving fraud or moral turpitude, and that disbarment as opposed to a suspension was excessive.

21. Mrs. Thebiad leaves her valuable fur coat in the reception room of the beauty parlor without drawing her action to the attention of the proprietor or staff. While she is having her hair done, an unknown thief enters and takes her coat. Mrs. Thebiad alleges that a bailment relationship existed with the proprietor and he is liable for her loss.

22. Stephen and William Valentine break and enter a warehouse looking for valuables to steal. They find a slot machine which they carry off. Apprehended later, they deny that they are guilty of burglary because the slot machine could only be used for gambling which is illegal in that state.

23. Carol Chapel seeks a divorce from Paul Chapel on grounds of cruelty. Her husband frequently administered severe beatings to their young son in her presence, heedless of her protests and wishes, and without justification. Paul Chapel defends against the action by alleging that his treatment of their son is not "cruelty" in law.

24. Arthur Cruz is dismissed from a high paying position in Chicago. After a lengthy search for new employment he finds a job in Tulsa which does not pay as well. His wife Mabel refuses to move to Tulsa with him because his new salary will not enable her to live in the same style as she had previously. He sues for divorce alleging desertion.

25. Yazoo City passes an ordinance authorizing the flouridation of the City's water supply. Malcom Sharpe seeks a court order against its enforcement claiming that the City is not licensed to practice dentistry and that flouridation of the water supply would be the practice of dentistry.

ASSIGNMENT 5
A.L.R.2D DIGEST:
USE OF THE A.L.R. 2D
DIGEST TO LOCATE ANNOTATIONS ON POINTS
OF LAW APPEARING IN A.L.R.2D

Method:

　　Refer to A.L.R.2d Digest. Locate and cite, in proper form, the A.L.R.2d annotation on each of the following points of law.

Example:

　　QUESTION:　　Due process of law as violated by statute or ordinance providing for destruction of dogs without notice or hearing.
　　ANSWER:　　Annot., 56 A.L.R.2d 1037 (1957).

Questions:

1. Failure of artisan or construction contractor to procure occupational or business license or permit as affecting validity of contract.

2. Civil liability for use of firearm in defense of habitation or property.

3. Landlord's duty under express covenant to rebuild or restore, where property is damaged or destroyed by fire.

4. Fact that gun was unloaded as affecting criminal responsibility.

5. Right of owner of housing development or apartment houses to restrict canvassing, peddling, solicitations of contributions, etc.

6. Alteration of figures indicating amount of check, bill or note without change in written words as forgery.

7. Liability for statement or publication representing plaintiff as cruel to or killer of animals.

8. Truant or attendance officer's liability for assault and battery.

9. Criminal responsibility of husband for rape, or assault to commit rape on wife.

10. Character and duration of tenancy created by entry under invalid or unenforceable lease.

11. Danger or apparent danger of great bodily harm or death as condition of self-defense in civil action for assault and battery.

12. Partial payment on private building or construction contract as acceptance of defective work.

13. Validity and construction of zoning regulations requiring garage or parking space.

14. Vacancy or non-occupancy of building as affecting its character as "dwelling" as regards arson.

15. Validity and enforceability of contract in consideration of naming child.

ASSIGNMENT 6
A.L.R.2D LATER CASE SERVICE:
USE OF A.L.R.2d, LATER CASE SERVICE TO LOCATE RELEVANT DECISIONS
APPEARING SUBSEQUENT TO ANNOTATIONS PUBLISHED IN A.L.R. 2d

Method:

Refer to A.L.R. 2d, Later Case Service. For each of the following annotations give the name and citation, according to the latest edition of A Uniform System Of Citation, of the described subsequent case. You may have to refer to the actual case you located in order to provide the complete citation.

Example:

QUESTION: 14 A.L.R.2d 7
Subsequent common-law marriage does not raise presumption that former marriage terminated in divorce.
ANSWER: Lumberments Mut. Cas. Co. v. Reed, 84 Ga. App. 541, 66 S.E.2d 360 (1951).

Questions:

1. 5 A.L.R.2d 874.
Trial court properly awarded counsel fees to city where taxpayer's case so clearly lacked merit that public interest was not clearly vindicated or served by such litigation.

2. 5 A.L.R.2d 1143.
Under common law, where offense occurred February 25, 1967 at 4:30 P.M. and defendent was born February 25, 1950 at 6:32 P.M., defendant had reached 17 years of age at time of offense.

3. 6 A.L.R.2d 859.
Allegations that divorced wife used alimony payments for alcohol and drugs and had been arrested 50 or more times and confined in jail on many of these occasions did not justify modification of decree for alimony, at least in absence of allegation on part of divorced husband of inability to continue payments or lack of need on part of wife.

4. 64 A.L.R.2d 100.
Recovery was allowed for subsequent illness resulting from plaintiff discovering unpackaged prophylactic in remaining contents of bottle of Coca-Cola after having drunk a portion thereof.

5. 64 A.L.R.2d 301.
   Misconduct while practicing law in another state which included among other things borrowing and failing to return books from the county law library warranted denial of admission to bar.

6. 64 A.L.R.2d 600.
   Where spectator at pretrial hearing in Black Panther criminal prosecution disrupted proceeding and was summarily adjudged guilty of contempt, judge was not required to refer contempt proceeding to another judge.

7. 78 A.L.R.2d 905.
   Results of breathalyzer test were properly suppressed where officer failed to advise defendant of his right to have additional tests administered by any qualified person of his choosing.

8. 7 A.L.R.2d 8.
   Presumption of gratuity need not apply where adult or emancipated child, by prearrangement with parent, gives up established home and moves into home of parent, not for purpose of reestablishing family relationship, but for purpose of rendering services of an extraordinarily burdensome nature over long period of time.

9. 22 A.L.R.2d 244.
   Alien who admitted homosexual practices with 6 women was not of good moral character as the ordinary man or woman sees it.

10. 24 A.L.R.2d 873.
    Acts of cruelty occurring after his wife became insane could not be relied upon by husband as ground for divorce.

11. 24 A.L.R.2d 1288.
    Where client's mental incompetence was well-known to attorney, it was his duty to insist that she procure independent advice before deeding her home to him, and his failure to do so rendered the deed void.

12. 25 A.L.R.2d 315.
    Discharge of waitresses who walked off job in protest against discharge of friendly supervisor was not unfair labor practice.

13. 27 A.L.R.2d 498.
    Congress never intended dependency exemption to be construed so literally as to allow exemption for individual whom taxpayer maintains in an illicit relationship in violation of criminal law of state.

14. 37 A.L.R.2d 551.
    Cost of trip to Lourdes shrine in hope of physical improvement not deductible as medical expense.

15. 91 A.L.R.2d 1120.
Claim that juror stated that decision was based upon racial prejudice because defendant was Negro and "that all those people had Cadillacs" was not ground for new trial where there was no showing that any statement by a juror as to race influenced any other juror.

ASSIGNMENT 7
A.L.R. BLUE BOOK OF SUPPLEMENTAL DECISIONS:
USE OF THE A.L.R. BLUE BOOK OF SUPPLEMENTAL DECISIONS
TO LOCATE LATER DECISIONS AND ANNOTATIONS SUPPLEMENTING OR
SUPERSEDING ANNOTATIONS PUBLISHED IN A.L.R. FIRST SERIES

Method:

Refer to the A.L.R. Blue Book of Supplemental Decisions bound volumes 1-5 only. Give the full case name and citation according to the latest edition of A Uniform System of Citation of the first case appearing there subsequent to the publication of each of the following annotations (one case only). Cite all supplementing annotations and any superseding annotation.

Example:

    QUESTION: 83 A.L.R. 127
    ANSWER: Davis v. Mississippi, 394 U.S. 721 (1969).
                  Division III superseded 46 A.L.R.3d 900.

Questions:

1. 3 A.L.R. 1682.

2. 56 A.L.R. 666.

3. 23 A.L.R. 1402.

4. 46 A.L.R. 792.

5. 79 A.L.R. 688.

6. 100 A.L.R 814.

7. 109 A.L.R. 892.

8. 109 A.L.R. 1148.

9. 133 A.L.R. 11

10. 70 A.L.R. 817.

11. 10 A.L.R. 1137.

12. 58 A.L.R. 737.

13. 66 A.L.R 439.

14. 77 A.L.R. 1165.

15. 78 A.L.R. 766.

ASSIGNMENT 8
POCKET SUPPLEMENTS:
USE OF A.L.R. 3D POCKET SUPPLEMENTS TO LOCATE RELEVANT DECISIONS
SUBSEQUENT TO ANNOTATIONS PUBLISHED IN A.L.R. 3D.

Method:

Refer to the pocket part in the appropriate volume of A.L.R. 3d for each of the following annotations. Give the name and citation, according to the latest edition of A Uniform System Of Citation, of the described subsequent case. You may have to refer to the actual case in order to obtain necessary information for the complete citation.

Example:

QUESTION: 92 A.L.R.3d 545
Testimony as to assault by defendant upon woman occuring 75 feet from where body of victim in homicide prosecution was found, in remote area, was properly admitted against defendant, even though assault occurred two years after homicide.
ANSWER: State v. Ellis, 208 Neb. 379, 303 N.W.2d 741 (1981).

Questions:

1. 11 A.L.R.3d 907.
Where an attorney living in one state gave legal advice to his sister living in another state in which he was not admitted, recovery in suit for fee was not barred.

2. 3 A.L.R.3d 829.
Law school expenses incurred by taxpayer to maintain and improve skills as forensic pathologist held deductible.

3. 1 A.L.R.3d 849.
Calling rabbi a "crook" was not actionable per se.

4. 7 A.L.R.3d 1040.
Finding that juror took one drink with her lunch during noon recess was insufficient to require setting aside conviction of defendant where nothing in record reflected incapacity of juror to perform her duties.

5. 14 A.L.R.3d 1201.
High school student's suspension for wearing Confederate flag on jacket did not violate First and Fourteenth Amendments.

6. 14 A.L.R.3d 993.
Promoter of wrestling match held not liable for injuries to patron from being inadvertently bumped by policeman while expelling another patron.

7. 6 A.L.R.3d 1446.
Attorney who split legal fees for referrals from person supposedly a member of the bar in Cuba, but not a member of bar in any state in the U.S. was in violation of Code of Professional Responsibility.

8. 21 A.L.R.3d 116.
In prosecution for murder by running over deceased with automobile, conviction was sustained where evidence showed that accused intended to kill two other persons at time of act, although there was little or no evidence that he intended to kill the deceased.

9. 21 A.L.R.3d 603.
Owner of wild animal (a chimpanzee) was liable to one injured by animal under strict or absolute liability doctrine.

10. 21 A.L.R.3d 641.
Operating boarding house for mentally retarded persons for financial consideration as violation of covenant restricting use to residential purposes.

11. 27 A.L.R.3d 1274.
Surgeon's action in performing operation upon wrong person, while admittedly negligent, did not warrant award of punitive damages where surgeon did not know that he was operating upon wrong patient.

12. 27 A.L.R.3d 794.
If one who was beneficiary under insurance policies upon lives of his wife and daughter was insane when he killed them, he would be entitled to proceeds.

13. 17 A.L.R.3d 1442.
In malpractice action alleging that attorney failed to file personal injury action within the statute of limitations period, expert testimony as to reasonable settlement value or verdict value was inadmissable.

14. 38 A.L.R.3d 419.
Although square dancer might have assumed risks inherent in square dancing, such as being kicked by another dancer, she did not assume risk of faulty and dangerous floor.

15. 40 A.L.R.3d 444.
    Word "child" as used in statute means unborn child whose heart is beating, who is experiencing electronically measurable brainwaves, who is discernably moving, and who is so far developed as to be capable of surviving trauma of birth with aid of usual medical facilities.

ASSIGNMENT 9
POCKET SUPPLEMENTS:
USE OF POCKET SUPPLEMENTS (POCKET PARTS) TO A.L.R.3D, A.L.R.4TH, AND A.L.R. FED. TO LOCATE LATER CASES THAT SUPPLEMENT THE ANNOTATION.

Method:

    Refer to the pocket supplement of the appropriate volume of A.L.R.3d, A.L.R.4th or A.L.R. Federal and provide the name of the first case that supplements the A.L.R. volume and section number in the following problems.

Example:

    QUESTION: 2 A.L.R. Fed. 18 §9(a)
    ANSWER: Andrews v. Maher

Questions:

1. 2 A.L.R. Fed. 376 §6(e)
2. 1 A.L.R.4th 411 §2(b)
3. 50 A.L.R.3d 1311 §9(a)
4. 2 A.L.R.4th 27 §8(g)
5. 13 A.L.R. Fed. 145 §2(b)
6. 8 A.L.R.4th 70 §3(b)
7. 42 A.L.R.3d §6(a)
8. 13 A.L.R.4th §5
9. 3 A.L.R.3d §4(b)
10. 20 A.L.R.4th §4
11. 18 A.L.R.4th 249 §7
12. 23 A.L.R. Fed. 895 §4(a)
13. 15 A.L.R.4th 294 §6(a)
14. 4 A.L.R. Fed. 123 §18(a)
15. 68 A.L.R.3d 7 §6(a)

16. 8 A.L.R.Fed. 415 §4(c)

17. 53 A.L.R.3d 748 §6

18. 10 A.L.R. Fed. 15 §8

19. 47 A.L.R.3d 398 §5

20. 19 A.L.R. Fed. 492 §3

21. 28 A.L.R.4th §19(e)

22. 56 A.L.R.3d 14 §11(b)

23. 28 A.L.R. Fed. 584 §2(b)

24. 9 A.L.R.4th 633 §2(b)

25. 32 A.L.R. Fed 155 §14

26. 7 A.L.R.3d 8 §9(a)

27. 15 A.L.R Fed. 771 §7(a)

28. 20 A.L.R.3d 1127 §6(a)

29. 5 A.L.R.4th 234 §10(a)

30. 37 A.L.R.3d 464 §29(a)

ASSIGNMENT 10
A.L.R. FEDERAL TABLES:
USE OF THE A.L.R. TABLES VOLUME TO LOCATE CASES,
STATUTES AND REGULATIONS IN A.L.R. FEDERAL.

Method:

    Refer to the A.L.R. Federal Tables Volume. Give the first listed citation to a place in A.L.R. Federal where the following federal laws, regulations, and cases are cited.

Example:

    QUESTION: Adler v. Nicholas
    ANSWER: 10 A.L.R. Fed. 874

Questions:

1. 5 U.S.C. sec. 73b.

2. 7 U.S.C. sec. 612.

3. 8 U.S.C. sec. 43.

4. 8 U.S.C. sec. 144.

5. 10 U.S.C. sec. 802.

6. 5 C.F.R. sec. 151.122.

7. 7 C.F.R. sec. 1.51.

8. 7 C.F.R. sec. 273.

9. 10 C.F.R. sec. 50.

10. 20 C.F.R. sec. 3.4.

11. 1 Stat. 73.

12. 5 Stat. 614.

13. 43 Stat. 253.

14. 62 Stat. 163.

15. 74 Stat. 196.

16. 22 U.S.C. sec. 1203.

17. 34 U.S.C. sec. 1200.

18. 35 U.S.C. sec. 11a.

19. 39 U.S.C. sec. 201.

20. 40 U.S.C. sec. 258.

21. Rule 30 (Fed. Rules of Civil Procedure).

22. Rule 36 (Fed. Rules of Civil Procedure).

23. Rule 59 (Fed. Rules Of Civil Procedure).

24. Rule 26 (Fed. Rules of Criminal Procedure).

25. Rule 27 (Rules of U.S. Supreme Court).

26. <u>King v. Greenblatt</u>

27. <u>Howard v. Grant</u>

28. <u>Petteys v. Butler</u>

29. <u>Freemon v. United States</u>

30. <u>Lynn v. Caraway</u>

ASSIGNMENT 11
WORDS AND PHRASES:
USE OF QUICK INDEXES, A.L.R. DIGEST, AND BLUE BOOK
OF SUPPLEMENTAL DECISIONS TO LOCATE
DEFINITIONS OF WORDS AND PHRASES

Method:

Refer to the Words and Phrases Section of the A.L.R. Quick Indexes, Digests, and Blue Book of Supplemental Decisions to locate definitions or annotations on point for the questions in each subset below.

Example:

    QUESTION: Declaration
    ANSWER: 60 A.L.R.2d 124

Questions:

A. Using the A.L.R.2d Quick Index; the A.L.R.3d & 4th Quick Index; and the A.L.R.2d 1-100 Digest, Words and Phrases section (Volume 12) and locate a definition of the following words and phrases. Give the citation to the annotation or annotations on point.

    1. Flag desecration

    2. Operation

    3. Usual Place of Abode

    4. Securities "dealer"

    5. Pilferage

    6. "Personal belongings" in a will

    7. Sickness

    8. Interception

    9. Competent witness

   10. Slander

   11. Will-Call plan

   12. Blood heirs

13. Any

14. All

15. Compound interest

16. Zoning

17. Vandalism

18. De Bene Esse

19. Final submission

20. Suit

21. Train

22. Struck by

23. Scaffold

24. Valid Defense

25. Occupying

B. Using the A.L.R. Digest, A.L.R. Blue Book of Supplemental Decisions, Permanent vols. 4 (1959-67) and 6 (1976-1983) and cite an A.L.R. annotation on point for each of the following words appearing under "Words and Phrases." Include in your answer any supplementing or superseding annotations which have appeared in A.L.R. or A.L.R.2d.

1. Poor person.

2. Endangering life.

3. Nepotism

4. Warranty

5. Successful parties.

6. Accord and satisfaction

7. Accession.

8. Action for the recovery of money only

9. Actual doubt

10. "As is"

11. Barratry
12. Blood relations
13. Born out of wedlock
14. Death by own hand
15. Duration of war
16. Double derivative suits
17. End of war
18. Habitual drunkeness
19. Lobbying
20. Member of a family
21. Natural flow
22. Real estate board
23. Slot machine
24. Severance pay.
25. Standing timber

ASSIGNMENT 12
THEME PROBLEMS

Theme Problem I:

A. Using the Quick Index to A.L.R.3d and 4th, answer the following:

   1. Give the title and citation of an A.L.R. Annotation on the defacto segregation of the races in public schools.

   2. On what case is the Annotation based?

   3. Where are open enrollment plans discussed?

   4. Cite a related law review article by Fiss.

   5. In what section can a California case be found?

   6. Cite a federal case from Texas that comments on § 2(b).

   7. Has this Annotation been superseded or supplemented?

   8. Where might one look in Am. Jur. 2d for a related discussion?

   9. Where can one find an A.L.R.2d Comment-Note on Racial Segregation?

   10. Where is Brown cited in this Annotation?

B. Using the same volume of A.L.R.3d, answer the following:

   1. Give the name and citation of an annotation that discusses marriage or pregnancy of a public school student as grounds for expulsion or exclusion, or of restriction of activity.

   2. In what section is there discussion of situations where exclusion and expulsion have been upheld?

   3. What earlier annotation does this annotation supersede?

   4. On what case is this annotation based?

   5. Where could one find a related annotation on the application of state law to sex discrimination in sports?

   6. Who wrote the briefs of counsel for appellant?

C. Using the same volume, give the citations for the following cases:

1. McCrossen v. United States

2. Yarrington v. Thornburg

3. Russell v. Casebolt

Theme Problem II:

A. Use the Quick Index to A.L.R.3d and 4th, answer the following questions:

1. Give the title and citation of an annotation dealing with the right of a woman to have an abortion against the wishes of the child's father.

2. What case is the annotation based on?

3. Has the annotation been superseded or supplemented?

4. In the same volume, find an annotation that discusses what constitutes a church for purpose of worship.

B. Using the annotation found in A.4 answer the following:

1. Where would the issue of whether the home of a priest should be considered as part of the Church be discussed?

2. Where are Wisconsin cases discussed?

3. What treatise is suggested as a reference?

4. Where in Am.Jur. 2d is the same topic discussed?

5. What case is it based on?

C. Using the same volume, give full citations for each of the following cases:

1. Ventress v. Rice.

2. Grinnel v. Sard.

3. State v. Bagenehl.

D. Using the same volume, answer the following:

1. Cite an Annotation, including the title, dealing with damages caused by dredging.

2. Cite an Annotation, including the title, dealing with the conviction of narcotics offenders due to unlawful entrapment.

Theme Problem III:

A. Using the A.L.R.2d Quick Index, answer the following.

1. Give the full title and citation to an annotation discussing a Gideon v. Wainwright issue--right of an indigent to counsel in a state court proceeding.
2. Who authored it?
3. Has it been superseded or supplemented?
4. Cite an annotation in the same volume on drive-in movie theaters as a public nuisance.

B. For the annotation noted in A.4, answer the following:

1. What annotation does this one supersede?
2. Where in Am. Jur. 2d will you find related discussion?
3. On what case is it based?

C. Using the same volume, give citations, including the title, for annotations on the following topics:

1. Killing a protected (i.e. endangered) game to defend property.
2. How long a judge can keep a criminal jury deliberating.
3. The validity of an expert's opinion of how fast an auto was going based on its post-crash appearance.

D. Using the Later Case Service bound volumes, answer the following:

1. What related annotation to 93 A.L.R.2d 1366 is cited?
2. What case updated § 18 of 94 A.L.R.2d 788?

ASSIGNMENT 13
DRILL PROBLEMS

Drill Problem I:

A. Turn to 69 A.L.R.3d 845 (1976) and answer the following:

    1. What sections of this annotation cite Louisiana cases?

    2. Where could one find discussion of the incapacity of a plaintiff to sue?

    3. Where in Am. Jur. 2d could you find a related discussion?

    4. On what case is this annotation based?

    5. Are there any new cases on § 6 since the annotation was published

    6. Where could one find a related annotation on the power of a court to vacate or modify an order granting a new trial in a civil case?

B. Cite annotations of the following cases:

    1. Vermont v. Grant.

    2. Restifo v. McDonald.

    3. Abdulla v. Pittsburgh & Weirton Bus Co.

C. Locate annotations on the following topics:

    1. The validity of traffic regulations requiring motorcyclists to wear protective headgear.

    2. The attempt to commit assault as a criminal offense.

    3. The liability of Roy Rogers if Trigger kicks someone.

D. Specify any annotations that supplement or supersede any of the following:

    1. 25 A.L.R.2d 1077.

    2. 41 A.L.R. 1437.

    3. 75 A.L.R.3d 1000.

E. Use the A.L.R. Blue Books (Permanent Edition and Supplements) to answer the following:

1. Cite a case in 379 N.Y.S.2d that updates 90 A.L.R. 101-116.

2. Is there a 1977 Louisiana decision related to 52 A.L.R. 935-941? If so, give citation.

F. Use the A.L.R.2d Later Case Service to answer the following:

1. Cite a case updating 12 A.L.R.2d 524-573, § 10 that involves beer barrels.

2. Cite a Pennsylvania case in 227 Pa. Super. that updates § 26 of 55 A.L.R.2d 554-638. (639)

G. Use the pocket parts of A.L.R.3d ~~and A.L.R. Fed~~. to answer the following:

1. Cite a Conn. case that updates § 25 of 72 A.L.R.3d 131-239.

2. Cite an Arizona case that updates §10 of 67 A.L.R.3d 824-889.

3. Cite two Am. Jur. 2d sections that discuss 31 A.L.R.3d 1448-1454.

Drill Problem II:

A. Turn to 84 A.L.R.3d 665 and answer the following:

1. Where in this annotation can one find discussion of the waiving of a guardian's consent?

2. Where in Am. Jur. 2d could one find a discussion of the same topic?

3. Where are any Oklahoma cases cited?

4. Where could one find related discussion on the adoption of an adult?

5. On what case is this annotation based?

B. Cite annotations on the following cases:

1. Labbee v. Anderson.

2. Cherry v. State.

3. Giroux v. Lassier.

C. Locate annotations on the following topics:

   1. Statutes related to sexual psychopaths.

   2. Exemption from taxation of a municipally owned auditorium.

   3. The application of zoning ordinances [public laws] to a research laboratory.

D. Specify any annotations that supplement or supersede any of the following:

   1. 163 A.L.R. 1188.

   2. 153 A.L.R. 329.

   3. 1 A.L.R. 148.

E. Use the A.L.R. Blue Books (Permanent Edition and Supplements) to answer the following:

   1. Cite a case in 324 N.E.2d that cites to the annotation at 10 A.L.R. 1591-1594.

   2. What is the latest information on 15 A.L.R. 125-145?

F. Use the A.L.R.2d Later Case Service to answer the following:

   1. Cite a Conn. case updating § 3 of 15 A.L.R.2d 11-94.

   2. Cite a Washington case that updates § 39(b) of 70 A.L.R.2d 268-335.

G. Use the pocket parts of A.L.R.3d and A.L.R. Fed. to answer the following:

   1. Cite a 5th Circuit case from Texas that updates § 3 of 14 A.L.R. Fed. 806-818.

   2. Cite an Am. Jur. Proof of Facts 2d article on § 1, 60 A.L.R.3d, 880. 923.

   3. Cite a 6th Circuit decision updating § 6, 3 A.L.R. Fed. 569-586.

Drill Problem III:

A. Turn to 78 A.L.R.3d 339 and answer the following:

   1. Where in this annotation is there discussion of the negligence of a pedestrian?

   2. Where in Am. Jur. Trials would you find related material?

3. Where is a Rhode Island case cited?

4. On what case is this annotation based?

5. Cite a related law review article by Prof. Prosser.

B. Cite annotations on the following cases:

1. <u>Page v. Sherrill</u>.

2. <u>Lake County Bar Association v. Ostrander</u>.

3. <u>Ottavia v. Savarese</u>.

C. Locate Annotations on the following topics:

1. The duty and liability of one driving in or along a rut in the highway.

2. The criminal nature of turning in a false alarm to the fire department.

3. Sexual impotence as grounds for annulment.

D. Specify any annotations that supplement or supersede any of the following:

1. 31 A.L.R. 756.

2. 161 A.L.R. 382.

3. 11 A.L.R.3d 1231.

E. Use the A.L.R. Blue Books (Permanent Edition and Supplements) to answer the following:

1. Cite a case in 425 F.2d that modifies the annotation at 1 A.L.R. 39 136.

2. Cite a case in 534 F.2d that supplements the annotation at 174 A.L.R. 1010-1045.

F. Use the A.L.R.2d Later Case Service to answer the following:

1. Cite a Tennessee case in 520 S.W.2d that updates § 5 of 21 A.L.R.2d 472-535.

2. Where could one find forms relevant to 81 A.L.R.2d 350-376, § 3(a)?

G. Use the pocket parts of A.L.R.3d and A.L.R. Fed. to answer the following:

1. What C.F.R. section, discussed in § 1 of 33 A.L.R. Fed. 751-766, has been amended?

2. Cite a Mississippi case that updates § 6, 1 A.L.R.3d 208-272.

3. Cite an Oklahoma case that updates § 6, 62 A.L.R.3d 110-160.

Chapter 8

CONSTITUTIONS

ASSIGNMENT 1A
UNITED STATES CONSTITUTION

Sources: United States Code Annotated (Constitution volumes)

United States Code Service

Constitution of the United States of America (Library of Congress 1972 edition and the 1980 supplement.)

Method:

Briefly answer the questions, using one of the above source materials. List the applicable article, section, and clause of the Constitution, and if the question involves judicial interpretation of a constitutional provision, cite a case in point.

Questions:

1. The City of Burbank sought enforcement of its city ordinance prohibiting take-off by jet aircraft from an airport between the hours of 11:00 p.m. and 7:00 a.m. Lockheed Air Terminal, Inc. resisted. What result?

2. Is a member of Congress eligible to hold a commission in the Armed Forces during his continuance in office as a Congressman?

3. Would a Congressional committee's action in printing and distributing a committee report entitled "Limited Survey of Honoraria Given Guest Speakers for Engagements at College and Universities" be subject to challenge in the Federal courts?

4. What House of Congress has the sole power to try all impeachments?

5. What vote is required for a House of Congress to expel a member?

6. If the President vetoes a bill and returns it to the House of Congress in which it originated, what formalities are necessary to override the veto and make the bill a law?

7. For what Federal officials must the President have the advice and consent of the Senate to effect their appointment to Federal office?

8. What limitations does the Constitution provide as to the formation of new States of the Union?

9. What constitutional provision regulates interstate compacts?

10. What constitutional provision empowers the President to make treaties and what limitations does it provide?

11. Are treaties the supreme law of the land?

12. How is a treaty of the United States abrogated?

13. If a Vice President assumes the office of President in the first year of his predecessor's elected term, may he seek reelection on his own a second time?

14. Under what constitutional authority does the Supreme Court act in reviewing the judgments and decrees of the supreme courts of the several states when federal questions are involved?

15. Does Congress have power to impose higher taxes in one state than in another?

16. What rights does the 26th Amendment confer on citizens? Does it apply to states?

17. John Ramsey sprouted a handlebar mustache. The principal of the school in which he was a teacher issued a ruling prohibiting teachers from wearing mustaches. John challenged the principal in court. What result?

18. Did the order requiring an Army Reserve officer to participate in a parade to be held as part of a program of a national convention for a veteran's organization violate the Third Amendment?

19. A Washington state statute empowered judges to declare children dependent for the purpose of authorizing blood tranfusions. Parents of children objected on the grounds that the transfusions were contrary to their religion and the Court's action violated the Constitution. What result?

20. Was the defendant in a murder trial deprived of his constitutional rights by the fact that the oath taken by jurors did not include an oath to support the Constitution?

21. When there is a vacancy in the office of the Vice President, what steps are taken to install a new Vice President?

22. Is it within the power of Congress to prohibit the importation, manufacture, and sale of intoxicating liquors in territories acquired by the United States?

23. For what type of cases does the Supreme Court of the United States have original jurisdiction?

24. Can aliens domiciled in the United States be prosecuted for treason?

25. Must state courts follow decisions of the United States Supreme Court in extradition matters?

26. Every bill passed by both Houses must be presented to the President before it becomes law. Two courses of action by the President are prescribed by the Constitution, either of which will result in the bill becoming law. What are they?

27. A Wisconsin compulsory school attendance law requires that Amish children attend high school. Parents of Amish children challenge the statute on the ground that the statute is contrary to their religious beliefs. What result?

28. A juvenile is charged with delinquency which may result in commitment. The parents and child are unable to employ counsel. Do they have a right to court-appointed counsel?

29. Who determines when Presidential disability exists under the 25th Amendment?

30. A municipal ordinance in Washington prohibited masseurs who are not licensed physicians from performing massages upon members of the opposite sex. Did this constitute a violation of the equal protection law and constitute a discrimination based on sex?

31. What are the qualifications for President of the United States?

32. An elementary teacher required the recitation of the verse: "We thank you for the flowers so sweet; We thank you for the food we eat; We thank you for the birds that sing; We thank you for everything." Is the compulsory recitation of this verse in a public school a violation of the Constitution?

33. Does the administration of corporal punishment by public schools, as authorized by Texas law, constitute cruel and unusual punishment?

34. May the salary of the President be lowered during the term for which he has been elected?

35. A dentist has a certificate to practice dentistry in one state. He maintains that under the full faith and credit clause of the Constitution he has the right to practice that profession in another state. Is he correct?

36. Under what circumstances may the federal writ of habeas corpus be suspended?

37. May a state grant property tax exemptions to religious organizations for religious properties used solely for worship?

38. May federal judges be removed from office by impeachment? Cite only the correct constitutional provision.

39. May the House of Representatives compel attendance of absent members?

40. An applicant for admission to the State Bar of Arizona is asked whether she has ever been a member of the Communist Party or any organization "that advocates overthrow of the United States by force or violence." Can exclusion from the bar be based on her refusal to answer the question?

41. A child was born on the high seas aboard an American vessel. The child's parents, at the time of his birth, were aliens residing in the United States. The child, now fully grown, seeks admission to the United States based on the ground he was "born in the United States." Is he a citizen?

42. The Constitution authorizes the removal of a President by impeachment, brought by the House of Representatives and tried by the Senate. What federal official presides over the trial?

43. Does the assignment of counsel to represent indigent defendants without compensation constitute involuntary servitude?

44. The House of Representatives can expel one of its members. May they exclude a person duly elected by his constituents, if the person was not ineligible to serve under any provision of the Constitution?

45. If ratified, when would the proposed Equal Rights Amendment have taken effect?

46. Can Congress limit the President's power of appointment of persons in the executive branch by providing that a certain named person cannot be appointed by the President?

47. A statute increasing the penalty for burglary and robbery was signed by the President at 3:05 p.m. and thus went into effect. The defendant's crime took place at 11:00 p.m. The defendant now challenges the statute as an ex post facto law because he did not have prior notice of the change. Must he have actual notice that the new legislation has passed?

48. Does the power of the President to grant reprieves and pardons take away from Congress the power to pass acts of general amnesty?

49. What section of the Constitution extends the judicial power of the United States to admiralty cases? Cite a 1943 case which deals with the power of Congress to legislate on maritime law.

50. What section of the Constitution deals with the federal judicial power to handle controversies between citizens of two different states? What 1965 case construes the purpose of this section?

51. What article and section of the Constitution deals with the power of Congress to declare war? Cite a 1944 California case which deals with the scope of this power.

52. Which section of the Constitution governs the issue of the impairment of contracts by states? Cite a 1935 case which deals with the question of whether Congress is also prohibited from impairing contracts.

53. What section of the Constitution prohibits cruel and unusual punishment? What 1972 Supreme Court case held that the death penalty as then used would constitute cruel and unusual punishment?

54. Due process of law is mentioned in what two sections of the Constitution? Is an alien a "person" subject to protection under these sections? With regard to the 14th Amendment, cite a 1915 Arizona case supporting your answer.

55. What section of the Constitution prohibits state denial of equal protection of the laws? Cite a 1974 Michigan case prohibiting employment discrimination on the basis of sex because it violated that section of the Constitution.

56. Where in the Constitution is one guaranteed the right to indictment by a grant jury for capital crimes? May this protection be waived? Cite a 1959 case supporting your answer.

57. What section of the Constitution protects freedom of the press? Cite a 1972 Louisiana case which discusses a court-imposed prior restraint on the publication of evidence from court proceedings.

58. Where would an office holder look in the Constitution to find out if he could accept gifts or emoluments from foreign states? According to an opinion of the Attorney General of the United States, may an office holder accept compensation from a foreign government under any condition? Give the citation to the appropriate Attorney General's opinion.

59. Treason is defined by which section of the Constitution? Can speech alone be treasonable? Cite a 1950 case supporting your answer.

60. Which section of the Constitution deals with women's suffrage? Does this section give women the right to vote? What 1938 case is on point?

ASSIGNMENT 1B
UNITED STATES CONSTITUTION

Method:

Using the tables and information contained in The Constitution of the United States of America (Library of Congress, 1972 edition and 1980 supplement), answer the following questions.

Questions:

1. How many amendments to the Constitution have not been ratified after being submitted to the states?

2. What is the subject of the most recent proposed amendment to the Constitution which was submitted to the states for ratification and failed to pass?

3. What is the subject matter of the proposed 28th Amendment to the Constitution?

4. In 1918 the Supreme Court held unconstitutional a statute prohibiting interstate shipment of articles made by child labor. What was the law and the case?

5. What case held unconstitutional the provisions of the Immigration and Naturalization Act of 1952, which provided for revocation of citizenship of those who had voted in a foreign election?

6. The Internal Revenue Code of 1954 had a provision which required gamblers to declare their gambling income. These provisions were held not to prevent the assertion of one's privilege against self-incrimination. Which cases held this?

7. What case held unconstitutional the section of the Voting Rights Act Amendments of 1970 that set the minimum age of 18 in state and local elections?

8. Shapiro v. Thompson, 394 U.S. 618 (1969), held what Act of Congress to be unconstitutional?

9. In what case did the Supreme Court hold that a Virginia statute which prohibited interracial marriages was unconstitutional?

10. What early case held that an Ohio statute levying a tax on the Bank of the United States was unconstitutional?

11. What 1956 case held that an indigent defendant is entitled to a free copy of the entire transcript of his criminal trial under some circumstances?

12. What justices concurred separately in the 1961 Cramp v. Board of Public Instructions decision which held unconstitutional a law requiring state and local employees to swear that they never lent support to the Communist Party?

13. Gideon v. Wainwright, 372 U.S. 335 (1963), overruled what prior case?

14. Wolf v. Colorado, 338 U.S. 25 (1949), was overruled in part by what 1961 case?

15. West Coast Hotel Co. v. Parrish, 300 U.S. 379 (1937), overruled what case?

ASSIGNMENT 2
COMPARISON OF STATE CONSTITUTIONS

Sources: The constitution of the states to which reference is made in each question.

Index-Digest of State Constitutions (Legislative Drafting Fund of Columbia University. 2d ed. 1959 with latest cumulative supplement).

Method:

Briefly answer the questions and cite the applicable constitutional provision.

Questions:

1. May divorces be granted by private, local or special law in:
    Arizona
    California
    Oregon

2. May a person under guardianship vote in:
    Louisiana
    Florida
    Massachusetts

3. May legitimation be authorized by local, private or special law in:
    Alabama
    Arkansas
    Florida

4. Is the property of public libraries exempt from taxation in:
    California
    Oklahoma

5. Is a state lottery legal in New York?

6. Do the Delaware and Idaho state constitutions define periods of emergency resulting from disasters caused by enemy attack?

7. What constitutional clauses provide a method of invoking initiative and referendum in:
    California
    Michigan
    Nevada

8. Are canals treated as public highways in Arkansas and Pennsylvania?

9. Does the Louisiana state constitution provide for the payment of a pension to a surviving spouse and minor children of law enforcement officers killed while engaged in the direct apprehension of persons during course of performance of duties?

10. Are military records and relics preserved in the office of the adjutant-general in Idaho?

11. May absconding debtors be imprisoned in Washington and Utah?

12. Are sheriffs commissioned by the governors in Arkansas and Delaware?

13. Is polygamy expressly prohibited by constitutional provision in Utah and Oklahoma?

14. Are perpetuities allowable for eleemosynary purposes in Montana and California?

15. Are retrospective laws permissible in:
    Colorado
    Tennessee
    Texas

16. How are claims brought against the state in:
    Arizona
    Washington
    Wisconsin

17. What constitutes a woman's separate property in:
    Alabama
    Michigan
    Utah

18. In case of suicide how does property descend in:
    Colorado
    Delaware
    Texas

19. What does the Michigan constitution provide with respect to findings of fact in workmen's compensation proceedings?

20. What does the California constitution provide with respect to home offices of insurance companies?

21. What does the Wyoming constitution provide with respect to the make up of Congressional districts?

22. Is life insurance exempt from the claims of creditors when wife and children are beneficiaries in North Carolina?

23. May the amount of damages recoverable by civil action for death by wrongful act, neglect or fault of another be limited by law in:
    Arizona
    Kentucky
    Ohio

24. Under what circumstances may the writ of habeas corpus be suspended in:
    California
    Illinois
    New York

25. Can titles of nobility be conferred by law in Oregon or Pennsylvania?

26. May timber in public forests (in New York, forest reserves) be sold in:
    Montana
    New York
    Washington

27. What state constitution requires that the metric system be taught in its public schools?

28. How do the constitutional provisions differ with respect to the affirmative vote required to pass a bill over the governor's veto in:
    Missouri
    Texas

29. Do the Hawaii and New Jersey constitutions provide expressly for collective bargaining by public employees?

30. Concerning what questions may the state supreme court issue advisory opinions in:
    Rhode Island
    South Dakota

31. What is the term of office for state treasurer in:
    Delaware
    Georgia

32. Do Arizona, Florida, and South Dakota have right to work provisions?

33. A man is conscientiously opposed to sending his child to a school in Kentucky. Can he be compelled to do so?

34. What officers are impeachable in:
    Delaware
    Oregon
    Utah

35. Do women have all the civil, political, and religious rights enjoyed by men in Wyoming and Utah?

36. Generally a person may not be imprisoned for debt. What exception to this rule is in the constitutions of:
    Indiana
    Washington

37. Is the legislature authorized to provide for compulsory voting in North Dakota?

38. In what Arkansas city is horse racing and pari mutuel betting constitutional?

39. May interest rates be regulated by local, private or special law in:
    Alabama
    Kentucky
    New Mexico

40. Compare the constitutional provisions concerning the bribery of officers in Colorado and West Virginia. Which provision defines bribery?

41. Are perpetuities allowed for charitable purposes in Montana?

42. Does the power of the governor and council to grant pardons include juvenile delinquency in Maine?

43. What is the minimum age for members of the Senate in:
    Iowa
    Oregon
    Tennessee

44. Do the Vermont and New Jersey constitutions provide for the impeachment of persons after leaving office?

45. In Louisiana, is it against public policy to deal in futures of agricultural products, where no bona fide delivery is intended?

46. Compare the constitutional provisions for the abolition of justice of peace courts in Louisiana and Missouri. How do they differ?

47. Does the Georgia constitution declare lobbying a crime?

48. In Nebraska and Montana, must the oath of office for public officials include a statement that bribes have not been and will not be taken?

49. Do the boundaries of California and Washington extend into the ocean three miles from the coast including all islands?

50. Can the legislature in Missouri or Oklahoma establish local laws concerning ferries?

51. Are notaries public appointed by the governor in these states:
    Alabama
    Georgia

52. In what state may the legislature restrain publication of obscene books by suitable penalties?

53. Is the Secretary of State of Pennsylvania appointed by the governor with the advice and consent of 2/3 of the members of the senate?

54. Cite the poll tax amendment to the Texas Constitution.

55. At what age must judges retire in Missouri?

56. Does the state of New Hampshire retain the right of revolution?

57. Cite the first Alabama Constitution to ban lotteries.

58. What is the residency requirement in order to vote for electors for president and vice president in Michigan?

59. How long must a person have been a citizen of the United States to be eligible for the office of state treasurer in these states:
    Alabama
    Arizona

60. Does the Alaska Constitution contain a statement of policy regarding natural resources?

61. What article or amendment of the Massachusetts Constitution provides for the joint election of governor and lieutenant governor and when was this article approved by the voters of the Commonwealth?

62. Does the constitution of Utah provide for the election of lieutenant governor?

63. Is the Maine legislature authorized to appropriate moneys for the payment of mortgage loans for Indian housing?

ASSIGNMENT 3
STATE CONSTITUTIONS -- INDEXES

Sources: The general index to the appropriate state statutes, index to the constitution, topical analysis of separate articles, and notes to the decisions of each state to which reference is made.

Method:

Using the above sources, cite the applicable constitutional provision for each question below. Cite in accord with the latest edition of A Uniform System of Citation.

Questions:

1. Cite the Maine constitutional provision dealing with construction of buildings for industrial use.

2. The Maine legislature's authority to insure Maine veterans' mortgage loans up to eighty percent.

3. The Maine constitution includes a provision which amends the apportionment of senatorial districts beginning in 1983.

4. Is there a section concerning police power in the Maine constitution?

5. Cite the Wyoming constitutional article dealing with changing the names of persons or places.

6. Can a woman under the age of fourteen do clerical work at a mine in Wyoming?

7. Is there a limitation on municipal indebtedness for the purpose of building sewers in Wyoming?

8. Does the U.S. government have jurisdiction over Indian land in Wyoming?

9. Does the schedule of the Tennessee constitution of 1870 provide for the appointment of a state reporter?

10. In Tennessee, can the size of an existing county be reduced to less than 275 square miles?

11. Which section of the Tennessee constitution deals with the pay and allowances for members of the General Assembly?

12. Which article and section of the New Mexico constitution gives Spanish-American children the right to equal education in New Mexico?

13. What is the length of the term of the "state mine inspector" in New Mexico?

14. How many members per county are there in the state senate of New Mexico?

15. In 1950 in New Mexico, was the state highway commissioner required to live within the highway district from which he was appointed?

ASSIGNMENT 4
STATE CONSTITUTIONS -- CONSTRUCTION

Method:

Using bound volumes, bound supplements, specific pamphlet supplements, pocket parts, and general pamphlet supplements to the appropriate state statutes, cite the cases and answer the questions given below, according to rules in the latest edition of A Uniform System of Citation.

Questions:

1. With reference to your answer of Question 1, Assignment 3 above, cite the Maine authority fixing the minimum limit on percentage of voters who may authorize issuance of municipal bonds, below which the Legislature may not go.

2. Cite a 1975 Maine authority construing Article IV, part 1, section 8 of the Maine Constitution.

3. With reference to your answer to Question 4, Assignment 3 above, cite the Maine case holding that proper regulation under the police power does not amount to a taking of property which could require the payment of just compensation by the state.

4. With reference to your answer to the same section of the Wyoming Constitution given in your answer to Question 5, Assignment 3, cite a Wyoming case holding that because a statute applies only to one city it is not necessarily unconstitutional as special legislation.

5. Article 9 of the Wyoming Constitution has a section which discusses the position of inspector of mines. In the "cross references" annotation to the section, two cases are listed. When were these two cases decided? Cite the older case.

6. With reference to the same section of the Wyoming Constitution given in your answer to Question 7, Assignment 3 above, cite a 1966 Wyoming case discussing storm sewers and additional bonded indebtedness.

7. With reference to your answer to Question 8, Assignment 3 above, cite the case which discusses power dam construction on former Indian lands.

8. With reference to the Sixth Amendment of the United States Constitution, cite the Tennessee case holding that a defendant's right to a speedy trial was not prejudiced even if he was not arrested immediately, because the evidence clearly showed that efforts were initiated to locate him within hours after the crime was committed.

9. With reference to the same section of the Tennessee Constitution given in your answer to Question 10, Assignment 3 above, cite the 1917 Tennessee case indicating whether the size of a county of less than 500 square miles could be further reduced.

10. With reference to your answer to Question 11, Assignment 3 above, cite the 1974 Tennessee case which discusses the state general assembly.

11. With reference to Article 16, Section 3, of the New Mexico Constitution, cite the 1974 case which lists several factors used in calculating "duty."

12. With reference to Article 12, Section 13 of the New Mexico Constitution, cite a recent case indicating whether a taxpayer has standing to enforce by mandamus the duty of the regents.

13. With reference to your answer to Question 14, Assignment 3 above, cite the number of a 1972 opinion by the Attorney General of New Mexico.

14. When (if ever) was that section of the New Mexico Constitution dealing with the right to bear arms most recently amended?

ASSIGNMENT 5
STATE CONSTITUTIONS -- CITATION PROBLEMS

Method:

Using the the latest edition of Uniform System Of Citation provide the correct citation for the following questions.

Questions:

1. Article 1, Section 6A of the Maine Constitution contains that state's due process clause.

2. Section 1 of article XXI of the New Mexico Constitution relates to the toleration of religious sentiment.

3. Part 2, Section 1 of article IV of the Maine Constitution states the number of senators to be elected to the state legislature.

4. Page 783 of the Index-Digest Of State Constitutions 2d (1959) has a section which indicates that South Carolina prohibits prize fighting.

5. Collective bargaining by public employees in New Jersey is provided for in Section 19 of article I of the New Jersey Constitution.

ASSIGNMENT 6
THEME PROBLEMS

Theme Problem I:

1. What parts of the U.S. Constitution does Brown v. Board of Education (347 U.S. 483) discuss?

2. Name four places where one could locate those sections.

3. What is the advantage of an annotated constitution?

4. Using U.S.C.A., find discussion of the Brown decision under the Equal Protection point of the 14th Amendment. Under what heading and number does it appear?

5. How can one get into such specialized areas when there are so many cases digested?

6. Using U.S.C.S., find discussion of the Brown decision under the Equal Protection Clause of the 14th Amendment. Under what heading and number does it appear?

7. Where could one find cases on discrimination in colleges and universities?

8. Does the bound volume cite any Annotations on the topic of Brown?

9. If one wanted to find related law review articles, where could one look?

10. Using the Library of Congress Constitution of the United States of America, locate discussion of the Brown case. On what pages is it discussed?

11. How does the discussion found in Question 11 differ from those found in U.S.C.A. and U.S.C.S.?

12. What problems would be presented by using the Library of Congress edition?

Theme Problem II:

1. What part of the Constitution does Roe v. Wade (410 U.S. 113) rely upon?

2. Name four places where you could find the text involved.

3. What would be the advantage of using an annotated constitution?

4. Using the U.S.C.A. Constitution volumes to answer Questions 4-7, where can one find discussion of the Roe case under the heading of Abortions - generally?

5. What case is noted before it?

6. How many places would you have to check to be sure you have all current cases on the subject?

7. Where could one find cases on the regulation of the advertising of contraceptives?

8. Using the Constitution volumes of U.S.C.S. for Questions 8-11, where in the notes could you find the Roe decision digested as a criminal matter?

9. Where could one find related law review articles?

10. Cite a relevant Annotation.

11. What does the abbreviation "LC" mean?

12. Contrast the information found through U.S.C.A. and U.S.C.S.; which is more useful and why?

13. Is Roe v. Wade discussed in the Constitution of the United States of America (1972 ed.) by the Library of Congress?

14. What problem with this source is highlighted in answering Question 13?

15. Does your home state have a constitutional provision on abortion? If so, cite and state its status.

Theme Problem III:

1. Upon what part of the Constitution does Gideon v. Wainwright, 372 U.S. 335 (1963) rely?

2. Name four places where you could find the text of that part.

3. What would be the advantage of using an annotated constitution?

4. Using U.S.C.S. for Questions 4-7, where can one find cases on the right of indigent defendants to have counsel appointed for them?

5. Where could one find cases on a request for counsel by a defendant in a foreign prison?

6. Where could one find citations to law review articles that relate to this topic?

7. What does "OSHD" stand for?

8. Using U.S.C.A. for Questions 8-11, where in the notes on the 6th Amendment would you find cases on:
   (a) an indigent's rights to counsel?
   (b) the retroactivity of the Gideon decision?

9. Why is there no pocket part in the main U.S.C.A. volume on Amendment 6? What must you do to locate all recent cases?

10. When were the first 10 Amendments ratified?

11. What does the abbreviation "C.C.P.A." stand for?

12. Using the Library of Congress Constitution of the United States of America (1972 ed.), locate discussion of the Gideon case. On what page is it discussed?

13. What problems might one face by relying on the Library of Congress tool as a current statement of the law?

14. Does your state have a constitutional provision guaranteeing representation to all defendants in all actions? If so, give the citation.

ASSIGNMENT 7
DRILL PROBLEMS

Drill Problem I:

A. Using the Library of Congress Constitution of the United States of America (1972 ed.), answer the following:

1. The 1941 decision in United States v. Classic, 313 U.S. 299, overruled what former decision?

2. What is the only place in the Constitution where the writ of habeas corpus is mentioned?

3. What case held the Act of Aug. 24, 1935 (49 Stat. 750) unconstitutional as beyond the taxing power?

4. What doctrine did the Court establish in the case of Luther v. Borden, 48 U.S. 1 (1849)?

5. Which was the only pending amendment submitted to the states for ratification as of 1973?

B. Use the Constitution as printed in the U.S.C.A. or the U.S.C.S. to answer the following:

1. What article and section of the Constitution deals with the power of Congress to declare war?

2. What provision empowers Congress to define what constitutes piracy and to set punishments for it?

3. What provision prohibits states from keeping ships of war without the consent of Congress?

4. Which provision guarantees a trial by jury in criminal cases? Locate a 1953 decision from the Sixth Circuit which holds that the elements of a constitutional jury trial that require 12 jurors and a unanimous verdict are procedural and not jurisdictional.

5. What provision gives Congress the power to grant copyrights?

C. State Constitutions

1. Using the constitution for the jurisdiction in which you currently reside, cite the provisions (if any) that deal with the following questions:
    (a) The publication of judicial opinions.
    (b) The appointment/election of justices to the state's highest court.
    (c) Granting of municipal charters.

Drill Problem II:

A. Using the Library of Congress Constitution of the United States of America, answer the following:

1. The 1890 decision of Leisy v. Hardin, 135 U.S. 100 (1890) overruled an Iowa law dealing with what subject matter?

2. Where can discussion of Ng Fung Ho v. White, 259 U.S. 276 (1922) be found?

3. Has there been a great deal of judicial commentary concerning the Third Amendment?

4. Which Supreme Court case dealt with the conviction of a man wearing a flag sewn to the seat of his trousers?

B. Use the Constitution as printed in U.S.C.A. or U.S.C.S. to answer the following:

1. Which Amendment prevents a criminal defendant from having to face the same charges twice?

2. Cite a 1978 federal decision from an Alabama case holding that intent is a necessary element in an action for racial gerrymandering under the XV Amendment.

3. Where is it specified that two witnesses are needed to convict a person of treason?

4. What provision prevents a religious test from ever being applied as a requirement for any office in the federal government?

Drill Problem III:

A. Using the Library of Congress Constitution of the United States of America, answer the following:

1. What was the first territory (later a state) to accord full suffrage rights to women in 1869, presaging the Nineteenth Amendment?

2. How many amendments to the Constitution have been submitted to the states and have failed to be ratified?

3. What is the object of the clause requiring Congress to keep a journal?

4. Was a statute that denied polygamists the right to vote in territorial elections unconstitutional as an ex post facto law when applied to one who had not contracted a polygamous marriage since the passing of the act?

5. Where can one locate discussion of the doctrine of prior restraint as it applies to the First Amendment?

B. Use the Constitution as printed in U.S.C.A. or U.S.C.S. to answer the following:

1. What part of the Constitution mandates the taking of a national census at 10 year intervals?

2. What provisions deal with taxation of native Americans?

3. Where is the pardon power of the President created?

4. Which clause of the Constitution deals with habeas corpus?

CHAPTER 9

FEDERAL LEGISLATION

ASSIGNMENT 1A
FEDERAL LEGISLATION - PARALLEL REFERENCE TABLES:
U.S.C.

Method:

Using the parallel reference tables of the United States Code, the United States Code Annotated, the United States Code Service, give the U.S.C. citation for each of the following public laws.

Questions:

1. 92-230
2. 93-387
3. 93-361
4. 93-182
5. 91-586
6. 90-81
7. 90-619 sec. 1
8. 89-589
9. 89-29
10. 86-591
11. 94-209
12. 94-217
13. 94-241
14. 87-2
15. 86-719

ASSIGNMENT 1B
FEDERAL LEGISLATION - PARALLEL REFERENCE TABLES:
U.S.C.C.A.N.

Method:

Using the Table of Classifications in the U.S. Code Congressional and Administrative News, give the U.S.C. citation for each of the following public laws:

1. 89-360
2. 89-408
3. 89-586
4. 89-615
5. 89-771
6. 90-66
7. 90-118
8. 90-183
9. 90-194
10. 90-215
11. 90-330
12. 90-427
13. 90-498
14. 90-524
15. 90-597
16. 91-5
17. 91-35
18. 91-154
19. 91-167
20. 91-183
21. 91-233
22. 91-252
23. 91-300
24. 91-442
25. 91-549

ASSIGNMENT 2
UNITED STATES CODE CONGRESSIONAL AND ADMINISTRATIVE NEWS:
USE OF THE INDEX TO LOCATE ACTS

Method:

Using the index to the U.S. Code Congressional and Administrative News, give the number of the Senate or House bill, the Public Law number and the approval date of the Act.

Questions:

A.   1966 volumes:

1. Providing for the participation of the United States in the Asian Development Bank.

2. Authorizing the disposal of ruthenium from the supplemental stockpile.

3. Establishing the District of Columbia Bail Agency.

4. Authorizing a work release program for persons sentenced by the courts of the District of Columbia.

5. Extending coverage of the State Technical Services Act of 1965 to the territory of Guam.

B.   1967 volumes:

1. Termination of the Indian Claims Commission.

2. Establishment of the Golden Spike Centennial Celebration Commission.

3. Establishing a National Commsision on Product Safety.

4. Retirement of District of Columbia public school teacher on full annuity at age 55 after thirty years of service.

5. Prohibition of age discrimination in employment.

C.   1968 volumes:

1. Proclamation of National Jewish Hospital Save Your Breath Month.

2. Providing for the election of members of the Board of Education of the District of Columbia.

3. Authorizing the Secretary of Agriculture to convey certain lands to the city of Glendale, Arizona.

   4. National inspection system for grain.

   5. Creation of the North Cascades National Park.

D. 1969 volumes:

   1. Providing for a national center on educational media and materials for the handicapped.

   2. Protection of children from hazardous toys.

   3. Establishing a national policy for the environment.

   4. Establishment of a Commission on Government Procurement.

   5. Increasing the rates of dependency and indemnity compensation payable to widows of veterans.

   6. Special packaging to protect children from ingestion of poisons.

   7. Disposition of geothermal steam resources.

   8. Prohibiting the movement in interstate commerce of "sored" horses.

   9. Rate of duty on parts of stethoscopes.

   10. Continuation of the International Coffee Agreement Act of 1968.

ASSIGNMENT 3A
LOCATING A RECENT STATUTE IN
THE U.S. CODE BY USE OF THE INDEX

Sources: United States Code, 1982 Edition

United States Code Annotated

United States Code Service

Method:

(1) Briefly answer the question.

(2) Use any of the above sources and cite the relevant title and section of the United States Code and the latest Statutes at Large.

Questions:

1. What is the maximum penalty for violation of the labeling requirement of the Public Health Cigarette Smoking Act of 1969?

2. Who fixes the per annum rates of basic pay of positions on the National Zoological Park police force?

3. Is the Secretary of Agriculture authorized to eradicate the golden nematode?

4. May a sixteen year old alien file a valid petition for naturalization?

5. May Coast Guard warrant officers be temporarily promoted to higher warrant officer grades?

6. Are the natives of the Pribilof Islands entitled by law to receive free dental care from the United States government?

7. What is the maximum penalty for impersonating, falsely and with intent to defraud, an agent for the 4-H clubs?

8. May the Secretary of the Smithsonian Institution authorize the employment of aliens?

9. What is the minimum age at which Indians have the right to receive annuity money due them?

10. How many judges on the United States Court of International Trade can be from the same political party?

11. Do provisions of the Occupational Safety and Health Act of 1970 apply to employment performed in the Canal Zone?

12. Do provisions of the Age Discrimination in Employment Act of 1967 apply to persons between the ages of 35-39?

13. Geothermal leases are for a primary term of how many years?

14. Can instructors of the National Guard use public buildings for their offices?

15. How many members are authorized for the National Advisory Committee on Oceans and Atmosphere?

16. May the Paralyzed Veterans of America promote the candidacy of a person for public office?

17. The United States Postal Service was established as an independent establishment of which branch of the U.S. government?

18. May an employee of the Capitol Guide Service accept a gratuity for his official services?

19. Can the Secretary of State accept money and property as gifts to carry out the purposes of the Center for Cultural and Technical Interchange between East and West?

20. Is California considered a Colorado River Basin State under provisions of the Colorado River Basin Project Act?

21. How many members of the general public are selected to sit on the Technical Pipeline Safety Standards Committee, which deals with natural gas?

22. What is the maximum amount of reward possible for furnishing information to the U.S. regarding the illegal introduction of atomic weapons into the U.S.?

23. Under provisions of the Federal Contested Elections Act, must service of the notice of contest upon contestee be made only by delivering a copy to him personally?

24. Is the Convention on the Recognition and Enforcement of Foreign Arbitral Awards enforceable in the U.S. courts?

25. May loans guaranteed under provisions of the Emergency Loan Guarantee Act be renewed?

ASSIGNMENT 3B
LOCATING A RECENT STATUTE IN
THE U.S. CODE BY USE OF THE INDEX

Method:

Give the U.S.C. citation of the law which does the following:

Questions:

1. Creates the courts of bankruptcy.

2. Creates the Federal Deposit Insurance Corporation.

3. Makes unlawful the showing of sored horses.

4. Limits the use of the free bathhouse at the Hot Springs National Park.

5. Provides the method of computing the good time allowances for federal prisoners.

6. Establishes the National Foundation on the Arts and Humanities.

7. Creates the schedules of controlled substances.

8. Limits billboards along interstate highways.

9. Establishes the diameter of a dime as .705 inches and the weight as 2.268 grams.

10. Makes unlawful the advertisement of cigarettes on television.

11. Makes unlawful the transportation of refrigerators without safety devices enabling the door to be opened from the inside.

12. Provides for extradition hearings to be held publicly in a room or office easily accessible to the public.

13. Prohibits the operation of a gambling ship.

14. Prohibits the publishing of counterfeit weather reports.

15. Establishes the Appalachian Trail as a National Scenic Trail.

ASSIGNMENT 4
TABLES OF POPULAR NAMES OF FEDERAL ACTS

Sources: United States Code, 1982 edition, Index of Acts Cited by Popular Name.

United States Code Service, Lawyer's Edition. Tables.

United States Supreme Court Reports, Lawyer's Edition. Index to Annotations.

Shepard's Acts and Cases by Popular Names.

Method:

(1) Using source No. 1 above, give the citation to the first Statutes at Large enactment and to the U.S. Code, by title and first section, as well as the page number of the table where the Act is located.

(2) Using sources 2 and 3 above, indicate only the page on which the Act is located in each source.

(3) Using source 4 above, list the first reference which is provided.

Questions:

1. Age Discrimination in Employment Act of 1967.

2. Bilingual Education Act.

3. Commodity Credit Corporation Charter Act.

4. Environmental Education Act.

5. Export Apple and Pear Act.

6. Federal Contested Election Act.

7. Foreign Military Sales Act.

8. Gambling Devices Act of 1962.

9. Handicapped Children's Early Education Assistance Act.

10. International Organizations Immunities Act.

11. Jury Selection and Service Act of 1968.

12. Motor Vehicle Air Pollution Control Act.

13. National Commission on Libraries and Information Science Act.

14. National Portrait Gallery Act.

15. National Trails System Act.

16. Newspaper Preservation Act.

17. Public Broadcasting Financing Act of 1970.

18. Radiation Control for Health and Safety Act of 1968.

19. Service Contract Act of 1965.

20. Special Drawing Rights Act.

21. Standard Reference Data Act.

22. Uniform Time Act of 1966.

23. Vaccination Assistance Act of 1962.

24. Volunteers in the Parks Act of 1969.

25. Wild and Scenic Rivers Act.

ASSIGNMENT 5
FEDERAL LEGISLATION - CODE ANNOTATIONS

Method:

Each of the problems below contains a reference to a particular title and section of the United States Code. Each such section has been interpreted by the courts. Annotations on a case interpreting a particular section will follow that section in the United States Code Annotated. Using these annotations, answer the questions in the problems below. Cite a case supporting your answer.

Questions:

1. Categories of priorities for visas for potential immigrants to this country are set out in 8 U.S.C. Sec. 1153. Subsection (a)(3) gives the third priority to immigrants who are members of the professions. Who bears to burden of proof with respect to a third preference visa?

2. The hunting of migratory birds, except as provided by regulation, is outlawed by 16 U.S.C. Sec. 703. Is the red-tailed hawk a migratory bird?

3. A remedy is provided by 25 U.S.C. Sec. 229 for U.S. citizens who have suffered injuries to their property at the hands of an Indian belonging to a tribe in "amity" with the United States. What constitutes "amity" as it is used in this section?

4. Certain disruptive students are disqualified by 20 U.S.C. Sec. 1088f from participation in federal student assistance programs. Has the constitutionality of this section ever been tested?

5. All citizens of the U.S. are given the same right to buy and sell property as the white citizen has by 42 U.S.C. Sec. 1982. Has this section ever been held to apply to a cemetery lot?

6. Voting qualifications which are designed to deny citizens the right to vote on account of race are prohibited by 42 U.S.C. Sec. 1973. Has this section ever been given retroactive effect?

7. Slavery in the United States was abolished by 42 U.S.C. Sec. 1994. Would that provision outlaw assignment of attorneys to represent indigents without compensation?

8. Discrimination and segregation in public places are prohibited by 42 U.S.C. Sec. 2000a. Would this prohibition apply to a skating rink?

9. In order to collect social security disability benefits, one's disability must fall within the definition of "disability" given in 42 U.S.C. Sec. 423(d). Could a psychosomatic impairment satisfy this definition?

10. Those persons who may be punished as principals for violations of federal criminal statutes are set out in 18 U.S.C. Sec. 2. Could an officer who agreed to protect a criminal be punished as a principal?

11. Is laches likely to be a good defense to a charge of conspiracy under 18 U.S.C. Sec. 371?

12. In determining the eligibility for parole under 18 U.S.C. Sec. 4202, is it proper to aggregate sentences which are being served consecutively?

13. Would 18 U.S.C. Sec. 1341, outlawing the use of the mails to execute a scheme to defraud, include premarital promises?

14. The procedure for removal of cases from state courts to federal district courts is provided by 28 U.S.C. Sec. 1446. May the bond required by this section be waived?

15. It is provided by 28 U.S.C. Sec. 2246 that on an application for a writ of habeas corpus, evidence may be taken by deposition. What law governs the taking of such a deposition?

ASSIGNMENT 6
USE OF U.S.C.S., UNCODIFIED LAWS AND TREATIES VOLUME

Source: United States Code Service, Lawyer's Edition. Notes to Uncodified Laws and Treaties.

Method:

    Cite a case interpreting the uncodified Federal law.

Questions:

1. The words "hereby granted" in the settlement and preemption proviso of the Joint Resolution, approved May 31, 1870, 16 Stat. 378, applied only to lands within the place limits in the State of Montana and not to lands acquired by the Northern Pacific Railway within the "second indemnity strip" in that state.

2. Note given to the United States and representing feed and seed loan made pursuant to the Joint Resolution, approved December 20, 1930, c. 21, 46 Stat. 1032, was not barred by state statute of limitations or by laches.

3. The three mile limit of territorial waters jurisdiction of the United States in preventing the smuggling of intoxicating liquors are limited by a treaty with Great Britain to a three-mile limit in territorial waters and seizure 20 miles from shore is unlawful (43 Stat. 1761).

4. United States succeeded to sovereignty of California by the Treaty of Guadalupe Hidalgo and had authority to impose a registration act on claimants to California land, under Act of March 3, 1851, c. 41, 9 Stat. 631.

5. The Menominee Indians, being dissatisfied with an arrangement made in 1822 to cede a large tract of land for the use of other tribes, agreed by a treaty at 7 Stat. 303 (1827) to refer the issue to the President.

6. The Wyoming Admission Act of July 10, 1890, c. 664, 26 Stat. 222 did not give the title to the lands identified as sections 16 and 36 upon the approval and acceptance of the official resurveys made by the general land office designating the lands in question as sections 16 and 36.

7. One charged with a sale of less than a gallon of intoxicating liquor can be compelled to submit to finger printing under the Jones Act amendments, 46 Stat. 1036 (1931).

175

8. An agreement between the City of San Francisco and the Secretary of the Interior, relieving the obligation to reimburse the U.S. for maintenance of certain roads in Yosemite National Park, under the Act of Dec. 19, 1913, c. 4, 38 Stat. 242, was void and the U.S. was not estopped from disaffirming the agreement.

9. Where Select Committee on Presidential Campaign Activities sought declaration from District Court pursuant to Pub. L. No. 93-190, 87 Stat. 736 (1973), that President Nixon had a legal duty to comply with a subpoena duces tecum directing him to produce five taped conversations and had its dismissed complaint affirmed.

10. The House Committee on Un-American Activities was not authorized under the Legislative Reorganization Act of August 2, 1946, c. 753, 60 Stat. 816, Section 121 to conduct an investigation in Puerto Rico.

11. Act of June 14, 1926, ch. 582, 44 Stat. 744 (1926) gave all title and interest in the bridge across Port Washington Narrows to the state by purchase or condemnation proceedings.

12. The property of the City of Dubuque Bridge Commission established by the Act of July 18, 1939, c. 318, 53 Stat. 1051 is not immune from state real estate tax.

13. Tax paid under protest under the Act of Feb. 10, 1936, c. 42, 49 Stat. 1106, could be recovered upon the tax and the act being held unconstitutional.

14. Section 9(a) of the Teton Dam Disaster Assistance Act, 90 Stat. 1211 (1976), was intended to establish independence of claims under the Act from those that might exist under any other provision of applicable law and does not waive the filing requirements of the Federal Tort Claims Act.

15. The State of New Mexico may pledge lands to carry out provisions of the Act of May 28, 1928, c. 812, 45 Stat. 775.

16. A bridge across Sandusky Bay was held taxable as real property under the Act of May 5, 1926, c. 245, 44 Stat. 402.

17. The provision as to search of private dwellings under the Willis-Campbell Act of Nov. 23, 1921, c. 134, 42 Stat. 223, Section 3 applied to Alaska.

18. The Soldiers' and Sailors' Civil Relief Act of March 8, 1918, c. 20, 40 Stat. 440, Section 102, was held to apply to proceedings in state courts.

19. The Food Control, "Lever Act" of Aug. 10, 1917, c. 53, 40 Stat. 276, was held not to have suspended operation of state antitrust laws.

20. The Indian Depredation Claims Act of Jan. 11, 1915, c. 7, 38 Stat. 791, did not reinstate claims previously dismissed on grounds other than alienage of claimant.

21. In acquiring the Alaska Northern Railway Co. under authority of the Act of March 12, 1914, c. 37, 38 Stat. 305, the U.S. was acting in its capacity as a sovereign and could not be sued in tort without its consent.

22. A certificate of furlough granted under the Act of Aug. 24, 1912, c. 391, 37 Stat. 569, Section 2, to one who had served three years in the U.S. Army, was not an honorable discharge, entitling him to apply for citizenship.

23. The Act of August 5, 1909, c. 8, 36 Stat. 130, was not repealed by the Organic Act or by the Independence Act.

24. Under the Act of June 11, 1906, c. 3072, 34 Stat. 231, the State of Washington and King County, not the federal government, were responsible for work in lowering levels of Lake Washington.

25. The Port of New York Authority, created by a compact between New York and New Jersey at 42 Stat. 174 (   ) is the immediate agency of two sovereigns.

ASSIGNMENT 7
USE OF TABLES FROM STATUTES
AT LARGE CITATION TO U.S. CODE CITATION

Source: <u>United States Code Annotated</u>. 1970 Tables Volume and latest supplements.

Method:

Give the U.S. Code citation and present status.

Questions:

1. Act of April 29, 1968   P.L. 90-297 Sec. 1   82 Stat. 110
2. Act of Dec. 31, 1970   P.L. 91-609 Sec. 212   84 Stat. 1779
3. Act of Dec. 9, 1969   P.L. 91-143 Sec. 8(b)   83 Stat. 323
4. Act of Oct. 1, 1969   P.L. 91-79 Sec. 6   83 Stat. 127
5. Act of Oct. 24, 1968   P.L. 90-639 Sec. 2(a)   82 Stat. 1361
6. Act of Oct. 21, 1968   P.L. 90-612 Sec. 4   82 Stat. 1202
7. Act of Oct. 17, 1968   P.L. 90-580 Sec. 541   82 Stat. 1136
8. Act of Oct. 16, 1968   P.L. 90-576 Sec. 304   82 Stat. 1096
9. Act of Aug. 16, 1968   P.L. 90-490 Sec. 301(d)   82 Stat. 788
10. Act of Aug. 1, 1968   P.L. 90-448 Sec. 1714(b)   82 Stat. 607
11. Act of June 29, 1968   P.L. 90-368 Sec. 1(1)   82 Stat. 278
12. Act of Apr. 29, 1968   P.L. 90-297 Sec. 1   82 Stat. 110
13. Act of Dec. 16, 1967   P.L. 90-206 Sec. 205(d)   81 Stat. 629
14. Act of Dec. 4, 1967   P.L. 90-170 Sec. 6   81 Stat. 530
15. Act of Nov. 14, 1967   P.L. 90-137 Sec. 302(q)   81 Stat. 462
16. Act of Nov. 6, 1966   P.L. 89-774 Sec. 3   80 Stat. 1352
17. Act of Nov. 3, 1966   P.L. 89-750 Sec. 181   80 Stat. 1209
18. Act of Oct. 29, 1966   P.L. 89-698 Sec. 104   80 Stat. 1068

19.	Act of Sept. 23, 1966	P.L. 89-601 Sec. 604	80 Stat. 844
20.	Act of Aug. 24, 1966	P.L. 89-544 Sec. 18	80 Stat. 352
21.	Act of May 24, 1966	P.L. 89-429 Sec. 8	80 Stat. 167
22.	Act of Mar. 15, 1966	P.L. 89-368 Sec. 202(a)	80 Stat. 66
23.	Act of Oct. 29, 1965	P.L. 89-301 Sec. 4(d)	79 Stat. 1114
24.	Act of Oct. 22, 1965	P.L. 89-287 Sec. 7	79 Stat. 1039
25.	Act of Aug. 19, 1964	P.L. 88-448 Sec. 401(g)	78 Stat. 490

ASSIGNMENT 8
USE OF TABLES FROM FORMER TITLES
OF U.S. CODE TO PRESENT TITLE

Source: United States Code Annotated. 1984 Cumulative supplement Tables volume.

Method:

Refer to Title 11 in Revised Titles Table. The problems relate to former sections. Give either the current section number of the revised title or the present status of the former section.

Questions:

1. 53
2. 1(4)
3. 76(e)
4. 32(b)
5. 112
6. 101
7. 208
8. 401(1)
9. 406
10. 418
11. 501
12. 513
13. 533
14. 556
15. 573
16. 590
17. 642(2)
18. 664(a)
19. 676
20. 731
21. 751
22. 753
23. 872(1)
24. 908
25. 926

ASSIGNMENT 9
USE OF HISTORICAL INDEXES

Sources: Index to the Federal Statutes 1874-1931

U.S.C. Tables 1976, and other applicable volumes of U.S.C.

U.S.C.A. Tables, and other applicable volumes of U.S.C.A.

Method:

Give the Revised Statutes or first Statutes at Large citation with section of Act and date and, when available, the U.S.C. citation. Then search for the present status of the Act and in case of title revisions in the code give the new title and section; and in case of repeal, the citation to the Statutes at Large of the repealing Act.

Questions:

1. Joint Resolution declaring that a state of war exists between the United States and the German Empire in World War I.

2. Light-house officers will be reimbursed for rations furnished to shipwrecked persons.

3. Words implying masculine gender, in statutes generally, apply to females.

4. Widows of diplomatic or consular officers dying abroad were entitled to allowances equal to the allowance made to such officers for returning to their residence in the U.S.

5. Whaling vessels are exempt from the requirement for slop-chests specified in 23 Stat. 56.

6. Widows of veterans buried abroad are not required to pay passport fees, when the journey is undertaken to visit the graves of their husbands.

7. Citizenship requirement of seamen on vessels in ocean mail service.

8. Free uniforms will be furnished to inmates of the Soldiers' Home.

9. Penalties are authorized for threatening the President of the U.S. by mail.

10. Soldiers are prohibited from selling liquor to Indians.

11. The Star-Spangled Banner was designated the national anthem of the U.S.

12. Guano may be taken from Guano Islands only for use of residents of the U.S.

13. Reimbursement will be made for property lost in firefighting under contract with the National Park Service.

14. Fort Smith Jail, Arkansas, is declared to be a national jail.

15. Portraits of living persons may not be used on paper money.

16. Copyrighted religious music obtained from public libraries may be performed for charitable purposes without infringing on the copyright.

17. Dismissal for hazing at the Military Academy disqualifies a cadet for reappointment.

18. The penalty for maliciously injuring springs on arid public lands is a fine of not more than $1000 or imprisonment for not more than three years, or both.

19. Unclaimed money in dead letters will be deposited as postal revenue.

20. Machine gun units in the Army are included in field artillery.

21. The maximum penalty for the unauthorized wearing of a U.S. letter carrier's uniform is a fine of $100 and six months imprisonment.

22. Licenses will not be granted for the sale of intoxicating liquors within one mile of the Soldiers' Home.

23. Gold certificates of the U.S. shall be legal tender for all debts and dues.

24. All glass shall be excluded from the mail.

ASSIGNMENT 10
THEME PROBLEMS

Theme Problem I:

A. 18 U.S.C. 245 proscribes willful interference with anyone's right to a public education on the basis of race. Using the U.S.C., locate that provision and answer the following:

   1. What was the Public Law number of this legislation?

   2. Give its Statutes at Large citation.

   3. What is the fine imposed if bodily injury results?

   4. If you own and occupy a home with four rooms for hire, are you bound by the law in renting the other units?

B. Using U.S.C.A., find the same provision and answer the following:

   1. Have any cases been decided under Sec. 245?

   2. Cite a case that involved threats to a presidential candidate.

   3. Has Title 18 been enacted into positive law?

C. Using U.S.C.S., find the same provision and answer the folowing:

   1. Into what three sets does it give you research entry?

   2. Does 18 U.S.C. Sec. 245 create a civil cause of action? Cite a case.

   3. Does U.S.C.A. or U.S.C.S. seem more useful? Why?

D. The 93rd Congress, 2nd Session, passed legislation that all children, regardless of race, color, sex, or national origin, are entitled to equal educational opportunities in the public schools. Find this legislation and answer the following using the appropriate U.S. Statutes at Large volume.

   1. What is the short title of this Act?

   2. What is the name and citation of the larger Act of which it is a part?

   3. What was the bill number of the Act?

   4. Where is Title II codified in U.S.C.?

Theme Problem II:

A. The plaintiffs and intervenor in Roe v. Wade appealed to the U.S. Supreme Court under 28 U.S.C. Sec. 1253. Examine that provision in the U.S.C. and answer the following:

   1. What was the U.S. Statutes at Large citation for this legislation?

   2. Where would one look for related sections on writs?

   3. Where else in the title is this section referred to?

   4. What are the appendices to Title 28?

B. Using U.S.C.A., look up the same provision and answer the following:

   1. What Key Numbers apply?

   2. Where are cases on the question of "mootness" noted?

   3. Where are cases on the courts of Puerto Rico noted?

C. Using U.S.C.S., look up the same provision and answer these questions:

   1. Cite a law review article by Rosenberg on this topic.

   2. To what two sets of forms are you given citations?

   3. Where are cases on the order of a single judge court noted?

D. Compare and contrast the advantages of the three tools used above.

E. The 94th Congress, 1st Session, passed legislation which forbade any officer or employee of the United States to coerce anyone to have an abortion. Find that legislation using the appropriate U.S. Statutes at Large volume and answer the following:

   1. What is the name and citation of the act?

   2. What was its Senate bill number?

   3. Where will the section on coercion appear in U.S.C.?

Theme Problem III:

A. What is the provision of the U.S.C. which deals with the adequate representation of criminal defendants through authorizing each U.S. District Court to draw up a plan?

B. Turn to that provision in U.S.C. and answer the following:

1. What is the maximum total amount an appointed attorney may receive in a felony case?

2. What was the U.S. Statutes at Large Act upon which this section is based?

3. What was the effective date of the 1974 amendment?

4. Where in Title 48 is this section referred to?

C. Using U.S.C.A., locate this provision and answer the following:

1. What Key Number will lead to relevant cases?

2. Does the pocket part contain new text? If so, what legislation is the changed text based upon?

3. Cite a case that decides if the defendant had the right to have an urban sociologist appointed to aid in his defense.

D. Using U.S.C.S., locate the same provision and answer the following:

1. Cite a relevant law review article by Professor Tague.

2. Find a case that decides if the "expert services" made available under subsection 18(e) comprehend psychiatric assistance.

E. Compare and contrast U.S.C., U.S.C.A., and U.S.C.S. as to how easy you find them to use.

F. The 91st Congress, 2nd Session, passed legislation that changed the name of the D.C. Legal Aid Agency and redefined its structure and function. Find that legislation using the appropriate U.S. Statutes at Large volume and answer the following:

1. What is the title and citation of the act of which it is a part?

2. Which title of the act deals with the Public Defender Service?

3. Where will these provisions be codified?

ASSIGNMENT 11
DRILL PROBLEMS

Drill Problem I:

A. Using either the U.S.C., U.S.C.A., or U.S.C.S., answer the following:

   1. Where in the Code would one find the penalty for the forgery of a passport?

   2. Where in the Code is the law affecting the issuance of commercial licenses by the Nuclear Regulatory Commission?

   3. What section of the Code gives the sentence for a U.S. ship captain who voluntarily surrenders his ship to a pirate?

   4. What section of the Code requires state legislatures and officers to declare allegiance to the Constitution of the United States?

   5. Where in the Code does it calculate the average rate of interest of the reserves of a life insurance company?

B. Using any of the popular name tables, locate the correct citation for the following (it may be necessary to consult more than one):

   1. White Russian Act

   2. Dawson Act

   3. Wetback Act

   4. Maritime Extension Act

   5. American Fire Act

C. For each of the questions in this section, provide:

   (1) The Public Law (or Chapter) number and Statutes at Large citation for the original legislation described.

   (2) The location of the legislation in the U.S. Code. (Note: if it has not been codified, write "none." If it has been codified in several Code locations, list the citation for the earliest part of the Act codified.)

   1. What 1975 act provides indemnity for creative works that are displayed in exhibitions?

2. What act passed by the 90th Congress prescribes penalties for the violation of certain federally protected rights of an individual?

3. What act passed by the 93rd Congress enables females to participate in National Little League baseball?

4. What act passed by the 85th Congress authorizes construction of the U.S.S. Arizona Memorial?

5. What act passed by the 93rd Congress provides financial assistance to prevent child abuse?

Drill Problem II:

A. Using U.S.C., U.S.C.A., or U.S.C.S., answer the following:

1. What are the factors determining whether a particular piece of work could be reproduced under the "fair use" doctrine?

2. What section of the code declares United States cooperation with other countries in the control of narcotics?

3. What section of the code specifies the age limits of those liable for training and service in a military draft?

4. What is the punishment for the disclosure of information involving U.S. communication of intelligence to aid a foreign country?

5. What sections of the code authorize the Secretary of Labor to recruit agricultural workers from Mexico?

B. Using any of the popular name tables, locate the correct citation for the following:

1. Bloody Bill Act

2. Shingles Quota Act

3. Sac and Fox Allotment Act

4. Refugee Assistance Act

5. Failing Newspaper Act

C. For each of the questions in this section, provide:

  (1) The Public Law (or Chapter) number and Statutes at Large citation for the original legislation described.

  (2) The location of the legislation in the U.S.C. (Note: if it has not been codified, write "none." If it has been codified in several locations in the Code, list the citation for the earliest part of the Act codified.)

  1. What act passed by the 93rd Congress provides job training for the economically disadvantaged and underemployed?

  2. What act was passed in 1954 to modify and extend the existing national defense laws?

  3. What act restored citizenship, posthumously, to Robert E. Lee in 1975?

  4. What act provides for the establishment of an American Folklife Center in the Library of Congress?

  5. What act of the 93rd Congress provides for the protection of human subjects in biomedical research?

Drill Problem III:

A. Using U.S.C., U.S.C.A., or U.S.C.S., answer the following:

  1. What are the testing requirements to determine whether a substance causes cancer?

  2. Where in the code is a study of the protection of whales?

  3. Where in the code is the definition of "misleading advertisement"?

  4. Where in the code is an employee's right to organize a labor union affirmed?

  5. What section of the code allocates money for legal clinical education programs?

B. Using any of the popular name tables, locate the correct citation for the following (it may be necessary to consult more than one):

  1. Chace Act

  2. Stowaways Act

3. Coercive Practices Act

4. Sunshine Law

5. Filled Cheese Act

C. For each of the questions in this section, provide:

    (1) The Public Law (or Chapter) number and Statutes at Large citation for the original legislation described.

    (2) The location of the legislation in U.S.C. (Note: if it has not been codified, write "none." If it has been codified in several parts of the code, list the citation for the earliest part of the Act codified.)

1. What 1973 Act amends the Public Service Act in order to encourage the operation of health maintenance organizations?

2. What 1972 Act authorizes the Atomic Energy Commission to issue temporary operating licenses for nuclear power plants?

3. What 1942 joint resolution declared a state of war against the government of Hungary?

4. What 1975 Act established the Hells Canyon National Recreation Area?

5. What Act of the 85th Congress allowed the duty-free importation of religious regalia when it was presented free of charge to a church?

Chapter 10

FEDERAL LEGISLATIVE HISTORIES

Introduction:

The questions presented here were developed to involve the use of the five sources for legislative histories most commonly found in small to medium-sized libraries. Students should become aware of other sources such as the U.S. Library of Congress, Congressional Research Service, Digest of Public General Bills; U.S. Congress, House of Representatives, Numerical Order of Bills and Resolutions which have passed either or both Houses, and Bills now pending on the Calendar; U.S. Congress, Senate, Library, Cumulative Index of Congressional Hearings, Bill Number Index; Public Laws (slip laws); and Information Handling Services, Legislative History Service. The questions were set up to include long and short questions in each section so that students may be assigned a long and a short question in each section as well as one or more of the general questions appearing at the end.

ASSIGNMENT 1
CONGRESSIONAL INFORMATION SERVICE

Method:

Use Congressional Information Service Annuals, 1970-75, Index volumes and tables of bill numbers, Abstract volumes and legislative histories. Answers to all questions should be cited according to rules in the latest edition of A Uniform System Of Citation, limiting citations to information found in C.I.S. Include volume, year, and pages where answers are found.

Questions:

1. In 1976 legislation was enacted to extend the United States fishing limit to 200 miles to prevent foreign over-fishing off the United States coast. President Ford supported the legislation on the condition that its effective date would be delayed so that the Law of the Sea Conference could complete its work. To trace the history of the current legislation, find the following in the 1975 CIS volumes:
   (a) Senate Report of H.R. 200, 94th Congress, 1st Session. Cite report and name of committee reporting.
   (b) What CIS Abstract number would you use to find the special oversight report on H.R. 200 on microfiche?
   (c) What are the numbers of the three House bills requiring the employment of straight baselines in charting fishery zone boundaries?

2. The Environmental Protection Agency was authorized to conduct research on the effects of noise on animals, humans and property, and one of the provisions of H.R. 11,021, as cleared by Congress on October 18, 1972, made it unlawful to import excessively noisy products. You wish to read some of the testimony presented before the Senate Committee by John Tyler, head of the technical committee of the National Organization to Insure the Sound Controlled Environment, and the floor debates on the bills. Cite:
   (a) Public Law number.
   (b) Date of enactment, Statutes at Large and Congressional Record citation, Senate Hearings wherein Mr. Tyler's testimony is recorded, the Presidential Statement of October 28, 1972.
   (c) Name of the House committee which reported on H.R. 11,021 and the House report number.

3. Organized crime control legislation (Bomb Threat Act) was proposed in S. 30 in 1969 and 1970. You wish to read the congressional hearing of June 11, 1970, during which examples of activities of organized crime which could be prevented under the bill's provisions, such as the racketeering operations of the Mafia, the Marcello organization in New Orleans, and newspaper articles on infiltration of legitimate business by organized crime were introduced. Find:
   (a) Public Law number of the Act.
   (b) Date of enactment, Statutes at Large and Congressional Record citations. State the name of the Senate committee reporting, and the CIS Abstract number of the House hearing.
   (c) Cite House Report and Congress which recommended passage of the bill, and the name of the member of the House of Representatives from New York who stated that the bill was unconstitutional.

4. In 1968 Congress repealed the authority which had been given to the National Science Foundation in 1958 to require persons engaging in weather modification activities to report such activities. This was repealed, and in 1971 legislation was enacted to require reporting of weather modification activities to the Federal government. To research the need for H.R. 6893, and the possibility of future legal and international problems arising from weather modification, find the following:
   (a) Public Law number.
   (b) Statutes at Large and Congressional Record citations. CIS Abstract numbers for the House hearings.
   (c) Cite the hearings.

5. In 1973 legislation was enacted to amend the Lead Based Paint Poisoning Act to prohibit the use of lead based paint in construction of facilities and in the manufacture of certain toys and utensils. Cite the following legislative materials in connection with S. 607:
   (a) Public Law number.
   (b) Date of enactment, Statutes at Large and Congressional Record citation, Number of 1973 Senate Report, and CIS Abstract number for microfiche.
   (c) Cite the House Conference Report which included agreements to differences concerning definitions of lead content constituting a hazard, and Congress.

6. One of the purposes of the Deepwater Port Act of 1974 is to authorize and regulate the location, ownership, construction, and operation of deepwater ports in waters beyond the territorial limits of the United States. Any adjacent coastal state directly connected by pipeline to a deepwater port is affected by the Act. You are required to research further reasons for the legislation introduced in H.R. 10,701 and H.R. 11,951. Cite:
   (a) Public Law number.
   (b) Date of enactment, Statutes at Large citation. CIS Abstract number of the 1974 House committee print. The Presidential Statement.
   (c) Cite Senate committee before which hearings were held.
   (d) Title of Senate committee print on policy issues.

7. In December, 1971, legislation was enacted to amend the Fishermen's Protective Act of 1967 to enhance the effectiveness of international fishery conservation programs. The legislation, which had been proposed in H.R. 3304 and related bills, authorized the President to prohibit importation of fishery products from nations conducting fishery operations in a manner that diminishes effectiveness of international fishery conservation programs. Cite legislative materials in support of the above:
    (a) Public Law number.
    (b) Date of enactment, Statutes at Large and Congressional Record citations. To read the House hearings on microfiche, which CIS Abstract number would you need? Cite the House report.
    (c) The hearings also included oversight of Soviet fishing violations in the Atlantic. Where were the hearings of April 14, 1971 held, and before which House committee and subcommittee?

8. Find a discussion of the 1973 planned cut in United States aid to the United Nations, and the extent of and need for assistance to smaller international organizations. Cite Congressional hearing and CIS Abstract number for microfiche.

9. To support their argument that plaintiff satisfied the first requirement for determining a cause of action to be implied in 18 U.S.C. Sec. 610, the U.S. Circuit Court of Appeals, in a 1975 case, referred to the intent of the 1971 legislation which led to the Federal Election Campaign Act. To read Richard G. Kleindienst's testimony regarding political campaign spending before a Senate committee in March 1971, cite the hearing and the CIS Abstract number of the microfiche.

10. In 1972, H.R. 9936 was enacted to provide for a current listing of each drug manufactured. What is the Public Law number? What is the name of the President of the Pharmaceutical Manufacturers' Association who testified in support of the bill? Cite the hearing.

11. Nuclear critics are advocating the use of solar power, and the Energy Research and Development Administration has called for increased use of solar energy for heating and cooling for the period 1985-2000. Having found a brief history of the legislation which led to the Solar Energy Research, Development, and Demonstration Act of 1974 as a result of S. 3234, give the Public Law number of the Act, Congress, Statutes at Large and Congressional Record citations.

12. In 1971 Roslyn McDonald, Acting Director of the Division of Youth, New York, testified before Congress during a hearing on H.R. 6247 which proposed amendments to the Juvenile Delinquency Prevention and Control Act of 1968. Cite the House committee and subcommittee hearings, give the Public Law number and Statutes at Large citation for the 1971 Act.

13. In March 1976, Senator Walter F. Mondale (D. Minn.) recommended that the Senate Committee on Labor and Public Welfare print a committee document to include the Senate bill of 1975 proposing the Child and Family Services Act of 1975, together with a response to an allegedly fraudulent propaganda campaign aimed at preventing passage of the legislation. Cite the number of the bill, the name of the subcommittee of which Senator Mondale was chairperson, and the Senate committee.

14. Cite the Public Law number and title of the legislation, enacted at the end of 1974, which removed social service programs from their prior close connection with cash public assistance programs, and set up a separate title in the Social Security Act. Where can you read the Presidential Statement in connection with this legislation?

15. The idea of extending cargo preference to oil imports appeared in the 1960s, and the result of studies of the United States shipping industry conducted by the Maritime Evaluation Committee led to the passage of the Merchant Marine Act Amendment of 1970. Give the Public Law number, the date the act was considered and passed by the House, and the CIS Abstract number of the hearing on microfiche.

ASSIGNMENT 2
UNITED STATES MONTHLY CATALOG

Method:

Use the subject, title, author index entry numbers of the United States Monthly Catalog, 1970-76, to find Congressional hearings, reports, documents, committee prints, and publications issued by the United States Government Printing Office for the various agencies and departments. Give complete citations in accordance with the latest edition of A Uniform System Of Citation.

Questions:

1. In December 1975, Public Law No. 94-135, Older Americans Amendments of 1975, was enacted to improve legal representation for older Americans. You wish to procure copies of the congressional material dealing with legislation on the aged and the aging from your congressman. Use the 1976 subject index and cite:
   (a) The Senate committees before which joint hearings were held. Include Congress, session, and date.
   (b) Locate a committee print in the title index which deals with doctors and nurses in nursing home care. Give complete citation.

2. In 1971 Congressional hearings were released on the establishment of a seaward boundary of the continental shelf, and on the emplacement of nuclear weapons on the ocean floor. Cite:
   (a) The hearings on the seaward boundary.
   (b) The Senate Executive Document containing the text of a message from the President on the seabed arms control treaty.

3. The only major Congressional action in 1973 on the busing of school children to eliminate racial segregation was in the form of proposed constitutional amendments prohibiting busing. Give complete citations for both publications.
   (a) A list of publications on constitutional rights was prepared by a subcommittee of the Senate Committee on the Judiciary.
   (b) A list of leading court decisions on public school desegregation was printed for the House Committee on the Judiciary.

4. In 1974 the House failed to act on H.R. 12,462, which established procedures for judicial enforcement of Congress's right to obtain information from federal officials by amending the Freedom of Information Act (Pub. L. No. 89-487). The bill raised the question of whether Congress should set up a statutory mechanism for dealing with claims of executive privilege and thereby implicitly recognize that privilege in law. Cite the following materials on the proposed amendments:
   (a) The report from the committee to accompany H.R. 12,462.
   (b) Hearings on government information involving national security.

5. In fiscal year 1975 business failures were 45% higher than in the previous year. New York's financial crisis and the great increase in the number of business and individual bankruptcies caused Congress to review the bankruptcy system. Legislation which was introduced in two important bills met with strong resistance from creditors. Many hearings were held in both Houses of Congress. To read the legislative materials on the Bankruptcy Reform Act which were available at the end of 1975, find complete citations for:
   (a) The hearings held on February 19 and April 24, 1975.
   (b) The committee report on revision of salary fixing procedure for referees.

6. In 1971 and 1972 hearings were held before the Senate Committee on the Judiciary on diversity jurisdiction, multiparty litigation, choice of law in Federal courts and an amended version of the Rules of Civil Procedure for United States District Courts was prepared by the House Committee on the Judiciary. Give complete citations to the hearing and the committee print.

7. (a) Cite the hearing which was held on the preventive detention of criminals in 1970.
   (b) The report of March 25, 1970, by the Committee on the District of Columbia to amend the D.C. Bail Agency Act.

8. Cite the 1970 hearings on the proposal to amend the Constitution to lower the voting age to 18.

9. Give the name of the Commission which compiled a list of the decisions on radiation injuries and workmen's compensation which were issued in 1972.

10. In 1976 Congress reconsidered the Public Works and Economic Development Act and held hearings on the status and implementation of Title 10, Job Opportunities Program. Cite the hearings.

11. In 1973 legislation was introduced to create a testimonial privilege for newsmen. Cite the numbers of two House bills. Include Congress and session.

12. In 1971 hearings were reported on legislation regarding he establishment of the seaward boundary of the continental shelf, and federally-owned oil and gas lands on the outer continental shelf. Give dates of the hearings on the seaward boundary and cite the bill number. Cite the name of the committee dealing with the federally-owned oil and gas lands.

13. Which two Senate committees reported on the bills proposing legislation popularly known as "Government in the Sunshine Act?"

14. In June 1972, Senator Walter F. Mondale (D. Minn.) addressed a Senate committee on the nation's failure to meet the needs of its children. Give complete citation to the Senate committee print containing this address.

15. Cite the number of the Senate bill introduced in connection with the Sixth Amendment right to a speedy trial, and the name of the Committee before which the April 17, 1973 hearing was held.

ASSIGNMENT 3
UNITED STATES CODE CONGRESSIONAL
AND ADMINISTRATIVE NEWS

Method:

    Use index, acts by popular names table, classification and legislative history tables, U.S. Code amendment and repeal tables, etc., in the United States Code Congressional And Administrative News volumes for the 88th Congress, 2d Session through the 94th Congress, 2d Session, to locate citations. Include Congress and session in your answers and cite in accordance with the latest edition of A Uniform System Of Citation. State volume and page where answers were located.

Questions:

1. Legislation continues to be introduced in an effort to prevent the tremendous increase in juvenile crime in the hope that this is the key to controlling crime in the United States. It is said that what has been done so far has failed miserably to instill in juveniles any respect for the law through either fear or confidence. Lawyers are paid to get juveniles off just as though they were in adult criminal court and, according to recent newspaper articles, the juvenile court as it is now set up is a standing joke in the juvenile community. Your state is in the process of rewriting its juvenile code and you have been asked to summarize the legislation which led to the Juvenile Delinquency Prevention and Control act of 1968. Cite the following:
   (a) Public Law number and Statutes at Large citation.
   (b) U.S. Code citation.
   (c) Date of approval, House bill number, full names of House and Senate committees reporting, and Congressional Record citation.
   (d) Who did Mr. Javits quote in connection with this legislation?

2. On July 6, 1976, President Ford signed S. 2853 (Pub. L. No. 94-339) to tighten up the accountability of food stamp vendors. On signing the bill, the President expressed disappointment that it was not a major revision of the program and stated that each day that goes by without congressional action to reform the food stamp program costs taxpayers about three million dollars. You have some questions about the integrity of the program. To research the legislation which led to the 1964 Act, cite the following:
   (a) Public Law number of the 1964 Act and the Statutes at Large citation.
   (b) House bill number, Congress and session. Congressional Record citation. Date House considered passage of the bill, and the name of the committee reporting.
   (c) Find the analysis of the House bill and cite the number of the section dealing with the redemption of coupons.

3. Major legislation was enacted in 1976 to revitalize the nation's railroads, and a new government agency was created to take over the operations of some of the bankrupt Northeast and Midwest railroads. You wish to research the background of the legislation which was enacted in 1973 to salvage the rail services operated by seven insolvent railroads in the same regions. Cite:
   (a) Public Law number of the 1973 Act and the Statutes at Large citation.
   (b) United States Code titles which were affected.
   (c) Date of approval, House bill number, Committee and Congress, Congressional Record citation.
   (d) The names of the four members who stated that, in their view, this legislation wrote into law a detailed collective bargaining agreement negotiated between railway management and labor, and paid for out of the Federal treasury.

4. On July 22, 1975, Attorney General Edward H. Levi presented to the Senate Judiciary Subcommittee on Juvenile Delinquency the Ford Administration's proposed gun control bill, which was intended to correct the flaws in the 1968 Gun Control Act. By September, 1975, the House Judiciary Subcommittee on Crime had 127 bills pending before it and both committees had held extensive hearings on gun control. To research the "flaws" in the 1968 Act find and cite the following:
   (a) Public Law number and Statutes at Large citation.
   (b) United States Code classification for Title I, Secs. 101-105 of the Act.
   (c) The Senate Report, the name of the committee reporting and the Congressional Record citation.
   (d) In Conference Report No. 1956 the title proposed for the Act by the Senate was adopted in lieu of that proposed by the House. Cite the title provided in the House bill.

5. A 1965 study entitled "The Older Worker - Age Discrimination in Employment" was reported by the Secretary of Labor. In 1967 legislation was introduced to correct this, and during Congressional hearings concerning the age limitation witnesses representing airline stewardesses revealed an apparent gross and arbitrary employment distinction based on age alone. To read the history of the 1967 Act cite the following:
    (a) Public Law number and Statutes at Large citation.
    (b) United States Code classification.
    (c) Bill number, Congress, and House committee reporting. Congressional Record citation.
    (d) How many states were cited as having age discrimination legislation of the type proposed in the House bill?

6. The coastal zone management concept which evolved some time in the mid-1960s led to the passage of federal legislation in 1972. Under the Act, and subsequent amendments, after a state has adopted a program and has it federally approved, federal actions are to be consistent with that state's program, giving the state additional leverage over federal agency actions. There is a developing legal area that is a major concern of the states, and you wish to evaluate the key issues and incentives in the coastal management program. Cite the following:
    (a) Public Law number of the 1972 Act, Statutes at Large citation.
    (b) United States Code classification.
    (c) Date of approval of the Act. Senate bill number, Congress, and name of Senate Committee reporting, date of passage, Congressional Record citation.
    (d) In his letter to Mr. Magnuson dated April 21, 1970, Mr. Robert F. Keller, Assistant Comptroller General of the United States, suggested a change in the bill regarding the acquisition of real property. What change did he suggest?

7. In his October 1973 anti-inflation message to Congress, President Ford requested new penalties for persons and corporations violating the antitrust laws. A bill to amend the antitrust laws with regard to the conduct of consent decree procedures resulted in legislation in 1974. Cite the following:
    (a) Public Law number and Statutes at Large citation.
    (b) The titles of the United States Code affected.
    (c) The number of the bill introducing the legislation and Congress. Date the House passed the bill and the name of the committee reporting, Congressional Record citation.
    (d) Having found a discussion of the legislation, state name of the person who introduced the first of the three bills relating to Antitrust Procedures and Penalties.

8. Cite the proper title of the 1975 Hazardous Materials Transportation Act, amendment, and Public Law number.

9. Cite the popular title of the provisions enacted under Public Law No. 93-638.

10. Give the Public Law number and the Statutes at Large citation of the legislation which was enacted as a result of H.R. 19,436 in 1970.

11. Cite a 1973 Executive Order dealing with the transfer of certain functions to the Office of Emergency Preparedness.

12. One of the major bills enacted in 1972 concerned dollar devaluation. From the 1972 U.S.C.C.A.N tables, cite the number of the bill and the Public Law number of the Act.

13. For the Act popularly known as Medical Device Amendments of 1976, provide the Public Law number and Statutes at Large citation.

14. Find the number of the House bill which was passed in lieu of S. 917, and approved on June 19, 1968, in the U.S.C.C.A.N. tables, and cite the Public Law number.

15. In 1974 the United States District Court ruled that infringement for criminal purposes exists under 17 U.S.C. Sec. 1(f) for tapes made by re-recording copyrighted tapes, even though slight changes were made by adding echoes or synthesizer sounds. This section of the United States Code applies to songs fixed after February 15, 1972. Check the 1971 U.S.C.C.A.N. tables and give the Public Law number and Statutes at Large citation, amending 17 U.S.C. to provide for the above.

16. Cite legislative material supporting the inclusion of American Samoa in territories covered by the Federal Aid in Wildlife and Fish Restoration Act of 1970.

17. Under the Disabled Veterans' and Servicemen's Automobile Assistance Act of 1970, the automobile allowance was raised to $3,000. Cite legislative material justifying this raise.

18. In considering the bill which, when enacted, created Voyageurs National Park in 1970, the Committee on Interior and Insular Affairs received assurances that the Governor of Minnesota favored the bill. Cite legislative material supporting that statement.

19. Cite legislative material which indicates the Department of the Interior's attitude toward passage of the Mining and Minerals Policy Act of 1970.

20. The Clean Air Amendments of 1970 authorize the Secretary of HEW to establish limitations on ingredients of motor fuels which endanger public health. Cite legislative material which claims that automotive pollution constitutes in excess of 60 per cent of our national air pollution problem.

21. The Poison Prevention Packaging Act of 1970 was passed in response to a national need. Cite legislative material which indicates that over 105,000 ingestions of drugs and toxic products occurred in 1968.

22. Cite legislative material which indicates that the New York Times endorses legislation of the type embodied in the National Environmental Policy Act of 1969.

23. The Child Protection and Toy Safety Act of 1969 was passed to protect children from toys which are hazardous due to electrical, mechanical, or thermal hazards. Cite legislative material which indicates that "Little Lady Oven" is considered hazardous.

24. The act which created the Desolation Wilderness in California in 1969 permits grazing in the area. Cite legislative material which supports this contention.

25. Cite legislative material which indicates that excessive radiation from color television sets was one hazard considered before passage of the Radiation Control for Health and Safety Act of 1968.

26. The act which created the Mount Jefferson Wilderness in Oregon in 1968 prohibited the further development of recreation facilities at Marion Lake. Cite legislative material which holds that preservation of the wilderness at Marion Lake is more important than the installation of such facilities.

27. The National Trails System Act of 1968 did not prohibit the use of bicycles. Cite legislative material which supports this contention.

28. The Wild and Scenic Rivers Act of 1968 was not intended to prohibit boating on the Rogue River in Oregon. Cite legislative material which supports this contention.

29. Cite legislative materials which indicate that the Animal Drug Amendments of 1968 were not intended to weaken the authorities of the Food and Drug Administration with respect to the regulation of new animal drugs.

30. The Consumer Credit Protection Act of 1968 restricts the garnishment of wages. Cite legislative materials which state that the garnishment of wages is the greatest single pressure forcing wage earners into bankruptcies.

31. Cite legislative materials which indicate that the number of buildings in use is expected to double by the year 2000, necessitating passage of the Fire Research and Safety Act of 1968.

32. The National Commission on Product Safety was established in 1967. Cite legislative materials which state that wringers on washing machines are potentially hazardous to children.

33. The Food for Peace Act of 1966 was not intended to provide commodities which the recipient country could obtain through its own resources. Cite legislative materials which support this statement.

34. Cite legislative material which indicates that Congress took action in the early 1800s similar to that embodied in the Disaster Relief Act of 1966.

35. The Child Protection Act of 1966 was enacted to deal with such hazardous objects as "cracker balls," small torpedo-like firecrackers. Cite legislative materials supporting that statement.

36. Cite legislative materials which indicate that the Fair Packaging and Labeling Act of 1966 does not inhibit innovation in design, as demonstrated by the attractive and imaginative bottles in which liquor is marketed.

37. Cite legislative materials which indicate that the act which established Wolf Trap Farm Park in Virginia in 1966 intended for not more than 145 acres to be included in the park.

ASSIGNMENT 4
COMMERCE CLEARING HOUSE CONGRESSIONAL INDEX

Method:

Use CCH Congressional Index, 1971-1972 (92d Congress, 1st Session) through 1973-1974 (93d Congress, 1st Session) to locate authors and numbers of Congressional bills, companion bills, names of committees to which bills are assigned and committee chairpersons, voting records, status and current status of bills. Cite answers in accordance with the latest edition of A Uniform System Of Citation.

Questions:

1. In the Juvenile Justice and Delinquency Prevention Act of 1974, provisions were made to establish a matching grant program within the Department of Health, Education and Welfare for local and private agencies to develop facilities and programs for runaway youths. A major controversy arose over the decision of who would run the expanded federal aid programs as members of Congress criticized the leadership of LEAA, HEW, and the effectiveness of social service facilities in juvenile delinquency control. Cite:
   (a) The number(s) of the Senate bill(s) which were introduced in connection with the controversy.
   (b) The numbers of any companion or identical bills.
   (c) The House committee(s) to which the first bill listed in a) above was referred.
   (d) The names of the House committees' chairpersons.

2. In 1975 the House reported a bill to amend the Immigration and Nationality Act so as to include a three-step procedure for imposing sanctions against employers who knowingly hire illegal aliens. To compare similar legislation which was passed in 1972, locate the earlier legislation and cite the following:
   (a) The two main sponsors of H.R. 16,188.
   (b) The name of the chairman of the committee to which it was assigned.
   (c) Number of the House report.
   (d) When was the bill sent to the Senate committee?

3. Since the late 1950s there has been agitation for reform of the existing motor vehicle insurance system. In 1974 legislation was proposed which would require all motorists to carry insurance providing compensation for bodily injury regardless of who caused the accident. To check the status of the proposed legislation at the end of the 1st Session of the 93d Congress, find the following:
   (a) The number(s) of the bill(s).
   (b) Numbers of companion or identical bills.
   (c) Who introduced the first bill in (a) above? To which committee was the bill assigned?
   (d) What action had been taken on the bill at the end of 1974?

4. Because of the lack of federal legislation, the only control of surface mining in 1973 rested with the laws enacted by 30 states, and strip mining has inflicted severe damage on the land in Appalachia and the Midwest due to the nation's hunger for power. During the first session in 1973, Congress considered legislation to regulate surface mining of coal. To determine the status of the legislation on land reclamation at the end of the first session, find the following:
   (a) The number(s) of the Senate bill(s).
   (b) Are any companion or identical bills listed?
   (c) The name of the standing House committee to which the Senate bill was referred, and the Senate Report number.
   (d) Date the bill was sent to the President.
   (e) Find a description of the Senate bill and name the sponsor(s).
   (f) How did Senator Mondale vote on the further amendment of October 9, 1973?

5. In April 1972, the Senate had before it a bill to amend the Truth-in-Lending Act of 1968 to protect consumers against unfair billing practices, and to help them resolve credit billing disputes. To determine the outcome of the legislation find the following:
   (a) The number of the Senate bill.
   (b) Are any companion bills listed? Number(s).
   (c) Find a description of the bill, and name the sponsor(s) and the committee to which it was assigned.
   (d) What was the name of the committee chairman?
   (e) Date of passage of the amended bill by the Senate.
   (f) Did Senator Hatfield (R. Or.) vote in favor of the bill?

6. In 1974 Congress found that the prolonged Federal domination of Indian service programs had served to retard rather than enhance the progress of Indian people and their communities by depriving them of the full opportunity to develop leadership skills crucial to the realization of self government, and it has denied them an effective voice in the planning and implementation of programs for their benefit which are responsive to the true needs of Indian communities. That year legislation was introduced to promote maximum Indian participation in the government and education of the Indian people. Cite:
   (a) Number of bill and Congress.
   (b) Date of Senate hearing. Name of Committee to which the bill was assigned, and the number of the House report.
   (c) Public Law number and the date approved.
   (d) Find a description of the bill and name the sponsor(s).
   (e) Was there a companion bill?
   (f) Name of Senate committee chairperson.

7. One of the most heated issues in Congress in 1972 was the conflict over busing elementary and secondary school children to eliminate racial segregation in education. In 1973 anti-busing constitutional amendments were proposed. To determine the status of the proposed legislation at the end of the first session of the 93d Congress find the following:
   (a) The numbers of the four bills.
   (b) The numbers of the identical bills to the second bill listed above.
   (c) Were any hearings held on the second bill listed in (a) above?
   (d) To which committee(s) were the bills asigned?
   (e) Who suggested the amendment proposed in the House Joint Resolution of April 1974?

8. During the 92d Congress a companion bill to H. 6978 was introduced in the Senate. Cite the number of the Senate bill and the subject matter of the proposed legislation. Who introduced the Senate bill?

9. Legislation was proposed in H. 1896, 93d Congress, to amend 15 U.S.C. 41 to provide that under certain circumstances exclusive territorial arrangements shall not be deemed unlawful. Give the number of an identical House bill. On which of the two bills was there a hearing? Who introduced the identical bill?

10. On what date was Public Law 92-159 approved? How did Representative Burleson of Texas vote? Give the Congressional Record citation.

11. During the 2d Session of the 92d Congress legislation was introduced regarding highway construction waste disposal and waste pollution control. Give Senate and House bill numbers. Who introduced the Senate bill?

12. Who introduced legislation to repeal the no-knock laws during the 93d Congress? Who was chairman of the committee to which the bill was assigned?

13. What was the subject matter of the legislation introduced in H. 1517 during the 92d Congress? Who was chairman of the committee to which the bill was assigned?

14. In lieu of which House bill was S. 607 passed in the 93d Congress? What is the subject matter of this legislation, and what was the number of the House resolution?

15. What is the number of the House bill (eventually Pub. L. No. 93-618) which proposed legislation during the 93d Congress to amend the Trade Reform Act to promote trade between the United States and the Soviet Union? How did Senator McGovern vote on the Conference Report on this bill?

ASSIGNMENT 5
CONGRESSIONAL QUARTERLY ALMANAC

Method:

Use table of contents, index, and tables in the <u>Congressional Quarterly Almanac</u>, volumes 28-31, 1972-1975, to research legislative highlights and summaries, bills, dates, congressional committees, presidential statements, voting records. Include volume and page numbers to indicate where the information was found.

Questions:

1. In February 1973, the Senate passed a bill that would provide new procedures to thwart aircraft hijackings. On the same day the United States and Cuba signed an agreement committing each nation to apply penalties to persons convicted of air or sea hijacking. Cite:
   (a) A discussion of the above in which the bill is described.
   (b) How did Senator Schweiker (R. Pa.) vote on the administration's regulations allowing searches?

2. The adverse impact on coastal states of the development of oil and gas resources resulted in the introduction of several bills proposing amendments to the 1953 Act to provide aid to the coastal states affected. Conflicting proposals caused some tension before one of the bills was passed in 1975, and you wish to read a discussion of the legislation. Find the following:
   (a) During the floor action there were complaints that the bill did not include aid to the inland states. What is the number of the bill which was later amended to include some inland states?
   (b) How did Senator Percy (R. Ill.) vote on the proposed amendments to narrow the uses to which states could put these aid funds?

3. In 1976 legislation was introduced to amend the 1972 Marine Mammal Protection Act in order to prohibit the taking of the killer whale, with certain exceptions. The basic thrust of the 1972 Act was to create a moratorium on the taking or importation of marine mammal products, but a controversial exception was given to a specific industry.
    (a) What is the number of the bill which was cleared for the President's signature, and the Public Law number of the Act?
    (b) In the Senate debate of July 25, 1972, on the issue of the moratorium, Harrison A. Williams, Jr. (D. N.J.) offered an amendment to prohibit the Secretary of the Interior or the NOAA Administrator from waiving for a five year period the provision of the moratorium. How did Senator Frank Church (D. Idaho) vote on this amendment?
    (c) Which industry was given the controversial exception?

4. In 1975 legislation was enacted to amend the Sherman Antitrust Act of 1890. There was a Presidential statement in connection with the legislation.
    (a) What was the number of the bill? State the popular name and Public Law number of the Act. What Federal exemptions were repealed?
    (b) During a discussion of the legislation a motion was made to suspend the rules and pass the bill. What was Representative Udall's position on the motion?

5. In May 1974 legislation was enacted to amend the Federal Revenue Sharing Act (State and Local Fiscal Assistance Act of 1972). The 1972 legislation provided for revenue sharing initially at an annual rate of $3.5 billion for local governments, and $1.8 billion for state governments, and it created three trust funds. Find a discussion of the 1972 legislation and cite the following:
    (a) The number of the House bill which was approved, and the Public Law number of the Act.
    (b) George Mahon (D. Tex.) made some vigorous comments. How did he vote when the time came for House floor action?

6. In September 1973, a House bill was introduced to amend the Immigration and Nationality Act of 1952, to impose a worldwide limit on United States immigration visas.
    (a) What was the ceiling on visas which the proposed legislation sought to impose?
    (b) How did Henry B. Gonzales (D. Tex.) vote?

7. In December 1975, the United States Senate delayed a final vote on the defense funding bill to discuss the growing controversy regarding American involvement in Angola. An amendment which would have enabled the United States to provide "some assistance resisting Soviet imperialism before it was too late" was rejected although its supporters argued that the Angolan situation was of symbolic importance and that an aid ban would strengthen elements in the Soviet leadership to whom detente was a guise behind which to pursue an expansionist policy without resistance from the United States.
    (a) Cite the names of the two members of Congress who introduced amendments.
    (b) How did Bella S. Abzug vote on the House bill?
    (c) The budget request for Central Intelligence Agency activities was reduced, and the Conference Report was adopted during the second session. State the Public Law number and the Congress.

8. When the Senate Select Committee on Nutrition and Human Needs held hearings in September 1972 on S. 76, which would broaden the definition of "food additives" under the Food, Drug and Cosmetic Act, Dr. John W. Olney of the Washington University School of Medicine, St. Louis, reported on studies of the effects of monosodium glutamate. What did he report?

9. What was the name of the witness representing the Association of the Bar of the City of New York when, on February 5-8, 1973, the House committee addressed the question of whether Congress has the right to enact legislation granting an absolute privilege to newsmen to resist demands for confidential or other unpublished information?

10. Two anti-abortion groups filed lobby registrations during the last two months of 1975. What were the names of the groups and what was each of the lobbyists seeking?

11. In 1972 the House and the Senate considered several bills concerning the control of predators and the preservation of endangered species. Give the numbers of the three main bills and names of sponsors.

12. Early 1974 a legislative bill was cleared which would authorize measures to be taken to prevent, mitigate, or eliminate grave and imminent danger to the United States coastline from pollution resulting from oil spills caused by ocean shipping. Cite bill number, Public Law number, and Congress.

13. During congressional action concerning the Federal Reserve System in 1974, one of the provisions of the banking insurance credit bill which was signed into law removed Puerto Rico from inadvertent coverage by a 1973 law (Pub. L. No. 93-100) putting a moratorium on state taxes on out-of-state banking institutions. Cite the bill, Congress, and Public Law number.

14. What was Harold V. Froehlich's (R. Wis.) amendment in 1973 on the issue of abortion and the involvement of legal corporation lawyers in helping women to procure non-therapeutic abortions?

15. Of the 537 votes taken in the House in 1974, which House members went on record as having been the two most frequent absentees?

ASSIGNMENT 6
DRILL PROBLEMS

Drill Problem I:

A. Using the array of research tools introduced in the chapter, answer the following. Provide full citations where appropriate.

1. What is the number of the Senate Report on Pub. L. No. 94-427, the Olympic Games Authorization Act of 1976?

2. On June 21, 1977, John J. Duncan made seven pages of testimony to a House subcommittee:
   (a) What bill did the testimony concern?
   (b) What is the CIS fiche code number?
   (c) What is its Superintendent of Documents number?

3. On what date did the Senate consider and pass Pub. L. No. 94-34?

4. What is the Statutes at Large citation for Pub. L. No. 95-209?

5. What does the abbreviation C.P.I. stand for?

B. Using the Index and Daily Digest volumes of the Congressional Record, answer the following for the First Session of the 93rd Congress:

   (a) Give the number of two Senate Reports on S-9.
   (b) What was the subject of S. 2534?
   (c) What legislation was passed in lieu of H.R. 9682?
   (d) What was the number of the bill that was enacted as Pub. L. No. 93-222?
   (e) What bills were introduced in the Senate on Monday, May 21, 1973?

C. Use the U.S. Code Congressional and Administrative News volumes to answer the following:

1. Using the 1978 U.S.C.C.A.N., answer the following:
   (a) What are the Committee assignments of Congressperson Jack Brinkley?
   (b) Why is there no excerpt printed of the Senate Report on the Presidential Records Act of 1978?

2. Using the 1972 U.S.C.C.A.N., answer the following:
   (a) What were the Committee assignments of Delbert Latta?
   (b) What documents are printed as part of the legislative history of the Equal Employment Opportunity Act of 1972?

3. Using the 1974 U.S.C.C.A.N., answer the following:
   (a) What is the Statutes at Large citation for Pub. L. No. 93-558?
   (b) What reports were made on the Egg Research bill?

D. Use CCH Congressional Index to answer the following:

1. Using the 1975-1976 Congressional Index:
   (a) What was the name of the woman who married Senator Mike Gravel?
   (b) What was the purpose of S. 1298?
   (c) Give the date of a hearing on H.R. 13,950.
   (d) Did Senator Schweiker introduce any bills dealing with the Library of Congress? If so, cite them.
   (e) What is the Committee to which H.R. 11,776 was assigned?

Drill Problem II:

A. Using the array of research tools introduced in the chapter, answer the following. Provide full citations where appropriate.

1. On what date did the President make a statement concerning Pub. L. No. 94-158?

2. On May 17, 1973, Rowland F. Kirks made a statement, and participated in discussion during hearings on S. 1533.
   (a) What Committee and Subcommittee sponsored the hearings?
   (b) What document was discussed by Mr. Kirks during the hearings?

3. What was the number of the bill that became Pub. L. No. 94-68?

4. On what topic did Professor Shepard Forman testify on June 28, 1977?

5. Find a discussion of the 1974 planned cut in United States aid to the United Nations and the extent of and need for assistance to smaller international organizations. Cite the congressional hearing and CIS Abstract number for the microfiche.

B. Using the Index and Daily Digest volumes of the <u>Congressional Record</u> answer the following:

1. For the First Session of the 91st Congress:
    (a) What bill was the basis of Pub. L. No. 91-54?
    (b) What was the topic of H.R. 12,542?
    (c) What was the final disposition of H.R. 7206?
    (d) On what two subjects did the President submit messages to the Senate on August 6, 1969?
    (e) To what committee was H.R. 9198 referred?
    (f) What was the topic of Senate Joint Resolution 48?

C. Use the <u>U.S. Code Congressional and Administrative News</u> volumes to answer the following:

1. Using the 1978 U.S.C.C.A.N., answer the following:
    (a) Who is the Chairman of the House Standing Committee on Interstate and Foreign Commerce?
    (b) List the reports that accompanied the Amateur Sports Act of 1978.

2. Using the 1972 U.S.C.C.A.N., answer the following:
    (a) What was the subject of Presidential Proclamation No. 4169?
    (b) What is the number of the House Conference Report on the Coastal Zone Management Act of 1972?

3. Using the 1974 U.S.C.C.A.N., answer the following:
    (a) What is the subject of Presidential Proclamation No. 4331?
    (b) Who was the chairman of the Senate Foreign Relations Committee?

D. Use the CCH <u>Congressional Index</u> to answer the following.

1. Using the 1977-1978 <u>Congressional Index</u>:
    (a) Who introduced H.R. 11,774 and to what committee was it referred?
    (b) Give the date of a hearing on H.R. 13662.
    (c) What is the topic of S. 1520?
    (d) On what date did S. 3189 pass the Senate as amended?
    (e) Who was chairman of the Armed Services Committee?

Drill Problem III:

A. Using the array of research tools introduced in the chapter, answer the following. Provide full citations where appropriate.

1. What is the CIS code number for the House Veteran's Affairs Committee?

2. What is the CIS fiche code number for S. Rept. 93-338?

3. What House and Senate committees reported on Pub. L. No. 95-100?

4. What is the CIS fiche number for the Senate Report on Pub. L. No. 95-25?

5. Cite the Public Law number and title of the legislation, enacted at the end of 1974, which removed social service programs from their prior close connection with cash public assistance programs, and set up a separate title in the Social Security Act. Where can you read the Presidential statement in connection with this legislation?

B. Using the Index and Daily Digest volumes of the Congressional Record, answer the following.

1. For the First Session of the 92d Congress:
   (a) Give the Senate report number on S. 557.
   (b) What was the subject of H.R. 23?
   (c) How many private bills were enacted into law by this session of Congress?
   (d) What was the number of the bill that was enacted into Pub. L. No. 92-92?
   (e) To which committee was H.R. 248 referred?
   (f) On which page of the Congressional Record would you find an article about "Hoosier Hippies"?

C. Use the U.S. Code Congressional and Administrative News volumes to answer the following:

1. Using the 1978 U.S.C.C.A.N., answer the following:
   (a) Excerpts of what reports are printed as legislative history for Pub. L. No. 95-375?
   (b) On what date did the House finally pass on the Consumer Co-operative Bank Act?

2. Using the 1972 U.S.C.C.A.N., answer the following.
   (a) What is the number of the House Conference Committee report on the Pesticide Control Act? Is it included in U.S.C.C.A.N.?
   (b) What documents are published in U.S.C.C.A.N. as legislative history for the Volunteers in the National Forest Act of 1972?

3. Using the 1974 U.S.C.C.A.N., answer the following:
   (a) What documents are printed in U.S.C.C.A.N. to accompany the Education Amendments of 1974?
   (b) What reports on Pub. L. No. 93-383 are not published in U.S.C.C.A.N.?

D. Using the 1979-1980 Congressional Index:

1. What is Congressman Ron Dellums' birthday?

2. What is the purpose of H.R. 599?

3. What was the date of the House hearing on H.R. 2108?

4. When was Senate Resolution 51 reported without a written report?

5. Who was chairman of the Senate Armed Services Committee's Subcommittee on General Procurement?

Chapter 11

STATE AND MUNICIPAL LEGISLATION

ASSIGNMENT 1
STATE LEGISLATION - GENERAL

Method:

Answer all questions of this assignment using legislative sources for your own state. Cite in accord with the latest edition of A Uniform System of Citation. Cite either specific or illustrative authority as appropriate. Because the questions found in this assignment are cumulative, rather than repetitive, the student should answer each for his/her own jurisdiction.

Questions:

1. Identify the statutory compilation(s) within your jurisdiction.

2. What is the authoritative force of the compilation(s)?

3. Describe the method(s) of supplementation of the compilation(s).

4. Is there a general index to the compilation(s)? Are there separate indexes for individual volumes or titles?

5. What is the most significant difference between the scope of coverage of the general and the separate indexes?

6. Is the index to the compilation(s) arranged typically and factually? Or only typically?

7. Are the references in the general index to compilation sections or to page numbers?

8. In your jurisdiction is there an overall index to general, special, local and temporary acts which are not included in the statutory compilation(s)?

9. How, if at all, are the cases construing provisions of the compilation(s) located?

10. Does the compilation(s) include references or citations to opinions of the state attorney general? If so, where are they found?

11. Indicate the cross references, if any, to other non-statutory research aids found in the compilation(s).

12. Does the compilation(s) contain textual commentaries or general historical essays?

13. Describe the historical notes, if any, given for each section of the compilation(s).

14. Are there cross references to related sections of the compilation(s)? Where are they found?

15. Are cross references to comparable legislation in other jurisdictions given in the compilation(s)? If not, locate a compilation containing such cross references.

16. Is the effective date of each section of the compilation(s) given? If not, what date is given? Where would one find the effective date?

17. Is there a separate table of acts by popular names? If not, how are acts by popular names indexed?

18. Are there parallel references from earlier compilations to the present? Where are they located? If not, how does one traces from a prior compilation to a current compilation?

19. Is there a reference table from the session laws of the state to the compilation(s)? Where is the table located?

20. Does the index to your state constitution contain specific terms leading you directly to cases construing the constitution?

21. Describe the general procedure to be followed in locating specific cases construing a provision of your state constitution.

22. Locate and cite the "due process" clause of your state constitution.

23. Under the constitution of your state, can a minor traffic violation be used as justification to search the car of a defendant without a search warrant?

24. Does your state compilation(s) include the United States Constitution? If yes, is it annotated? Where is it located?

25. Does your state have a formalized procedure for advising one of pending legislation? If so, describe it.

ASSIGNMENT 2
STATE CODES--USE OF INDEXES

Method:

Using the index to the latest code of your state, locate the current statutory laws on the following subjects:

Questions:

1. Arbitration laws

2. Pollution laws

3. Powers of attorney laws

4. Landlord and tenant laws

5. Specific performance laws

6. Chiropractors laws

7. Fictitious name laws

8. Franchise laws

9. Gambling laws

10. Gifts to minors laws

11. Descent and distribution laws

12. Extradition laws

13. Fraud laws

14. Hunting laws

15. Insolvency laws

16. Municipal corporations laws

17. Drug laws

18. Mechanics' liens laws

19. Trademarks and tradenames laws

20. Trust companies laws

21. Attachment laws

22. Housing laws
23. Workmen's compensation laws
24. Birth certificates laws
25. Nursing home laws
26. Capital punishment, existence of
27. Next of kin, who is?
28. Homicide, definition of.
29. Homestead exemptions.
30. Legislation governing use of state flag.
31. Negotiable instrument, definition of.
32. Maximum highway speeds in your state.
33. Consumer protection statutes in your state.
34. Hauling combustible liquids on public ways.
35. Grounds for divorce.
36. Donation of one's eyes for medical purposes.
37. Sex as determinant of salary.
38. State agency authorized to set freight rates.
39. Agency charged with regulating admissions to the bar.
40. Age of majority.
41. Minimum number of directors required under corporation law.
42. Veto power of governor.
43. Rate of tax on retail sales.
44. Length of residency to make one eligible to vote in state elections.
45. General status of confidential communications between an attorney and a client.
46. Legislation prohibiting the discarding of litter in a public place.

47. Legislation stating general powers and duties of state attorney general.

48. Statute of limitations for written contract not under seal.

49. Agency charged with examining applicants for the practice of medicine.

50. Maximum loan issuable by a small loan company.

51. Definition of assault.

52. Financial aid to medical students who intend to practice in rural areas.

53. Abortion.

54. Uniform Anatomical Gift Act.

55. Pet licenses.

56. Reduction of prison sentence for blood donations.

57. State historian.

58. Definition of single family residence.

59. Definition of motor vehicle.

60. Definition of habitual offenders under the motor vehicle statute.

61. Conservation of endangered species.

62. State agency authorized to set freight rates.

63. Penalty for cock fights.

64. Funding of county law libraries.

ASSIGNMENT 3
STATE CODES - CONSTRUCTION

Method:

Using bound volumes, bound supplements, specific pamphlet supplements, pocket parts, general pamphlet supplements, and the tables of statutes construed from the appropriate reporter bound volumes and advance sheets, cite the most recent case construing the statutes located in Assignment 2.

ASSIGNMENT 4
STATE CODES - DERIVATION

Method:

Using the same sources employed in Assignment 2, locate and cite the oldest legislation noted as part of the history of each of the statutes found as a result thereof.

ASSIGNMENT 5
STATE SESSION LAWS - PARALLEL REFERENCE TABLES

Method:

Using parallel reference tables from the appropriate state codes, convert the following citations to their current equivalent.

Questions:

1. 1913 Ariz. Rev. Stat. sec. 626.

2. 1838 Ark. Rev. Stat. c. 129, sec. 22.

3. 1935 Del. Code sec. 575.

4. 1863 Ga. Code sec. 3796.

5. 1955 Hawaii Rev. Laws sec. 30-9.

6. 1919 Ida. Comp. Stat. sec. 3201.

7. 1874 Ill. Rev. Stat. c. 34, p. 302, sec. 67.

8. 1868 Kan. Gen. Stat. c. 105, sec. 39.

9. 1870 La. Rev. Stat. sec. 1154.

10. 1954 Maine Rev. Stat. c. 144, sec. 7.

11. 1930 Miss. Code sec. 4941.

12. 1942 N.H. Rev. Laws sec. 229:71.

13. 1929 N. Mex. Comp. Stat. sec 4-2103.

14. 1910 Okla. Rev. Laws sec. 7381.

15. 1939 S. Dak. Code sec. 5.0310.

16. 1858 Tenn. Code sec. 3369.

17. 1917 Utah Comp. Laws sec. 8296.

18. 1947 Vt. Stat. sec. 6831.

19. 1961 W. Va. Code (Michie) sec. 1467.

20. Ch. 405 §9 (1955) Me. Public Laws.

21. Ch. 205 (1975) Me. Public Laws.
22. Ch. 374 §4 (1967) Me. Public Laws.
23. Ch. 291 (1957) Me. Public Laws.
24. Ch. 84 (1965) W. Va. Acts.
25. Ch. 61 §1 (1937) W. Va. Acts.
26. Ch. 141 (1975) W. Va. Acts.
27. Sect. 1 (1967) Ill. Laws 3359.
28. Ch. 284 §1 (1963) N. M. Laws.
29. Ch. 340 §2 (1975) N. M. Laws.
30. Ch. 9 §4 (1941) N. M. Laws.

ASSIGNMENT 6
STATE CODES - COMPARATIVE RESEARCH

Sources: ALI-ABA Model Business Corporation Act Annotated (2d ed. 1971).

Uniform Laws Annotated (Master ed. 1968).

Martindale-Hubbell Law Directory (1984).

Book of the States, 82-83 (1982).

Method:

Using the sources listed above, answer the following questions. When required, cite sources in accord with A Uniform System of Citation (13th ed. 1981).

Questions:

A. Use the Model Business Corporation Act Annotated, 2d.

1. Locate and cite the section on voluntary dissolution by act of the corporation. Is this model act provision identical or comparable with that of your state? If so, cite your state's statute.

2. Locate and cite the appropriate section on failure of the corporation to hold annual meetings. Does any state have a provision identical in substance with this section? If so, cite that state's statute.

3. Locate the section dealing with payment of cash dividends; indicate whether the Model Act provision is identical with that of your state.

4. What is the minimum number of directors required for a corporation? What do the corporation laws of your home state and the states contiguous thereto require?

B. Use the Uniform Laws Annotated.

1. According to the Uniform Probate Code, what effect does the divorce of a testator have upon his/her previously executed will? What research references are given to legal sources outside the Code? Has the Code been enacted in your state? If so, what is its effective date?

2. According to the Uniform Partnership Act, how do partners share in a partnership's profits? Cite a 1977 New Jersey case concerning a partner's share in partnership profits. Has the Act been enacted in your state? If so, give its effective date.

C. Use the Uniform Laws Annotated (Master ed. 1968).

1. Has your state adopted the Uniform Partnership Act? If so, cite the applicable statute from your state and its effective date.

2. Locate and cite the text of the Uniform Fraudulent Conveyance Act. Has your state adopted this law? If so, cite the applicable state statute and its effective date.

3. Locate and cite the text of the Residential Landlord and Tenant Act. Has your state adopted this law? If so, when did it become effective?

4. According to the Uniform Eminent Domain Code, how is the fair market value of property which has no relevant market determined? Please cite the applicable section. Has your state adopted this uniform law? Cite your authority.

D. Use Martindale-Hubbell Law Directory (1984). For each answer, give the subject heading(s) under which the answer was found, the jurisdictions, and the authority specified in Martindale-Hubbell. Give answers for Alabama, Louisiana and Mississippi.

1. Age of majority.

2. Time specified by statute of limitations to recover damages for wrongful death.

3. Drug use as a ground for divorce.

4. Seat of the supreme court, i.e., highest court of appeal.

5. Notice to be given to terminate tenancy at will.

E. Use Book of the States 1982-83 (1982). For all answers, give the page on which the answers were found.

1. Identify the states having the highest and lowest individual income tax rates. Specify the rates.

2. What is the method of selecting Supreme Court Justices in Louisiana, Alabama and Mississippi?

3. According to the Am. Jur. 2d Desk Book (1979), do the courts of Kansas maintain an administrative office? If yes, what is the legal source of its authority?

4. Using the Book of the States 82-83, which state had the largest number of measures vetoed by the governor?

ASSIGNMENT 7
STATE CODES - CITATION PROBLEMS

Method:

Using the latest edition of A Uniform System of Citation, provide the correct citation for the following problems.

Questions:

1. On page 503 of the 1978 vol 7A of the Uniform Laws Annotated, the text of the Uniform Residential Landlord and Tenant Act begins.

2. In New Hampshire Revised Statutes Annotated, special provisions providing for the administration of small estates of deceased persons is found in sections 553:31 and 553:31a.

3. A California attorney general's decision which interprets Sections 1101 and 1151, West Annotated Harbor and Navigation Code is in volume 55, page 80 of the California Opinions of the Attorney General, dated February 9, 1972.

ASSIGNMENT 8
MARTINDALE-HUBBELL LAW DIRECTORY - FOREIGN LAW DIGESTS

Method:

Using the summaries of foreign legislation in the Law Digests volume of the Martindale-Hubbell Law Directory, ascertain whether alcoholism or drunkeness constitute grounds for either a divorce or a separation in the following countries:

1. Argentina
2. Australia
3. China (Taiwan)
4. Columbia
5. Costa Rica
6. El Salvador
7. Finland
8. France
9. Guatemala
10. Honduras
11. Ireland (Eire)
12. Italy
13. Mexico
14. New Zealand
15. Northern Ireland
16. Norway
17. Pakistan
18. Philippine Republic
19. Portugal
20. Scotland

21. Sweden
22. Switzerland
23. U.S.S.R.
24. Venezuela
25. Yugoslavia

ASSIGNMENT 9
MUNICIPAL CODES

Method:

Refer to the municipal code of the city in which your law school is located, or the one for your home town, or one that is readily available in the law library that you are using. Identify the code that you select for this exercise. Explain briefly the provisions of the ordinance as called for below and include a citation to the pertinent provision.

Questions:

1. Is there an ordinance relating to false or misleading advertising?

2. Is there an air pollution ordinance?

3. Is there an ordinance regulating door to door solicitors and vendors?

4. Is there an ordinance regulating the size of signs that may be used by merchants?

5. Is there an ordinance on drunk driving?

6. Is there an ordinance relating to false arrest?

7. Is there an ordinance on littering of streets?

8. Is there an ordinance relating to loitering near election polls on election days?

9. Is there an ordinance prohibiting pinball machines?

10. Is loud noise near hospitals prohibited by ordinance?

11. Is there an ordinance on consumption of alcoholic beverages in motor vehicles?

12. Is there a curfew ordinance for minors?

13. Does an ordinance give pedestrians the right of way at crosswalks?

14. Is there an ordinance relating to reckless driving?

15. Is there an ordinance relating to stealing or removing vehicle parts or accessories?

16. Is there an ordinance on taxicab parking?
17. Is there an ordinance on cruelty to animals?
18. Is there an ordinance relating to disturbing religious worship?
19. Is there an ordinance prohibiting U-turns?
20. Is there an ordinance regulating projections over street areas?
21. Is there an ordinance on the location of private swimming pools?
22. Is there an ordinance on vision clearance on corner lots in residential districts?
23. Is there an ordinance on the storage of readily combustible materials?
24. Is smoking in retail stores prohibited by ordinance?

ASSIGNMENT 10
DRILL PROBLEMS

Drill Problem I:

Locate the following:

1. The section of the Alabama code prohibiting policemen from improperly disposing of traffic tickets.

2. The section of the Alaska statutes prohibiting the ombudsman from charging an investigative fee.

3. The section of the Arizona statutes legalizing betting on horse and dog races.

4. The current state code cites for the following:

   (a) 1969 Ark. Acts No. 279 §1.
   (b) 1965 Ark. Acts No. 180 §3.
   (c) 1963 Colo. Rev. Stat. §37-2-1.

Drill Problem II:

Locate the following:

1. The code section designating the Azalea as Georgia's State Wild Flower.

2. The Hawaii Code section defining the rights of a buyer of a horse or mule with glandus.

3. The Idaho Code section giving business corporations the authority to issue no-par stock.

4. The current state code cites for the following:

   (a) 1965 Ill. Laws 1400 §1.
   (b) 1935 Ind. Acts Ch. 128 §1.
   (c) 1927 Iowa Code §13615.
   (d) Ky. Carroll's Civ. Code §460.

Drill Problem III:

Locate the following:

1. The section of the Maryland code requiring the clerks of county courts to microfilm each deed to real property.

2. The section of the Massachusetts code providing for a lower than normal minimum wage for theatrical ushers.

3. The section of the Michigan code providing for a study of sand dunes within the state.

4. The current state code cites for the following:

   (a) 1969 Minn. Laws Ch. 895 §1.
   (b) 1972 Mo. Laws, p. 605 §1.
   (c) 1942 Miss. Code §1186.
   (d) 1979 N.H. Laws Ch. 492 §1.

ASSIGNMENT 11
THEME PROBLEMS

Theme Problem I:

Using the indicated codes, locate the following matter:

1. (a) An Iowa statute making corporations operating railways liable for the torts of their employees.
   (b) The first Iowa case holding that although the duty of care to passengers of a railway is that of extraordinary care and caution, the duty to employees is only ordinary care.

2. (a) A Louisiana statute defining the duty of care owed by ambulance drivers.
   (b) A Louisiana case holding that a police officer was negligent in following 15 feet behind a suspect vehicle at an excessive rate of speed with the siren blaring.

3. (a) The definition of ordinary negligence in Oklahoma. Provide the citation as well.
   (b) An Oklahoma case holding that a plaintiff whose head may have smelled of cats did not negligently provoke the dog which bit the top of her head.

4. (a) The North Dakota statute making everyone responsible for injuries occasioned to others by their want of ordinary care of skill in the management of their property or persons.
   (b) A North Dakota case requiring a landlord to inform a tenant of dangerous latent conditions which create a foreseeable, unreasonable risk to persons.

Theme Problem II:

Using the indicated codes, locate the folllowing matter:

1. (a) A New York statute permitting claims for both damages and rescission in a complaint on an action based on misrepresentation in the inducement of a contract.
   (b) A New York case holding the fraudulent misrepresentation by a lessor of a hidden material defect may entitle the lessee to rescission as well as damages.
   (c) The New York case precluding recovery of damages in an action for rescission, which the statute overrules.

236

2. (a) A Virginia statute holding that a cause of action accrues for rescission of a contract based on mistake when the mistake should have been discovered by the exercise of due diligence.

   (b) A Virginia case holding that a person who, because of his own carelessness in failing to inspect his own cancelled checks, failed to notice his mistake in making a duplicate payment could not demonstrate due diligence under the statute.

3. (a) A Washington statute prohibiting minors from disaffirming contracts if their acts gave the other party good reason to believe them capable of contracting.

   (b) A Washington case holding that where a minor had $800, made his own contracts, collected his own wages, and did his own banking he could not deny liability on a contract.

4. (a) A Wisconsin statute permitting equitable reformation of deeds which fail to meet the formal statutory requirements.

   (b) A Wisconsin case permitting parol evidence to prove unjust enrichment to support imposing a constructive trust on property.

   (c) A law review commentary discussing equitable conversion.

Chapter 12

COURT RULES AND PROCEDURE

ASSIGNMENT 1
FEDERAL RULES OF CIVIL PROCEDURE

Method:

Use C. Wright, Federal Practice and Procedure, and/or J. Moore, Moore's Federal Practice. Briefly answer the question, citing the rule, the number and the section in Wright or Moore under which the answer is found. Supply case citation when asked.

Questions:

1. Under the rule of pleading in an action under Fair Labor Standards Act of 1938 to recover overtime wages (back-pay suit), is the pleader required to do more than make a "short and plain statement of facts"? Cite the pertinent rule.

2. (a) In an amendment in 1970 a quite important change was made in a rule to bring the Federal Rules into the computer age (production of documents) (use Wright).
   (b) Does this mean that respondent may have to supply a printout of computer data?

3. (a) How is the service of papers upon the opposing attorney or party to be made?
   (b) Cite a 10th Circuit case in support of the rule that service of papers is complete upon mailing.

4. (a) In the construction of Rule 6(a), is any other day appointed by the President or the Congress or by the state in which the district court is sitting also a legal holiday for purposes of computing time?
   (b) An amendment in 1971 added another holiday to this Rule. What holiday is this? Cite statute which changes the day on which certain holidays are to be observed.

5. (a) What is the purpose of a pretrial conference?
   (b) To how many subjects is the court encouraged to direct its attention at a pretrial conference?

6. (a) Whenever the physical or mental condition (including the blood groups) of a party is in controversy, the court in which the action is pending may require him to submit to a physical or mental examination by a physician. What rule number allows this?
   (b) The 1970 Amendment codifies the case law holding that blood tests are authorized. Cite a pre-1970 paternity case on point (use Moore).

7. (a) What Rule provides that a court appointed guardian ad litem is entitled to a reasonable fee for his services, usually paid out of the amount recovered? (Use Wright.)
   (b) Cite a 1982 case taxing the guardian's fee against the opposing party.

8. If interrogatories are served within 15 days after service of process, and served with the summons and complaint, how many days is defendant allowed in which to respond?

9. (a) Who must sign pleadings, motions and other papers in an action?
   (b) Must the address be stated and may the name be typewritten?

10. (a) What rule limits discovery to matter that is "not privileged?" Have the courts recognized a privilege for communications to clergyman, sometime referred to as priest-penitent privilege? (Use Wright.)
    (b) Cite pertinent case.

11. (a) What rule provides an opportunity to submit to the court requests for instructions to the jury on the key question in the case? When are these requests made?
    (b) Should these be in writing or may oral requests be sufficient if they clearly inform the court of the point involved?

12. (a) In the federal courts, when is a master appointed?
    (b) What does the word "master" include?

13. (a) What rule number sets forth the procedure to be used in taking a deposition by oral examination during the pendency of an action?
    (b) Must the notice of taking a deposition state the subject matter concerning which the examination will be made?

14. (a) Are alternate jurors subject to the same laws and requirements as regular jurors?
    (b) How many alternate jurors may the court impanel?

15. (a) If a trial by jury has been demanded as provided in Rule 38, what procedure is to be followed?
    (b) If the demand was untimely or otherwise not in compliance with Rule 38, can the jury trial deemed to have been waived?

16. (a) Are the disbarment proceedings of an attorney governed by the scope of the Federal Rules of Civil Procedure?
    (b) What rule describes the scope of application of the rules? Cite case in which disbarment is not an adversary proceeding (civil actions).

17. (a) Cite a pertinent case on the issue of price discrimination against a trading stamp company.
    (b) With apparent increasing frequency Rule 23(b)(3) is being used in antitrust and securities fraud suits. Is a class action proper if the alleged violation can be shown to arise out of a common course of conduct or have a general effect on the market?

18. (a) Cite the "two dismissal" or "second dismissal" rule.
    (b) Cite a case in which the court stated that the two dismissal rule should be strictly construed (use Wright).
    (c) Using Moore, cite a commentary in the Federal Rules Service on the "Two- Dismissal" Rule.

19. (a) The rule of admissibility of evidence creates a three-pronged test for the admissibility of evidence. It has often been remarked that this rule is a rule of admissibility, not a rule of exclusion. Cite pertinent rule.
    (b) Cite a 1970 case in the 5th Circuit supporting the remark that this rule is one of admissibility, not exclusion.

20. (a) Who serves a subpoena?
    (b) Is it sufficient to leave a copy of the subpoena at the dwelling place of the witness?
    (c) Must the fees for one day's attendance and the mileage allowed by law be supplied with the subpoena? Cite statute that fixes the compensation fee.

21. (a) What rule permits juries of less than 12 persons?
    (b) Cite a 1969 5th Circuit case in which the court stated that verdict in a federal civil case must be the unanimous verdict of 12 jurors unless otherwise stipulated by the parties (use Wright).

ASSIGNMENT 2
FEDERAL RULES OF CIVIL PROCEDURE

Sources: Title 28 United States Code Annotated or United States Code Service covering 1-86 of the Federal Rules of Civil Procedure.

C. Wright, Federal Practice and Procedure covering Federal Rules of Civil Procedure.

Cyclopedia of Federal Procedure (3d ed.) covering Federal Rules of Civil Procedure.

J. Moore, Moore's Federal Practice (2d ed.) covering Federal Rules of Civil Procedure.

Method:

   Briefly answer the questions. Cite to rule numbers, treatises and cases as required.

Questions:

1. Cite the section in Moore which discusses the Supreme Court's authority to promulgate rules of procedure under the Rule-Making Statute of 1934.

2. In what years have subdivisions (b), (d)(4), (d)(7), (e), and (f) of Rule 4 been changed?

3. What rule prescribes a uniform method of service upon the United States in all actions governed by the Federal Rules?

4. Cite the rule which indicates to what extent the Federal Rules of Civil Procedure are applicable to proceedings for admission to citizenship, habeas corpus, and quo warranto?

5. Cite the rule which indicates if it is a requirement that the signing of pleadings must always be verified or accompanied by an affidavit.

6. In what year was Rule 6(c) rescinded? Why was this rule rendered unnecessary?

7. Cite the rule regarding depositions pending appeal.

8. Using Wright, cite a 1958 6th Circuit case in which a bank sought a declaratory judgment that it would be unlawful for a state bank to open a branch in the same city. Cite also the section in Wright under which the case is cited.

9. If a party is served with a pleading stating a cross-claim against him, how much time does he have to serve an answer to the pleading? Cite pertinent rule.

10. If a court orders separate trials as provided in rule 42(b), judgment on a counterclaim or cross-claim may be rendered in accordance with what rule?

11. Rule 14 was modeled on what Admirality Rule?

12. Does Rule 17 govern procedure in adoption proceedings? Cite a case mentioned in U.S.C.A. which provides an answer to this question.

13. Rule 23(a) is a substantial restatement of what earlier Equity Rule?

14. Under the Federal Rules, does the court have the power to order a summary judgment without a hearing? Cite applicable rules and section in Wright.

15. Is shareholder-plaintiff in a successful derivative action entitled to reimbursement of attorney's fees? Cite applicable section in Wright.

16. A person who wishes to intervene in an action must serve a motion to intervene upon the parties. What must accompany this motion? Cite pertinent rule.

17. In 1970 some of the rule numbers of discovery rules were rearranged. Construct a table showing these changes.

18. Upon motion, the court may order that testimony taken at deposition be recorded by other than stenographic means. If so, should the order designate the manner of recording? Cite rule number.

19. Is Rule 74 currently in force? Briefly explain your answer.

20. Rule 4 remained as promulgated in 1937 until 1963. What subdivision(s) of this rule still remain unchanged?

21. Has Rule 47(b) ever been revised? If so, what was the effective date of the latest revision?

22. Under the Rules of Civil Procedure, is it always necessary to file pleadings and other papers with the clerk of the court? Cite pertinent rule.

23. Under what section of Wright should one look for a discussion of abolition in civil rules of the distinction between special and general appearance?

24. Section 41(5) of former Title 28 U.S.C. was changed to what section number under the new Title 28 U.S.C.?

ASSIGNMENT 3
FEDERAL RULES OF CRIMINAL PROCEDURE

Method:

Use C. Wright, Federal Practice and Procedure, volumes 1, 2, 3 and 3A covering the Federal Rules of Criminal Procedure. Briefly answer the question when necessary and cite the rule number under which the answer is found. Supply case citation when required. Give correct citation form for rule number, treatises and cases.

Questions:

1. During what hours do the rules require that a district court clerk's office be physically open?

2. Where may one find the 25 suggested forms to be used with the Federal Rules of Criminal Procedure?

3. (a) If the judge before whom a defendant is tried is disabled to perform the duties required of him after the finding of a guilty verdict, who may perform the duties?
   (b) Cite case in which the disability was the retirement of the trial judge.

4. If a witness violates a sequestration order (exclusion of witnesses), does the court have the discretion to decide whether the witness shall nevertheless be permitted to testify?

5. (a) What rule permits the court on motion of a defendant to strike surplusage?
   (b) Cite a case indicating that use of aliases in an indictment should not lead to dismissal absent indication in motion to dismiss that the aliases would not be proved at trial.

6. (a) If a defendant refuses to plead (standing mute) or a corporate defendant fails to appear, what must the court enter?
   (b) Cite a case pertaining to the corporate defendant where the court entered the plea of not guilty.

7. May a deposition be used at trial if it appears "that the witness is unable to attend or testify because of sickness or infirmity"?

8. (a) If a witness who is subpoenaed for trial does not appear, may he be punished for contempt of the court from which the subpoena was issued?
   (b) Cite a case where a person refused to comply with a subpoena for health reasons who in good faith believed that compliance with the subpoena would create a risk of harm to him.

9. (a) Is the jury bound by the opinions of expert witnesses?
   (b) Cite a case where Judge Winter said: "... We would unduly limit the ability of a court to find the truth in a criminal case where sanity is an issue were we to turn our backs on the tool of expert medical knowledge."

10. (a) May a defendant with the consent of the court enter a plea of nolo contendere?
    (b) The U.S. Court of Appeals for what circuit does not allow conviction on a plea of nolo contendere to be used for impeachment of a witness?

11. (a) May a defendant agree to be tried by a jury of fewer than twelve?
    (b) Cite applicable case in which it was held that the Sixth Amendment does not demand that a jury in a state criminal proceeding be of any particular size.

12. In computing time, once a warrant has been issued the Federal Rules of Criminal Procedure enumerate legal holidays which should be excluded in the computation. In 1971, by amendment, one more holiday was added to the list. What holiday was this?

13. Do the criminal rules apply to the District Court for the District of Puerto Rico?

14. (a) A grand jury should be composed of how many members?
    (b) How many jurors must concur in finding an indictment?

15. (a) What rule requires the clerk of the district court to keep records, including a book to be known as the "criminal docket"?
    (b) It has been said that once the case is within the jurisdiction of an appellate court, the district court cannot make changes in the record. Cite a 1968 pertinent case.

ASSIGNMENT 4
FEDERAL RULES OF CRIMINAL PROCEDURE

Sources: Title 18 United States Code Annotated or United States Code Service covering Rules 1-60 of the Federal Rules of Criminal Procedure.

C. Wright, Federal Practice and Procedure (1969) covering the Federal Rules of Criminal Procedure.

Cyclopedia of Federal Procedure (3d ed.) covering the Federal Rules of Criminal Procedure.

J. Moore, Moore's Federal Practice (2d ed.) covering the Federal Rules of Criminal Procedure.

Method:

Briefly answer the questions. Cite to rule numbers, treatises and cases as required.

Questions:

1. When used in the Federal Rules of Criminal Procedure, does the word "state" include the District of Columbia? Cite applicable rule.

2. May a defendant waive his right to preliminary examination? Cite applicable rule.

3. Is it proper for an attorney for the government to challenge a grand juror after the oath to the grand juror has been administered? Cite pertinent rule.

4. Must a motion raising defenses and objections based on defects in the institution of the prosecution always be made before trial? Cite pertinent rule.

5. Are statements made by accused in psychiatric examination admissible as evidence against the accused on the issue of guilt? Cite rule.

6. According to United States v. Anzelmo, is the record of prior criminal convictions of persons whom government intends to call as witnesses at trial discovered under Rule 16?

7. Rule 17(f) of the Federal Rules of Criminal Procedure is substantially the same as what rule of the Federal Rules of Civil Procedure?

8. Cite a rule which indicates if the indigent defendant in a criminal case has the right to secure attendance of witnesses at the expense of the Government.

9. When did the rule establishing a basis for pretrial conferences with counsel for the parties in criminal cases become effective? Cite pertinent rule.

10. Under what circumstances may a jury consist of less than twelve persons? Cite pertinent rule.

11. If a judge presiding over a case dies prior to sentencing, must the successor judge always order a new trial? Cite pertinent rule.

12. Are there special circumstances in which the court may appoint an expert witness even though he has not consented to act? Cite pertinent rule.

13. If the defendant has been found not guilty, does he still have the right to examine the report of the presentence investigation of him made by the probation service of the court? Cite pertinent rule.

14. A motion for a new trial based on grounds other than newly discovered evidence must normally be made within how many days of a verdict? Cite pertinent rule.

15. What rule gives a court discretion in deciding whether to stay an order placing a defendant on probation?

16. Who may request that a search warrant be issued? Cite pertinent rule.

17. If a judge certifies that he actually saw or heard conduct constituting contempt being committed in the actual presence of the court, is it necessary for the contempt to be prosecuted on notice? Cite pertinent rules.

18. An advisory committee was appointed by the Supreme Court of the United States in 1941 to assist in the preparation of the criminal rules.
    (a) Who was appointed Chairman of this Committee?
    (b) What was the exact date of the order upon which the appointment of this Committee was based?

19. Do the Federal Rules of Criminal Procedure apply to local crimes in the Virgin Islands? Cite a 1964 Court of Appeals case which is on point.

20. The Federal Rules of Criminal Procedure abolish all pleadings but five. What are they? Cite pertinent rule.

21. If a defendant is arrested in a district other than that in which an indictment against him is pending, does he have the right to request in writing that he wishes to waive trial in the district in which the indictment is pending and to ask that the trial be held in the district in which he was arrested? Cite pertinent rule.

22. Cite a circuit court case holding that the time limit for discretionary reduction of sentence on motion is jurisdictional and may not be enlarged or extended for any reason.

23. May a defendant, with the consent of the court, enter a plea of nolo contendere? Cite pertinent rule.

24. Do the criminal rules apply to the District Court for the Northern Mariana Islands? Cite pertinent Rule.

25. What rule permits the court on motion of a defendant to strike surplusage?

ASSIGNMENT 5
FEDERAL RULES OF CIVIL AND CRIMINAL
PROCEDURE IN UNITED STATES CODE ANNOTATED

Sources: Title 18 United States Code Annotated or United
           States Code Service covering Rules 1-60 of the Federal
           Rules of Criminal Procedure.

           Title 28 United States Code Annotated or United
           States Code Service covering Rules 1-86 of the Federal
           Rules of Civil Procedure.

Method:

   (1) Briefly answer each question supplying correct citations
       for court rules or other material as required.

   (2) Indicate which index subject headings were used.

Questions:

1. For what reason may a court dismiss an indictment, information or complaint and thereby terminate criminal prosecution?

2. What rule provides for a stay of sentence of death pending appeal?

3. What is the time limit for entering a motion for a new criminal trial based on any grounds other than newly discovered evidence?

4. How long does a court have to reduce a sentence it has imposed?

5. Can a harmless error in a criminal case ever be disregarded and if so, when?

6. In what circumstance is a party allowed permissive intervention in an action?

7. What rule states which pleas are permitted in a criminal action?

8. When, in a criminal proceeding, must the government furnish a defendant with the copy of his/her prior record (if any)?

9. The capacity of a corporation to sue or be sued is determined by what law?

10. Before accepting a guilty plea, must the court determine that the defendant understands the effect of any special parole term connected with the maximum possible penalty?

11. In criminal prosecutions, for what type of offenses is a defendant's presence not required (after he/she gives his/her written consent)?

12. How many prerequisites must be fulfilled for a class action suit to be possible?

13. In a criminal trial, who opens the argument after the closing of evidence, and do they have the opportunity for rebuttal?

14. Under what general power do the <u>Rules of Civil Procedure for the United States District Courts</u> govern the procedure of the condemnation of real and personal property?

15. Who may be present while a grand jury is in session?

ASSIGNMENT 6
USE OF FEDERAL PROCEDURAL FORMS

Method:

Use <u>West's Federal Forms</u>. Locate forms and cite volume and section number, observing <u>A Uniform System of Citation</u> (13th ed.) for style.

Questions:

1. (a) Attorney's application for admission to practice before the Supreme Court.
   (b) Is it necessary for attorney to appear in Court in order to be admitted to the Supreme Court bar?

2. An order granting motion for summary judgment and dismissing motion for preliminary injunction.

3. Claim of owner to articles seized under Food and Drug Act.

4. Order for writ of habeas corpus.

5. Affidavit for search warrant, counterfeiting of coins (under Rule 41).

6. A pre-trial order in a railroad crossing accident case.

7. A pre-trial order in a tort claim against the United States.

8. A jury instruction on alibi.

9. Questioning by court of prospective jurors in an air piracy charge.

10. Motion for new jury trial with statement of grounds [F.R.C.P. Rule 59(a)].

ASSIGNMENT 7
USE OF FEDERAL PROCEDURAL FORMS

Method:

   Use Nichols Cyclopedia of Federal Procedure Forms. Cite section number containing the form or relevant information.

Questions:

1. Some district courts require, by local rule, the filing of a brief or memorandum of authorities in support of a motion for new trial.

2. Complaint for trademark infringement.

3. Motion for new trial in action tried by jury.

4. Motion for appointment of a receiver

5. Libel complaint

ASSIGNMENT 8
USE OF FEDERAL PROCEDURAL FORMS

Method:

Use C. Wright, Federal Practice and Procedure, volume 3, appendix. Locate forms and cite form number. Give volume and page number on which the forms are found.

Questions:

1. Cite form number for motion in arrest of judgment.

2. Cite form number to be used in an indictment for mail fraud.

3. Cite form number for an indictment for receiving stolen motor vehicles.

4. Cite form number for warrant for arrest of witness.

5. Cite form number for motion for new trial.

6. Cite form number to be used in an indictment for sabotage.

7. What form number would you use if a form was needed for a summons?

8. Rule 41 of the Criminal Rules pertains to search and seizure. What form number should be used for a search warrant under this rule?

9. Cite the form number for an indictment for murder in the first degree of a federal officer.

10. Cite form number to be used in connection with bail bond or appearance bond

ASSIGNMENT 9
COURT RULES

Method:

Use the court rules volumes of United State Code Annotated (USCA) and/or United States Code Service (USCS) to answer the following questions, citing the rule number:

Questions:

1. In the Court of Appeals for the Fourth Circuit, within how many days must a party request a reconsideration of a non controversial order granted by the clerk?

2. In the Court of Appeals for the Fifth Circuit, is the clerk authorized to act upon a motion for leave to file amicus curiae briefs under Fed. R. App. P. 29?

3. Under the Federal Rules of Appellate Procedure, is leave or consent required for a state to file an amicus curiae brief?

4. Unless the Court has provided otherwise, at what time is the appendix to a brief to be filed in a United States Court of Appeals?

5. May anyone remove books from the Supreme Court Library?

6. Under the Federal Rules of Appellate Procedure, how is a request for postponement of oral argument made?

7. In the Supreme Court, how much time is usually allowed for oral argument?

8. Before the Supreme Court will admit an attorney applying to practice in the Court, she/he must have been admitted to practice in the highest court of a state, etc., for how long?

9. What rule provides for law students to appear in the United States Court of Appeals for the District of Columbia?

10. To whom should a complaint of misconduct by a Ninth Circuit judge be addressed?

11. Cite a 1979 Minnesota Eighth Circuit case in which the court declined to entertain a motion to dismiss based upon frivolity.

12. Name a 1974 Arkansas Eighth Circuit case in which the court exercised its Rule 9(a) authority and responsibility to consider jurisdiction whether raised by the parties or not.

13. What supplemental requirement to Fed. R. App. P. 35 exists in the First Circuit?

14. What is the Findex number covering subpoena of data compilations?

ASSIGNMENT 10
COURT RULES

Method:

    Use Callaghan's <u>Federal Rules Service</u> and <u>Federal Local Court Rules</u> to answer the following questions. Cite rule when answer is contained in a rule.

Questions:

1. Who is the clerk of the U.S. District Court for the Western District of Arkansas?

2. Motions for extension of time of not more than 15 days within which to answer a complaint may be routinely granted once under what Wyoming District rule?

3. Where does <u>Bangor and Aroostock R. Co. v. Bangor Punta Operations, Inc.</u> appear in <u>Federal Rules Service - Cases</u>?

4. What is the Findex number for the manner of raising an objection under Fed. R. Civ. P. 19(b)?

5. What is the headquarters of the U.S. District Court for the Southern District of Iowa?

6. What local rule treats requests for instructions to juries in the U.S. District Court for Maine?

7. In Rhode Island, what designation must appear on the complaint in a class action brought in the U.S. District Court?

8. Where does <u>Southern Ry. Co. v. Chapman</u> appear in <u>Federal Rules Service - Cases</u>?

ASSIGNMENT 11
COURT RULES

Sources: Federal Rules Service Finding Aids.

   Federal Rules Digests.

Method:

Cite the applicable court rule and the case required to answer the question. Methodology for locating the answers is as follows:

Read the section on How to Use Federal Rules Service in the Finding Aids volumes. Begin with the word index in the Finding Aids volume. Proceed to the Federal Findex to read explanation of rule number located in the Word Index. Locate appropriate section in the Federal Rules Digest. Check Current Volume where necessary.

Questions:

1. Cite a 1974 Supreme Court case on the effect of the running of the Statute of Limitations on the institution of class actions.

2. Cite a 1967 Court of Appeals case on possible penalties for contempt citations on the failure to respond to a court subpoena.

3. Cite a 1968 District Court case involving cross claims by third party defendants.

4. Cite a 1974 Court of Appeals decision in the 7th circuit which refers to claims of excessive damages as grounds for a new trial.

5. Cite a 1959 case involving the right to assert assumption of risk as an affirmative defense.

6. Husband and wife are granted the privilege of freedom from discovery. Cite a 1971 case on this subject of privilege.

7. The court has discretion to grant a motion for voluntary dismissal of an action only on the condition that plaintiff pay its discharged attorneys their reasonable fees. Cite a 1969 case on this subject.

8. Cite the 1973 case which sets out material which may be considered in the determination of proper foreign law application as evidence in federal courts cases.

9. Cite a 1975 District Court case dealing with the proper time for objecting to instructions given to the jury.

10. Cite a 1975 Court of Appeals case dealing with raising the issue as to capacity to sue or be sued.

11. Cite a 1968 case dealing with an attorney's admission to the bar as established by the rules of the District Court.

12. In placing limitations on completion of discovery, the District Court should consider other demands upon the time of counsel. Cite 1963 District Court case dealing with this subject.

13. Cite a 1956 case involving the necessity of the payment of filing fees in filing complaints with the court.

14. Cite a 1961 case involving depositions taken before action in regard to whose testimony may be examined other than the applicant.

15. Cite a 1966 case dealing with the effect of dismissal for improper venue.

ASSIGNMENT 12
WRIGHT'S FEDERAL PRACTICE AND PROCEDURE

Method:

    Using C. Wright, Federal Practice and Procedure, answer the following questions, giving citations where necessary.

Questions:

1. What 1952 Supreme Court case upheld the admissibility of evidence obtained through use of a "wired" undercover agent in a criminal case?

2. Where is there discussion of the meaning of the word "admissible" as used in Rule 402 of the Federal Rules of Evidence?

3. Where are the implications of "negative pregnants" in the Federal Rules of Civil Procedure discussed?

4. Where can one find the forms mentioned in Rule 84 of Federal Rules of Civil Procedure?

5. Which of the Federal Rules of Criminal Procedure gave government a right to discovery against criminal defendants for the first time?

6. Where is there discussion of pretrial conferences in complex cases?

7. May an injunction be binding on unnamed members of a labor union?

8. Where is there a discussion of Ex parte Young as it relates to relations of state and federal courts?

9. Where is there a discussion of the law controlling the question of immunity from service of process?

ASSIGNMENT 13
MOORE'S FEDERAL PRACTICE

Method:

Using J. Moore, Federal Practice (2d ed.), answer the questions, giving citations as necessary.

Questions:

1. Which court has original jurisdiction in federal question suits brought by Indian tribes?

2. Is an injunction subject to collateral attack?

3. After remand, may a trial court correct an error existing but not raised on an interlocutory appeal?

4. In criminal prosecutions, is a showing of irreparable injury a test allowed for the granting of an injunction?

5. If an attorney fails to object to instructions to the jury, is this a waiver of error?

6. Does one have a permissive right to intervene in a claim or defense when such claim or defense has a question of law or fact in common with the main action?

7. Applying conflict of law rules in non-federal matters, must state substantive law be applied?

8. Is "harmless error" grounds for disturbing a judgment if the error relates to evidence introduced at trial?

9. Which federal rule governs the alternatives available in personal service of a summons?

10. Can a party's deposition be used as original evidence and also for impeachment purposes if being used by an adverse party?

11. May a third-party defendant assert a counterclaim against a plaintiff?

12. At which paragraph is waiver by defendent of right to remove discussed?

13. The "final judgment rule" as to the appealability of any decree other than one that is a final judgment is a complex one. Where can one find some illuminating discussion of the general rule?

14. Where is there a discussion of venue in actions against the United States?

15. Where can one find discussion of the general history that surrounds Rule 62 of the Federal Rules of Civil Procedure?

16. Where can one find discussion of U.S. v. Vandetti?

17. Locate discussion of the availability of the sanction of a contempt citation for disobeying a subpoena?

18. Where can one find discussion of the Toucey Case?

19. Where is § 101.9 of Illinois Revised Statutes cited?

20. Where can discussion of removal based upon forum non conveniens be found?

21. Can the court accept admissions made at pretrial conferences without the necessity of proof being offered at the actual trial?

22. Once a complaint has been dismissed, is leave to amend the pleadings within the discretion of the Court or is this a matter of right?

23. Once a judgment by default has been entered in a civil case, can such judgment be set aside?

24. Is it necessary that a defendant be present at every phase of his trial or may he expressly waive his right?

ASSIGNMENT 14
WEST'S FEDERAL PRACTICE MANUAL

Method:

Use M. Volz, West's Federal Practice Manual:

(1) Consult the index. If necessary, check the table of contents in front of the particular sections of the book for indications of specific sections necessary to answer the questions.

(2) Answer the questions, checking both the main volumes and their pocket part. Cite to Volz. List the index subject heading under which you found the answer, if appropriate.

Questions:

1. During tax audits, is the taxpayer entitled to representation by an attorney?

2. When computing the taxable estate of a decedent, are attorney's fees deductible?

3. Which section of U.S.C. gives the General Accounting Office the authority to settle and adjust claims by or against the U.S. Government?

4. What is the statute of limitations with regard to claims against the government?

5. What requirements must an attorney meet for admission to practice before the U.S. District Court?

6. What is a prerequisite to filing a federal suit charging discrimination against an employer?

7. In which courts can condemnation proceedings be filed? Where is the jurisdictional authority found?

8. What are the judicial remedies for infringement of copyrights?

9. What is the proper venue in copyright cases?

10. Do the Federal Rules of Civil Procedure apply to the Court of Claims?

11. Is there a jurisdictional amount in the Court of Claims?

12. When applying for a refund of income taxes believed to have been improperly paid to the Internal Revenue Service, to which court would you apply for judicial remedies?

13. What are proper grounds for a change of venue in criminal cases?

14. Does adverse possession operate against the U.S. on federally owned lands under the jurisdiction of the Department of Interior?

15. Where is 42 U.S.C. § 417 cited in West's Federal Practice Manual?

16. Is the National Labor Relations Board a quasi-judicial agency?

17. What section in West's Federal Practice Manual discusses filing fees for the Court of Claims?

18. Is it always necessary for an attorney to be admitted to practice in the Supreme Court of the United States before he can be admitted to practice before the Court of Appeals for the Federal Circuit? (Cannot be answered through index.)

19. Under what code was the practice before Army, Navy, Coast Guard and Air Force Courts first unified? In what year was this Code enacted by Congress?

20. What is the correct address of the U.S. Court of Appeals for the Federal Court? (Cannot be answered through index.)

21. Under what section of U.S.C.A. is the Supreme Court authorized to prescribe rules of civil procedure for the district courts?

22. What publication outlines in detail procedures to be used in court martial practice?

23. Give the U.S.C. citation for a provision governing impleader motions in the Court of Claims.

24. On what date is statutory protection against age discrimination provided for District of Columbia employees?

25. The Eighth Circuit of the United States Court of Appeals generally holds court in what cities?

26. What rule first applied the title judge to referees in bankruptcy?

27. Within how many years must a claim of condemnation by inverse taking be asserted?

28. What must the caption to a complaint include under the Federal Rules? (List elements)

29. Where is § 6(c) of the Administrative Procedure Act cited in Volz?

30. Where can you find a "Findings and Judgment" form for a Federal condemnation proceeding?

31. Where is § 315 of the Communications Act cited in Volz?

32. Is it necessary for a person to be an attorney for admission to practice before the National Labor Relations Board? Are there any restrictions as to who may appear before the Board on behalf of clients?

33. To whom is aircraft wreckage released following an investigation by the National Transportation Safety Board?

34. Are the files, records, reports and other papers and documents related to claims with the Veterans Administration confidential and privileged?

ASSIGNMENT 15
WEINSTEIN'S EVIDENCE

Method:

Using J. Weinstein & M. Berger, Weinstein's Evidence, answer the following questions, giving citations where necessary.

Questions:

1. Where is there discussion of the degree of privilege that attaches to communications in a group therapy setting.?

2. Where is Burr v. Kase noted?

3. Where can one find discussion of the right of a judge to comment on the credibility of witnesses?

4. Where can one find discussion of admissibility of ballistic expert testimony linking defendant to the weapon used in a crime?

5. Where is Polen's "The Admissibility of Truth Serum Tests in Court" cited?

6. Where is Connecticut General Statute § 1443i mentioned in the text?

7. Where is the proper form of an offer of proof discussed?

8. Where is Pugh v. Cannon noted?

ASSIGNMENT 16
COURT RULES

Method:

Using the appropriate sets of federal court rules, answer the following, giving citations where necessary.

Questions:

1. What rule of the United States Claims Court governs joinder of persons needed for just adjudication?

2. Cite the rule which allows a Federal District Court Judge to choose an expert witness.

3. Using and citing to Callaghan's Federal Rules Service, find the case of Zdanok v Glidden.

4. Footnotes in briefs printed for the U.S. Supreme Court must have type no smaller than what size? Cite rule.

5. Is hearsay testimony admissible when it concerns the reputation of a person's character in the community? Cite rule.

6. Under the Federal Rules of Civil Procedure, can one make a solemn affirmation in lieu of an oath? Cite the rule.

7. Using Callaghan's Federal Rules Service, under what "Findex" number would one find cases under Rule 1 of the Federal Rules of Civil Procedure that deal with "joinder of claims"?

8. Can one impair the credibility of a witness by showing that the witnesse's religious beliefs are untenable? Cite rule.

9. In volume 71 of West's Federal Rules Decisions
   (a) Where is Rule E(6) of the Admiralty Rules discussed?
   (b) Where is Rule 17(b)(1) of the Federal Rules of Civil Procedure cited?
   (c) What article by the Honorable Harold R. Tyler, Jr. appears?

10. What provision in the Federal Rules of Criminal Procedure guarantees every defendant who is unable to obtain counsel the right to have counsel assigned?

11. Using and citing to Callaghan's Federal Rules Service, under Findex Number 26b.321, find a 1970 case holding that in a minimum wage action by the Secretary of Labor, the plaintiff is not required to furnish names of employees who requested the suit where it is not relevant to do so.

265

12. For what reason may a court dismiss an indictment, information or complaint and thereby terminate criminal prosecution? Cite the rule.

13. When are errors and irregularities in the notice for taking a deposition not waived? Cite the rule.

14. In civil proceedings, by whom shall service of process, other than a summons and complaint, be made and when can other special appointments be made? Cite rule.

15. When, in a criminal proceeding, must the government furnish a defendant with the copy of the defendant's prior record (if any)? Cite rule.

16. In criminal prosecutions, for what type of offenses is a defendant's presence not required (after giving written consent)? Cite rule.

17. Under what general power do the Federal Rules of Civil Procedure for the United States District Courts govern the procedure of the condemnation of real and personal property? Cite rule.

18. Using the Federal Rules of Civil Procedure and the Federal Rules of Criminal Procedure, answer the following, giving citations where necessary in proper Bluebook form:
    (a) What is the time limit for entering a motion for a new criminal trial based on any grounds other than newly discovered evidence? Cite rule.
    (b) In what circumstances is a party allowed permissive intervention in a civil action? Cite rule.
    (c) The capacity of a corporation to sue or be sued is determined by what law? Cite rule.
    (d) How many prerequisites must be fulfilled for a class action suit to be possible? Cite rule.

Chapter 13

ADMINISTRATIVE LAW

ASSIGNMENT
USE OF THE CODE OF FEDERAL REGULATIONS

Method:

Using the appropriate indexes to the C.F.R., locate and cite the appropriate title and section for each of the following problems:

Questions:

1. Where in the C.F.R. is it specifically stated that it is an unlawful employment practice to classify a job as "male" or "female" or to maintain separate lines of progression or separate seniority lists based on sex where this would adversely affect any employee unless sex is a bona fide occupational qualification for the job?

2. In which C.F.R. title and section does the Occupational Safety and Health Administration of the Department of Labor specify the amount of airborne concentrations of asbestos fibers to which an employee may be exposed in an eight hour period?

3. Under which C.F.R. title and part is the procedure for reporting natural gas pipeline leaks given?

4. Where in the C.F.R. is the provision requiring the giving of thirty days advance notice, when possible, to the National Science Foundation by anyone intending to engage in any weather modification activity?

5. What C.F.R. title and section governs the withholding of U.S. Government checks which are intended for delivery in certain countries where it has been determined that postal, transportation, or banking facilities are such that there is not a reasonable assurance that named payees in those areas will actually receive these checks and be able to negotiate them for full value?

6. What C.F.R. title and part is intended to effectuate the provisions of a portion of the Civil Rights Act of 1964 requiring equal employment opportunities in all programs or activities receiving Federal financial assistance from the U.S. Coast Guard?

7. Where in the C.F.R. is the provision establishing a maximum liability of fifty dollars per card for credit card holders in cases involving unauthorized use of such cards?

8. Where in the C.F.R. is it specified that misuse of the word "perfect" in describing a diamond is an unfair trade practice?

9. Where in the C.F.R. is the description of the signaling arrangements, i.e., the attention signal, whereby standard, FM, and television broadcast stations can actuate muted receivers for the receipt of cuing announcements as part of the Emergency Broadcast System?

10. Where in the C.F.R. are the provisions which deal with the "Warnings" which packages of antacid products for human use must carry to avoid being misbranded?

11. Where in the C.F.R. are the reporting requirements for accidents involving the transportation of radioactive materials?

12. Where in the C.F.R. are the provisions which deal with attempts to mail merchandise into the United States when it is subject to an absolute quota that has already been filled?

13. The Postal regulations provide that the Domestic Mail Manual is available for reference and inspection at various places including all U.S. Post Offices and branches. What portion thereof deals with Postage Meters and Meter Stamps?

14. Where in the C.F.R. is the provision governing the use of non-federal funds in federally sponsored vocational rehabilitation programs for the mentally retarded?

15. Where in the C.F.R. are the federal grade standards for frozen okra enumerated?

16. Where in the C.F.R. is the requirement that any food which is a substitute for another food of superior nutritional value shall be deemed to be misbranded unless its label bears the word "imitation" in conjunction with the name of the food imitated?

17. Where in the C.F.R. are the provisions as authorized by the Federal Truth in Lending Act which govern the determination of finance charges?

18. Where in the C.F.R. is the provision covering the pooling of reserve hops which are a part of domestic production?

19. Where in the C.F.R. are the provisions covering the labeling requirements for "Lemon juice?"

20. Where in the C.F.R. are the provisions governing the service of process and subpoenas upon personnel of the Department of the Navy?

21. Where in the Domestic Mail Manual are the provisions governing commemorative stamps?

22. Where in the Domestic Mail Manual are the provisions specifying what may be mailed?

23. Where in the C.F.R. are the provisions of the Social Security Administration covering insurance benefits for victims of black lung disease?

24. Where in the C.F.R. are the provisions of the Food and Drug Administration specifying the standard of fill for a container of canned applesauce?

25. Where in the C.F.R. are there provisions dealing with the rate of import tax on beer as of the time of its importation, or, if entered into customs custody, at the time of removal from such custody?

26. 42 U.S.C. § 263 is the federal law authorizing the U.S. Public Health Service to prepare certain biological products when not available from licensed establishments. Cite C.F.R. parts issued under this statute as shown in the C.F.R. Index and Finding Aids:

27. 43 U.S.C. § 641 authorizes certain conditional grants of federal desert land to the States for homestead use. Cite the C.F.R. parts which set out the regulations issued under this law. What federal bureau administers these rules?

28. What C.F.R. part cites Executive Order 1234 as one of the authorities for its adoption?

29. Find which of the assistant Secretaries of Defense is responsible for insuring that there be no unlawful discrimination in any Federally assisted program of the Department of Defense.

30. Pollution of navigable waters by the discharge of oil of all types is covered by what title and part of the C.F.R.? Set out the U.S. Code reference cited as authority for this part.

31. Locate the C.F.R. definition of "cable television system."

32. Cite the C.F.R. part covering the labeling or advertising of automobile tires.

33. Federal flood insurance regulations define the coverage of this insurance. Are mud slides covered? Cite the definition regulation for this.

34. Any person may bring to the attention of the Civil Rights Commission a grievance believed to fall within its jurisdiction. Should the complaint include the names and titles of the officials or other persons involved in acts forming the basis for the complaint?

35. What federal regulation bans hazardous toys? Of the two related citations you find in this area, which one exempts certain items from the "banned toys" classification?

36. The public use of records in the National Archives is subject to the terms of the Privacy Act of 1974. Under this act, the GSA has made provision for denials of access and for the appeal of such denials within that agency. Cite these regulations. Who has the authority to deny public use? Must the denials be made in writing? Cite the regulation for the latter.

37. Under certain circumstances, an official of the Indian Affairs Bureau having jurisdiction over particular tribal land may issue permits to prospect on such lands for minerals other than oil and gas. What action must the tribal authorities take before such permits may be validly issued? Give the citation for this.

38. Find and cite the C.F.R. part covering the advertising and labeling of wines. In compliance with these regulations how would a manufacturer label his grape wine made effervescent by some means other than the natural fermentation of the wine?

39. There are quarantine regulations which the U.S. Surgeon General administers. Cite the regulation which lists the various diseases that are "Quarantinable."

40. A table of Public Land Orders issued by the Bureau of Land Management is published in the C.F.R. Sometime between 1948 and 1972, Order No. 4373 was issued on the withdrawal of lands for national forest recreation areas in Arizona. Give as shown the citation to this order. What was date of the order?

41. Where in the C.F.R. is the provision of the Federal Trade Commission regulations specifying that it is an unfair or deceptive act or practice to sell, in commerce, any finished article of wearing apparel which does not have a permanently affixed label or tag clearly disclosing instructions for the care and maintenance of such article?

42. Alien spouses of American citizens can be naturalized under special laws. Regulations covering this in the C.F.R. include persons whose citizen spouse is employed abroad. Cite this regulation. What is the U.S.C. authority for this part of the C.F.R.?

43. The employees of the Department of Justice have regulations prescribing their standards of conduct. Cite the part of the C.F.R. defining these standards. Also give the citation to the specific regulation covering participation in a proceeding in which the employee has a financial interest.

44. Applications for authorizations to operate private short-distance citizens' radio services can be obtained from what offices? What standard form is used in applying for such an authorization as to a new base station of this general class?

45. Find the policy forms used by the Federal Crime Insurance Program and give the citation for the required Commercial Crime Insurance Policy form.

46. A major portion of the general information governing the day-to-day operations of the U.S. Postal Service is contained in the Domestic Mail Manual. What portion of such manual deals with nonmailable matter?

47. Regulations for the Historic Preservation of American Antiquities specify which Departmental Secretary to address for an application for permission to explore a site. If the area is within Federal forest reserves to whom shall the requester apply? What Federal agency then gets the application for recommendation?

48. Are consular or other foreign service officers permitted to celebrate marriages? What regulation covers the consular officer acting as an official witness to a marriage?

49. The Law and Order regulations for Indian reservations refers to a Court of Indian Offenses. Cite the regulation stating where these regulations are applicable. This regulation also states the conditions under which such a court will not be established on a reservation. Quote the pertinent words from it.

50. Tort claims against the United States involving an employee of the Department of Agriculture are covered by what U.S.D.A. regulation? This same regulation refers to other regulations of the U.S. Department of Justice. Cite this latter C.F.R. part.

Chapter 14

LOOSELEAF SERVICES

ASSIGNMENT 1
USE OF LOOSE-LEAF SERVICES OR REPORTERS

Method:

Briefly answer the question and give the citation requested using the form required by the latest edition of A Uniform System of Citation to the extent that the indicated source provides the information needed for such a citation.

Questions:

1. Source: C.C.H. Standard Federal Tax Reporter. Where a taxpayer does not establish a basis for measuring an alleged casualty loss of ornamental trees, will a deduction be allowed? Cite the C.C.H. paragraph on point

2. Source: C.C.H. Standard Federal Tax Reporter. Was a newspaper subscriber taxable on the value of an auto- mobile which he won on a lottery ticket received with his subscription as part of a campaign by the news- paper to increase its circulation? Cite a case on point.

3. Source: C.C.H. Standard Federal Tax Reporter. Are punitive damages awarded specifically for fraud and antitrust violations taxable income to the recipient? Cite the C.C.H. paragraph on point.

4. Source: C.C.H. Standard Federal Tax Reporter. May a member of the U.S. foreign service, i.e., a consular officer, take a business traveling expense deduction for transportation, meals, and lodging that is occasioned by being on "home leave?" Cite a Revenue Ruling on point.

5. Source: C.C.H. Standard Federal Tax Reporter. May letter carriers deduct the cost and maintenance expenses of uniforms? Cite a Revenue Ruling on point.

6. Source: C.C.H. Standard Federal Tax Reporter. Is the amount of a dissolved partnership debt paid by a former partner on behalf of a deceased partner's insolvent estate deductible? Cite a Revenue Ruling on point.

7. Source: C.C.H. Standard Federal Tax Reporter. In some cases may the cost of improvements made by business tenants in lieu of paying rent be deductible as rent? Cite the C.C.H. paragraph on point.

8. Source: C.C.H. Standard Federal Tax Reporter. Are travel expenses of teachers on sabbatical leave deductible if and to the extent that the travel is directly related to the duties of the teacher in his teaching position? Cite a Revenue Ruling on point.

9. Source: C.C.H. Standard Federal Tax Reporter. Were the legal fees incurred in an unsuccessful attempt to have a liquor license transferred from one bar to another building which the taxpayer owned deductible? Cite a case on point.

10. Source: C.C.H. Standard Federal Tax Reporter. Is a monthly charge or "tax" made by a city for the use of its sewer system a deductible personal expense as are property taxes? Cite the C.C.H. paragraph on point.

11. Source: P-H Federal Taxes. Was a payment by a congregation to a theological student serving as assistant pastor for services required in obtaining the theological degree nontaxable as a scholarship? Cite a Revenue Ruling on point.

12. Source: P-H Federal Taxes. Are penalties paid by truck operators for innocent violations of state size and weight limit laws deductible business expenses? Cite the P-H paragraph on point.

13. Source: P-H Federal Taxes. What is the Federal income tax status of subsistence and uniform allowances that are granted to personnel of the Public Health Service of the United States? Cite the pertinent section of the Income Tax Regulations.

14. Source: P-H Federal Taxes. Can a Jewish cantor who performs worship, training and educational functions on a full time basis for a congregation qualify as a minister of the gospel for the purpose of excluding compensation received as a rental allowance? Cite a Revenue Ruling on point.

15. Source: P-H Federal Taxes. By treaty with the Quinaielt Indian Tribe, tribal lands were transferred to the United States and an area was reserved for the exclusive use of members of the tribe. Later the Bureau of Indian Affairs of the United States Department of Interior sold the standing timber on this allocated land. Were the proceeds received by the Indians from this timber sale subject to income tax? Cite a United States Supreme Court opinion on point.

16. Source: P-H *Federal Taxes*. Was the cost of restoring a part of a trellis which collapsed on a hop ranch as a result of an extraordinarily large crop, rainfall, and wind deductible as a business expense? Cite a Board of Tax Appeals decision on point.

17. Source: P-H *Federal Taxes*. Where the taxpayer alleged in his complaint that but for the patent infringement asserted he would have been in receipt of large gains and profits, was the entire amount of damages received held to be income for purposes of taxation? Cite a First Circuit case on point.

18. Source: P-H *Federal Taxes*. Were payments made by a brewery to a state brewers association for the purpose of establishing trade practices and dealing with labor and labor matters, i.e., set up a strike fund, allowed as business expense deductions? Cite a Board of Tax Appeals decision on point.

19. Source: C.C.H. *Trade Regulation Reporter*. Does Supreme Court's failure to make specific attorney fee award for legal services performed at the appellate stages of a successfully prosecuted private antitrust suit preclude a district court from granting such an award after remand of the case to it? Cite a Supreme Court case on point.

20. Source: C.C.H. *Trade Regulation Reporter*. Does use of the word "reprocessed" on a container of reclaimed oil as required by North Carolina law meet the applicable Federal Trade Regulation Rule requiring disclosure of previous use? Cite a case on point.

21. Source: C.C.H. *Federal Securities Law Reporter*. Where the defendant wrote a letter to a woman purchaser of securities he was selling and stated, "if you know of some of your friends whom you can write to and simply state that if they still want some of it (interest in an electrical device represented to extract gold from water) you can get them some for a few days. . ." Was this construed as evidence to show that the defendant was offering units of interest to the general public? Cite a case on point.

22. Source: C.C.H. *Federal Securities Law Reporter*. Did a Federal District Court have jurisdiction to hear a case in which a stockholder sought enforcement of the proxy solicitation rules promulgated under section 14 of the Securities Exchange Act of 1934 notwithstanding the fact that the Securities and Exchange Commission had declined to institute a court action against the defendant for such purpose. Cite a case on point.

23. Source: C.C.H. Federal Securities Law Reporter. Did a bank which credited the account of a customer upon having endorsed to it the customer's draft on a third party, accompanied by a spurious warehouse receipt securing a like note, in subsequently receiving payment from the third party, effect a sale within the meaning of section 2(3) of the Securities Act? Cite a Third Circuit case on point.

24. Source: P-H Estate Planning. It appears to be well settled that installments of alimony which are due and owing, and unpaid, at the time of the husband's death constitute a valid claim against his estate. If, however, the award of alimony was made by a foreign decree, does this automatically render the wife's claim unenforceable? Cite a Washington (State) case on point.

25. Source: P-H Estate Planning. The question commonly arises as to the right of executors and trustees to receive attorney's fees (compensation) for legal services rendered to the estate. Cite an 1896 Alabama case in which the fiduciary who was also an attorney was entitled to recover attorney's fees for his services in a legal capacity.

26. Source: C.C.H. Standard Federal Tax Reporter. Must an outstanding player award in sports be included in the player's gross income? Cite a relevant case.

27. Source: C.C.H. Standard Federal Tax Reporter. Are legal expenses deductible where incurred by a husband in resisting his wife's suit for divorce deductible as such? Cite the U.S. Sup. Ct. cases on point.

28. Source: C.C.H. Standard Federal Tax Reporter. If a taxpayer overpaid his income by simply an erroneous calculation, is he entitled to interest on the refund by the federal government? Cite a case on point.

29. Source: C.C.H. Standard Federal Tax Reporter. Does the operation of a dining room, cafeteria, and snack bar by an exempt art museum for the use of its employees and members of the visiting public constitute an unrelated business activity? Cite the pertinent Revenue Ruling so determining.

30. Source: C.C.H. Standard Federal Tax Reporter. A stock purchase plan for an employee allowed him to buy stock with a current market value of $100 by paying only $85 per share for it. Will he be taxable on the $15 difference in value at the time he purchases this stock? What section of the Int. Rev. Code applies here?

31. Source: C.C.H. Standard Federal Tax Reporter. X is enrolled as a student in a recognized educational institution taking a full time day course for only five calendar months during 1972. Does this limited enrollment fit the definition of a "student" so that his parents may use him as a personal exemption? Cite regulation shown.

32. Source: C.C.H. Standard Federal Tax Reporter. A taxpayer wants to claim a loss on the sale of property to his son who paid him its fair market value at the time. Is this deductible? Cite pertinent I.R. Code section.

33. Source: C.C.H. Standard Federal Tax Reporter. Land and a warehouse, which taxpayer held for rental purposes was condemned and purchased by city. This was an involuntary conversion. Taxpayer then used the sale money to construct an automobile service station on other land that he owned that he likewise held for rental purposes. Was this station "similar or related in service or use" under the pertinent statute so as to qualify for the non-recognition of gain on the condemnation sale? Cite the Revenue Ruling on point and the I.R. Code section governing Involuntary Conversions.

34. Source: P-H Federal Taxes. Where professional entertainer was accompanied by his wife, a trained singer, who coached her husband and handled the essential business details of the trip, were her traveling expenditures deductible as business expenses? Cite a case on point.

35. Source: P-H Federal Taxes. Was the sale of raw gravel paid for by the cubic yard as taken a sale of gravel in place and treated as capital gains or was it income? Cite Battjes case on point.

36. Source: P-H Federal Taxes. Stock of a corporation was split-up and stockholder exchanged one share of old common for 25 shares of new common. Was there a gain recognized on this?

37. Source: P-H Federal Taxes. Was it an involuntary conversion when stock had to be sold because owner no longer met corporation restrictions upon ownership?

38. Source: P-H Federal Taxes. Can a partner deduct life insurance premiums paid on the life insurance policy of his partner? Cite the pertinent regulation.

39. Source: P-H Federal Taxes. Are the premium payments that an individual made on a whole-life insurance policy which he had assigned irrevocably to divorced wife under the divorce decree taxable as alimony and hence includable in her gross income? Cite the 1970 Revenue Ruling on point.

40. Source: P-H *Federal Taxes*. Find Revenue Ruling 70-413 in Main Table of Rulings and supply the *Cumulative Bulletin* location.

41. Source: P-H *Federal Taxes*. Find Revenue Ruling 70-454 in Main Table of Rulings and supply the *Cumulative Bulletin* location.

42. Source: C.C.H. *Trade Regulation Reporter*. A publishers agreement called for a lock-out of all pressmen if one of the publishers was prevented from publishing by a pressmen's strike. Was a union entitled have such a lock-out enjoined on the ground that an employer's compliance with this agreement was in violation of the Sherman Act? Cite case authority.

43. Source: C.C.H. *Trade Regulation Reporter*. Did the fact that various steel producers, at a time of short supplies, limited the amounts of their current sales to individual customers by reference to the extent of their respective prior sales to them as well as the urgency of each customer's needs support an inference of unlawful conspiracy? Cite Ninth Circuit Court case on point.

44. Source: C.C.H. *Trade Regulation Reporter*. Would fraudulent concealment by the defendant suspend the statute of limitations otherwise applicable to a private treble- damage suit under the Federal anti-trust laws? Cite Second Circuit case on point.

45. Source: C.C.H. *Trade Regulation Reporter*. Find the Agricultural Fair Practice Act of 1967 and give both Statutes at Large and *U.S. Code* citations for it.

46. Source: C.C.H. *Consumer Credit Guide*. Under "Charts" section find Home Solicitation Sales. Are insurance sales excluded from statutes giving buyers right to cancel within time limitations shown in the states of Florida, Michigan and Wisconsin?

47. Source: C.C.H. *Consumer Credit Guide*. What is the maximum liability that a credit card holder can incur under the Federal Reserve Board regulations with respect to the "unauthorized use" of his credit card? Give Federal Reserve Board regulation citation.

48. Source: C.C.H. *Consumer Credit Guide*. Find the Federal Reserve Board Regulation Z under Federal-Truth- In-Lending. Under what regulation section can you find a definition of "open end credit?"

49. Source: C.C.H. Poverty Law Reporter. Does section 514 of the Soldiers' and Sailors' Civil Relief Act entitle service men stationed in Connecticut but regularly domiciled and resident elsewhere to exemption from the payment of Connecticut sales and use taxes? Cite C.C.H. paragraph on point.

50. Source: C.C.H. Poverty Law Reporter. Publication of Poverty Law Reports for insertion in this Reporter has been discontinued. Give the date as of which the material therein was last updated.

ASSIGNMENT 2
USE OF LOOSE-LEAF SERVICE CITATORS

Method:

Answer the question by giving the citator reference as shown or otherwise providing the information requested.

Questions:

1. Source: C.C.H. Standard Federal Tax Reporter Citator. The Las Vegas Land and Water Co. case, 26 T.C. 881, was cited in a later opinion of the Tax Court. What is the Tax Court Reports citation for the citing case?

2. Source: P-H Federal Taxes Citator, 2d Series, vol. 1. Revenue Ruling 55-468, 1955-2 C.B. 501, was modified by what later Revenue Procedure?

3. Source: C.C.H. Federal Estate and Gift Tax Reporter, vol. 3. You are doing research in the estate tax area and have learned of a case in point entitled Elsie C. Emery v. U.S. Using this case as a finding aid, at what paragraph number in the loose-leaf reporter is the same topic discussed?

4. Source: C.C.H. Standard Federal Tax Reporter Citator. The case of Phillips v. Howe Films Co. was first decided by a Federal District Court for Pennsylvania. Was this decision affirmed or reversed by the Third Circuit?

5. Source: P-H Federal Taxes Citator, 2d Series, vol. 1. Income Tax Unit Ruling 3064, 1937-1 C.B. 94, was questioned in what case?

6. Source: P-H Federal Taxes Citator (Loose-leaf). The case of David v. Phinney, 16 A.F.T.R. 2d 5290, has been cited by two later cases for the topic of law which is treated in the first paragraph of the syllabus to the cited case. What are these cases?

7. Source: C.C.H. Federal Estate and Gift Tax Reporter, vol. 3. You are looking for the case involving the Estate of Frank Janson. What part of the official citation can be developed from the citator?

8. Source: P-H Federal Tax Service Citator, vol. 1. The case of Nicol v. Ames, 3 A.F.T.R. 2661, is cited by what later case for the topic of law which is treated in the second paragraph of the syllabus to the cited case?

9. Source: P-H Federal Tax Service Citator, vol. 3. Revenue Ruling 2, 1953-1 C.B. 484, was modified by what later Revenue Ruling?

10. Source: C.C.H. Standard Federal Tax Reporter Citator. Which federal courts heard the case of Rose E. Roybark?

11. Source: P-H Federal Tax Service Citator, vol. 1. The case of Edye v. Robertson, Head Money cases, 3 A.F.T.R. 2473, is cited by what later case for the topic of law which is treated in the fifth paragraph of the syllabus to the cited case?

12. Source: C.C.H. Standard Federal Tax Reporter Citator. Did the Commissioner of Internal Revenue indicate acquiesce in the holding of the Tax Court in the case involving Lola G. Bullard, 5 T.C. 1346? In what volume of the Cumulative Bulletin is the Commissioner's action reported?

13. Source: C.C.H. Standard Federal Tax Reporter Citator. The United States Court of Appeals affirmed the Tax Court in the case involving William E. Conroy. Did the action of the Court of Appeals appear in a full opinion or a per curiam opinion?

14. Source: P-H Federal Taxes Citator, 2d Series, vol. 1. The same case as was involved in Department of Labor Release, 9-6-56, 1956 P-H ¶76,702, was also involved in what Revenue Ruling?

15. Source: C.C.H. Federal Estate and Gift Tax Reporter, vol. 3. The case of Leonard D. Reeves, Admr. (Est. of T.K. Reeves) v. U.S., 57-2 U.S.T.C. ¶ 11,717, was cited in what 1971 Revenue Ruling?

16. Source: C.C.H. Standard Federal Tax Reporter Citator. Did the U.S. Court of Appeals for the Sixth Circuit reverse or affirm the Tax Court in the case involving George L. Sogg?

17. Source: C.C.H. Standard Federal Tax Reporter Citator. Who appealed the decision of the United States Board of Tax Appeals to the U.S. Court of Appeals in the case involving Little Gem Coal Company?

18. Source: P-H Federal Tax Service Citator, vol. 3. What is the American Federal Tax Reports citation for the opinion which reversed the Jerry Rossman Corp. case, 10 T.C. 468?

19. Source: C.C.H. Standard Federal Tax Reporter Citator (1983). The case involving Eugene M. Gideo was decided by a Federal District Court in Minnesota in 1970. Is the opinion in this case reported in the Federal Supplement? If not, is it reported in the Commerce Clearing House U.S. Tax Cases set, and if so, what is the citation?

20. Source: C.C.H. Federal Estate and Gift Tax Reporter Citator. What is the citation for the Snyder case which cited Worcester County Trust Co. (Est. of E.E. Aldrich) v. U.S.?

21. Source: P-H Federal Tax Service Citator, vol. 3. The case of Fruit Growers Supply Co. v. Commissioner, 10 A.F.T.R. 1277, was explained in what later case?

22. Source: P-H Federal Tax Service Citator, vol. 3. Was the Tax Court decision in a case involving Harry A. Kaufmann reversed on appeal by the Sixth Circuit?

23. Source: P-H Federal Taxes Citator, 2d Series, vol. 1. Revenue Ruling 59-277 was reversed by what later Revenue Ruling?

24. Source: P-H Federal Taxes Citator, 2d Series, vol. 1. Revenue Ruling 67-282 revoked what earlier Revenue Ruling?

25. Source: P-H Federal Taxes Citator, 2d Series, vol. 1. What action did the Fourth Circuit take relative to McAlister v. Cohen, 25 A.F.T.R. 2d 70-1072, when it was appealed? What is the Federal Reporter citation for the Fourth Circuit's opinion?

26. Source: P-H Federal Taxes Citator, 2d Series, vol. 1. Revenue Ruling 59-60 was modified by what later ruling?

27. Source: P-H Federal Taxes Citator, 2d Series, vol. 1. I.T. 2143, 1V-1 CB 214 was superseded by what Revenue Ruling?

28. Source: P-H Federal Taxes Citator, 2d Series, vol. 1. The William G. Lias case (24 T.C. 280) was affirmed by what decision of the federal appellate court?

29. Source: P-H Federal Taxes Citator, 2d Series, vol. 1. The Tax Court case involving Joseph L. Merrill, 9 T.C. 291, was followed in what later Tax Court memo?

30. Source: P-H Federal Taxes Citator, vol. 1. Headnote No. 3 of Guettel v. U.S., 95 F(2d) 229, was followed by what case?

31. Source: P-H Federal Taxes Citator, vol. 1. Shellabarger, Maud Dunlap v. Commissioner, 14 B.T.A. 695, was reversed by what appellate decision?

32. Source: P-H Federal Taxes Citator, vol. 1. What did Richmond Hosiery Mills v. Commissioner, 29 F.2d 262, do to the Richmond Hosiery Mills case, 6 B.T.A. 1247?

33. Source: P-H Federal Taxes Citator, vol. 1. What did I.T. 2968 do to I.T. 2472?

34. Source: P-H *Federal Taxes Citator*, vol. 1. T.D. 3911 was cited in a U.S. Supreme Court case. Give this citation without date.

35. Source: P-H *Federal Taxes Citator*, vol. 1. General Counsel's Memorandum 6667 was modified by a latter G.C.M. Cite the latter.

36. Source: *Pike and Fischer Radio Regulation Finding Aids Volume*. In 1954, the U.S. Court of Appeals for the District of Columbia Circuit released an opinion in *Zenith Radio Corp. v. FCC*, 211 F.2d 629. Give the later case reference to this opinion which appears in 45 R.R.2d in the form such reference is set out in the appropriate citation table.

37. Source: *Pike and Fischer Radio Regulation Finding Aids Volume*. Give the first citation of 27 F.C.C. 2d 743 that appears in 45 R.R. 2d.

38. Source: *Pike and Fischer Radio Regulation Finding Aids Volume*. The Fairness Doctrine Rules appeared in 10 R.R. 2d 1901. Find the last citation to these rules that appears in 24 R.R. 2d.

39. Source: P-H *Federal Tax Service Citator*. *Bob Jones University v. U.S.*, 468 F. Supp. 890 (D. S.C. 1979) was reversed by the 4th Circuit and appealed to the U.S. Supreme Court. Was it affirmed or reversed? Give the volume and page references to this latter decision just as they appear in the P-H Citator.

40. Source: C.C.H. *Standard Federal Tax Reporter Citator*. Did the Commissioner acquiesce in the Tax Court decision involving *John F. Lewis, Jr.*? Give as shown the action of the Third Circuit Court of Appeals in this case.

41. Source: C.C.H. *Standard Federal Tax Reporter Citator*. The Court of Appeals decision of *Mrs. Leonie G. Mayer v. Donnelly* was cited in a later decision, the *Swenson* case. What is the citation of such *Swenson* decision?

42. Source: C.C.H. *Standard Federal Tax Reporter Citator*. The *Everett Morss* case was first decided by a Massachusetts Federal District court in 1946. What later case cited this 1946 decision? On appeal was the *Morss* case affirmed or reversed?

43. Source: C.C.H. *Standard Federal Tax Reporter Citator*. Did the U.S. Supreme Court grant certiorari in the *Francis Doll* case? The Eighth Circuit *Doll* opinion was cited in *Northwest Security National Bank*. Give citator reference to this latter decision as shown.

44. Source: C.C.H. Standard Federal Tax Reporter at Case Table. Was the District Court decision in Ralph M. Currie, Jr. v. Internal Revenue Service affirmed by the Court of Appeals for the 11th Circuit? Give the U.S.T.C. citation for this latter decision.

45. Source: P-H Federal Tax Service Citator, vol. 2. Give the B.T.A. citation without date for the Rollin C. Reynolds case. What later case was "on all fours" with the Reynolds case?

46. Source: C.C.H. Federal Estate & Gift Tax Reporter Citator. Give as shown the Tax Court citation to the Estate of Mary H. Hays v. Commissioner. What did the Fifth Circuit, Court of Appeals do to the original Tax Court decision?

47. Source: C.C.H. Federal Estate & Gift Tax Reporter Citator. The Estate of Isaac G. Darlington case started in the Tax Court. What court reversed the Tax Court decision? This appellate decision was subsequently cited by the U.S. Supreme Court. Give the official reporter citator reference to Supreme Court case.

48. Source: C.C.H. Federal Estate & Gift Tax Reporter Citator. The case of Estate of Carrie Grossman, was decided by the Tax Court. Give the volume and page citation as shown for this decision. Cite also the 1970 Revenue Ruling which later referred to this Grossman decision.

49. Source: C.C.H. Federal Estate & Gift Tax Reporter Citator. Give as shown the citation to the Court of Claims case, Stewart P. Verckler, Exr (Estate of M.S. Verckler) v. U.S. In 1962 the Lorenz case in the Court of Appeals cited the Verckler decision. How was this reference to the Lorenz case set out in the citator?

50. Source: C.C.H. Federal Estate & Gift Tax Reporter Citator. The Estate of J.B. Weil went to the Court of Appeals from the Tax Court. Fully identify this Tax Court decision. What did the Court of Appeals do to the Weil case?

51. Source: C.C.H. Standard Federal Tax Reporter Citator. the United States Supreme Court denied certiorari in a case involving William H. Deck. Was a District Court opinion for this case ever reported? Is this case also listed in the Current Citator Table?

52. Source: P-H Federal Tax Service Citator, vol. 3. The case of C.G. Ganoplus, 39 B.T.A. 1120, was explained in what later Tax Court opinion? Is the cited case also listed in the most recent (looseleaf) Federal Taxes Citator?

53. Source: P-H *Federal Tax Service Citator*, vol. 3. The holding of the case involving Malcolm McDermott, 3 T.C. 929, was questioned in at least two later Tax Court opinions. What are the citations given in the citator for the questioning opinion which appears in volume 22 of the Tax Court Reports? Is the cited case also listed in the most recent (looseleaf) Federal Taxes Citator?

54. Source: P-H *Federal Taxes Citator*, 2d Series, vol. 1. The case of Hibler v. Commissioner, 20 A.F.T.R. 2d 5700, affirmed a Tax Court opinion. What is the proper citation for this affirmed opinion? Is the affirming case also listed in the most recent (looseleaf) Federal Taxes Citator?

55. Source: P-H *Federal Taxes Citator*, 2d Series, vol. 1. The case of Blanche A. Lockhart, 1 T.C. 804, was cited by what later case? Properly cite it in your answer. Is the cited case also listed in the most recent (looseleaf) Federal Taxes Citator?

56. Source: P-H *Federal Taxes Citator*, 2d Series, vol. 1. The opinion in the case of Superior Pocahontas Coal Co., 7 B.T.A. 380, was distinguished in the opinion of what later case? Is the cited case also listed in the most recent (looseleaf) Federal Taxes Citator?

57. Source: P-H *Federal Tax Service Citator*, vol. 1. The case of John B. Hittell, 33 B.T.A. 275, was followed in what later case? Is the cited case also listed in the latest (looseleaf) Federal Taxes Citator?

58. Source: P-H *Federal Tax Service Citator*, vol. 1. The case of F.A. Pease, 30 B.T.A. 17, was later followed by what other Board of Tax Appeals case? Is the cited case also listed in the latest (looseleaf) Federal Taxes Citator?

59. Source: P-H *Federal Tax Service Citator*, vol. 2. The case of Ocean Steamship Co. of Savannah v. Allen, 26 A.F.T.R. 584, was later affirmed on appeal by the Fifth Circuit. What is the American Federal Tax Reporter citation for this Fifth Circuit opinion? Is the cited case also listed in the latest (looseleaf) Federal Taxes Citator?

ASSIGNMENT 3
THEME PROBLEMS

Theme Problem I:

Many of the cases on discrimination that followed the Brown decision related to discrimination in labor. One of the most comprehensive, and to some, complex looseleaf services is the BNA Labor Law Reporter. Using the full set of this looseleaf, answer the following:

1. At what page and paragraph does the text of North Dakota labor laws begin?

2. What case is reported at 71 Labor Arbitration and Dispute Settlements 989?

3. What is the address of the Idaho Commission on Human Rights? (Hint - it serves as the state's fair employment practice agency.)

4. What is the Labor Relations Reference Manual?

5. What case appears at 18 Fair Employment Practice Cases 966?

6. Where could one find the text of the Export Administration Act?

Theme Problem II:

A. One way to track cases similar to Gideon would be through use of the BNA Criminal Law Reporter. Using volume 23 (1978) of this looseleaf, answer the following with case C.L.R. citation:

1. What is the Supreme Court docket number of Dungan v. Morgan Drive-Away?

2. Does the First Amendment preclude the search of a newspaper office for evidence pursuant to a particularly exact warrant?

3. According to the 7th Circuit, does one have a reasonable expectation of privacy against garbage collectors looking through one's trash at police request?

B. Using volume 22 (1977) of the Criminal Law Reporter, answer the following:

1. Can a defendant in a state trial for a non-petty criminal offense be convicted by a jury of less than six?

2. Can police properly stop two men carrying a T.V. though an alley in a high crime area at night? Cite the case on point.

3. What was the U.S. Supreme Court docket number of Zimmerman v. Eber?

ASSIGNMENT 4
DRILL PROBLEMS

Drill Problem I:

Using the 1984 CCH Standard Federal Tax Reporter or 1985 Prentice-Hall Federal Taxes as indicated, and the latest edition of A Uniform System of Citation, answer the following and properly cite to the looseleaf.

1. Is a nonresident alien individual who is a member of a partnership which is engaged in business in the U.S considered to be engaged in business in the U.S.? (CCH)

2. Where can one find commentary on the taxability of prizes and awards? (CCH)

3. Cite a case where a taxpayer's contributions to antiwar groups were not allowed as charitable contributions because a large part of the organization's activities were political. (CCH)

4. Where can one find a discussion of what constitutes "public charities?" (P-H)

5. Where can one find a discussion of the basic rules of collapsible corporations? (P-H)

Drill Problem II:

Using the 1984 CCH Standard Federal Tax Reporter or 1985 Prentice-Hall Federal Taxes as indicated, answer the following, indicating the paragraph number at which the answer is located.

1. Where can one find Reg. § 1.441-1(a) on the period for computation of taxable income? (CCH)

2. Where is there an explanation of the deduction of expenses for education? (CCH)

3. Cite a case where no tort claim for harassment against an IRS agent would lie because the agent gave the taxpayer sufficent time and warning before levying on the bank accounts. (P-H)

4. Under Reg. § 1.403(b)-1(f)(4), how can one determine whether an individual is employed full-time? (P-H)

5. Where is Revenue Ruling 74-298 discussed? (P-H)

Drill Problem III:

Using the CCH Copyright Law Reporter or BNA Family Law Reporter (volume 7 & reference file; give the page number instead of paragraph number) or 1981 Prentice-Hall Federal Taxes as indicated, and rules 18.1 and 18.2 of the latest edition of A Uniform System of Citation, answer the following and properly cite to the looseleaf.

1. Does a single performance of a dramatic work for an audience composed primarily of blind people merit an exemption from the copyright laws? (CCH)

2. Where is Nichols v. Universal Pictures Corp. discussed? Please provide the correct cite for the official version of this case. What play was claimed to have been infringed? (CCH)

3. Was Canada a signatory nation to the Buenos Aires Convention of 1910? If not, what is the basis of U.S. - Canadian copyright relations? (CCH)

4. Where can you find the text of North Carolina's Adoption Law? (BNA)

5. Is the Connecticut statute requiring that the party in a paternity suit requesting a blood test bear the cost of that test void as violative of the due process rights of indigents? (BNA)

6. At what conference did Donald Bross deliver an address? (BNA)

7. Is an organization formed to campaign on behalf of candidates for a schoolboard exempt? Cite to the looseleaf where you find the answer and to the official source of the answer. (P-H)

8. What did the Casper Ranger Construction Co. try to deduct? Cite properly to the looseleaf ¶ where you find the answer and to the official source of the answer. (P-H)

9. What is the subject of Revenue Ruling 81-81? Cite to the ¶ in the looseleaf where you find the answer. (P-H)

Drill Problem IV:

Using the CCH Blue Sky Law Reporter or the BNA Product Safety & Liability Reporter (volume 8) as indicated, and the latest edition of A Uniform System of Citation, briefly answer the following and properly cite to the looseleaf.

1. Is the sale of a single condominium unit exempted from the Hawaiian "blue sky" law? (CCH)

2. In the history of "blue sky" legislation, one case gave this peculiar name to the general type of statute. What was the case? (CCH)

3. Give the proper citation for Mifflin v. Cunningham. Also, give the cite where the case is mentioned in the looseleaf. (CCH)

4. Where did Ben Kelley give an address on research safety vehicles? (BNA)

5. Does the user of a fertilizer tank assume the risk of its exploding by not checking its air pressure gauge? Give the case name and cite to the page in the looseleaf where the case is discussed. (BNA)

6. Was the plaintiff's attorney disqualified in Reardon v. Marlayne? Properly cite to the looseleaf page where you found the answer. (BNA)

Drill Problem V:

Using the CCH Corporation Law Guide or BNA Environment Reporter as indicated, and the latest edition of A Uniform System of Citation, find the answers to the following and properly cite to the looseleaf service.

1. If deadlock of management threatens irreparable injury to the corporation, may a court order its liquidation? (CCH)

2. Did Curry v. McCanless deal with death taxes imposed on real property? (CCH)

3. Are tobacco tax laws usually held constitutionally valid? (CCH)

4. Where would one find Louisiana law on the surface mining rules of toxic materials? (BNA)

5. Who is to promulgate regulations governing bottled drinking water standards under the Federal Drinking Water Act? (BNA)

6. What agency administers the California Solid Waste Management Act? (BNA)

Chapter 15

SHEPARD'S CITATIONS

ASSIGNMENT 1
USE OF SHEPARD'S UNITED STATES CITATIONS
CONSTITUTION SECTION

Method:

   Refer to Shepard's United States Citations, Statute Edition, United States Constitution Section. Use bound volumes only. Answer the following questions with reference to the United States Constitution sections listed below. Cite as given in Shepard's.

   (1) Give the most recent citation to the official reporter of the Supreme Court of the United States which discussed the section (and clause).

   (2) Has the provision been noted in the American Bar Association Journal? If so, cite the most recent reference.

   (3) Give the latest A.L.R., A.L.R. Federal or Lawyers' Edition annotation in which the section (and clause) was noted.

Questions:

1. Art. I, § 8, cl. 10

2. Art. I, § 8, cl. 14

3. Art. I, § 8, cl. 18

4. Art. II, § 1

5. Art. III, § 2, cl. 3

6. Art. IV

7. Art. IV, § 1

8. Art. IV, § 2

9. Art. V
10. Art. VI
11. Art. VI, cl. 2
12. Amend. II
13. Amend. III
14. Amend. VII
15. Amend. VIII
16. Amend. IX
17. Amend. X
18. Amend. XII
19. Amend. XIV, § 5
20. Amend. XV
21. Amend. XV, § 1
22. Amend. XVII
23. Amend. XVIII
24. Amend. XXI
25. Amend. XXVI
26. Art. I, § 8, cl. 7
27. Art. I, § 10, cl. 3
28. Art. II, § 4
29. Art. IV, § 1
30. Art. I, § 9, cl. 4
31. Art. I, § 10
32. Art. III
33. Art. III, § 2
34. Art. VI
35. Art. VI, cl. 3

36. Amend. IX
37. Amend. XI
38. Amend. XIII
39. Amend. XIV
40. Amend. XIV, § 5
41. Amend. III
42. Art. 1, § 5, cl. 1
43. Art. 1, § 9
44. Art. 3, § 1
45. Art. 5
46. Amend. IV
47. Amend. VII
48. Amend. VIII
49. Amend. XXIV
50. Amend. V
51. Art. 1, § 2

ASSIGNMENT 2
USE OF SHEPARD'S UNITED STATES CITATIONS - 1964 CODE

Method:

Refer to Shepard's United States Citations, Statute Edition, Code Section. Use bound volumes only. Answer the following questions with reference to the 1964 United States Code sections listed below. Cite as given in Shepard's.

(1) Has the constitutionality of this statute ever been in question? If so, give the citation(s) of the case(s) holding the statute constitutional. For references to the Supreme Court of the United States, give only the official reporter.

(2) Give the latest citing of this statute by the Supreme Court of the United States, if any. Give only the official reporter.

Questions:

1. Title 2, § 264
2. Title 5, § 118K, subsec. c
3. Title 7, § 9
4. Title 7, § 511a
5. Title 8, § 1185
6. Title 8, § 1251
7. Title 11, § 203, subsec. s
8. Title 15, § 45, subsec. a
9. Title 22, § 1641d
10. Title 26, § 302
11. Title 26, § 2035
12. Title 26, § 4412
13. Title 28, § 1498
14. Title 28, § 2254

15. Title 29, § 152, subd. 3
16. Title 31, § 441
17. Title 33, § 702c
18. Title 40, § 258a
19. Title 41, § 38
20. Title 42, § 402, subsec. a
21. Title 42, § 1104
22. Title 42, § 1983
23. Title 46, § 808
24. Title 49, § 1382
25. Title 50, Appendix, § 1191, subsec. c, subd. 1

ASSIGNMENT 3
USE OF SHEPARD'S UNITED STATES CITATIONS - 1970 CODE

Method:

    Refer to Shepard's United States Citations, Statute Edition, Code Section. Use bound volumes only. Answer the following questions with reference to the 1970 United States Code sections listed below. Cite as given in Shepard's.

(1) Has the constitutionality of this statute ever been in question? If so, give the holding and the citation(s) of the case(s) so holding. For references to the Supreme Court of the United States, give only the official reporter.

(2) Give the latest A.L.R., A.L.R Federal or Lawyers' Edition annotation in which the provision was noted.

Questions:

1. Title 2, § 192
2. Title 5, § 1502, subd. 3
3. Title 5, § 7311
4. Title 8, § 1105a
5. Title 8, § 1182, subsec. e
6. Title 9, § 2
7. Title 10, § 934
8. Title 11, § 67, subsec. c
9. Title 15, § 78g
10. Title 18, § 287
11. Title 18, § 2511
12. Title 20, § 701 et. seq.
13. Title 21, § 321, subd. 3
14. Title 21, § 952
15. Title 26, § 165, subsec. c

16. Title 26, § 4412
17. Title 28, § 1821
18. Title 29, § 158, subsec. b, subd. 4, para. B
19. Title 29, § 217
20. Title 33, § 407
21. Title 33, § 933, subsec. i
22. Title 39, § 3008
23. Title 42, § 424a
24. Title 42, § 2651
25. Title 50 App., § 456, subsec. c, para. D

ASSIGNMENT 4
USE OF STATE SHEPARD'S

Method:

Refer to the Shepard's citator for your state. Use the bound volumes only unless the subject section of the information required can be located only in the temporary supplement to the bound volumes. Cite as given in Shepard's.

Questions:

1. Locate the section in your state citator covering your state's probate code. Select one article or section and answer the following questions:
    (a) Has it been amended, repealed, etc.? If so, answer with the latest citation as given in Shepard's.
    (b) Has it been discussed in legal periodical? If so, answer with citation as given in Shepard's.
    (c) If available, give the citation to the latest attorney general's opinion citing this article or section.

2. Locate the section in your state citator covering your state's code of criminal procedure. Select one article or section and answer the following questions:
    (a) Give the citation (National Reporter System and official, if available) to the latest case citing this article or section
    (b) Has it been amended, repealed, etc.? If so, give the latest citation as given in Shepard's.

3. Locate the section in your state citator covering the Uniform Commercial Code. Select one article and section and answer the following questions:
    (a) Has it been amended or repealed by the state legislature? If so, in what year?
    (b) Give the latest legal periodical citation to this section

4. Locate the section containing the official reports of the highest court of your state. Select one case from the earliest bound volume of your state's citator. "Shepardize" the case through all subsequent volumes by answering the following questions:
   (a) What is the National Reporter System citation to the same case?
   (b) Give the citation of the case if it is reprinted in another reporter.
   (c) Was the case appealed to the Supreme Court of the United States? If so, what was the result? Give the official citation only.
   (d) Has the holding of the case been criticized, distinguished, overruled, etc., by later decisions? Have these later cases cited the total case or only certain principles? In your answer, designate headnote numbers where necessary.
   (e) Has the opinion been cited by the attorney general of your state? If so, give the latest citation.
   (f) Has the cited opinion been noted in an A.L.R. annotation? If so, give the latest citation.
   (g) Has the case been cited in any legal periodicals? If so, give the citation(s).

5. Locate the section in your state citator containing the National Reporter System regional reporter for your area. Select one case and answer the following questions:
   (a) What is the official citation to the same case?
   (b) Has the case been overruled? If so, cite the overruling case.

6. Locate the section in your state citator containing the Table of Acts by Popular Names or Short Titles. Select one act and answer the following:
   (a) What is citation of the act?
   (b) Are amendments to the act listed in the Table?

7. Locate the section in your state citator covering the rules of the highest court. Select one rule and answer the following questions:
   (a) Has the rule been amended? If so, cite the source where the amendment can be found.
   (b) Has the highest court of your state ever cited this rule? If so, give the citation to the first case citing this rule.
   (c) Has the rule been cited in any legal periodicals? If so, give the citation(s) to the periodical(s).
   (d) Has this rule been cited in any A.L.R. annotation? If so, cite the annotation(s)

8. Locate the section in your state citator covering municipal ordinances or charters.
   (a) From the index to charters determine how many municipalities have been involved in litigation involving public utility rates.
   (b) Select one municipality from the previous question 8(a). Give all citations pertaining to one ordinance or charter provision.

9. Locate the section in your state citator covering the rules of your state bar. Select one rule and answer the following questions:
   (a) Has the constitutionality of this rule ever been questioned? If so, give all citations to that opinion.
   (b) Give the citation (<u>National Reporter System</u> and official, if available) to the latest case citing this rule.
   (c) Has the rule been discussed in legal periodicals? If so, cite one.

ASSIGNMENT 5
USE OF SHEPARD'S UNITED STATES CITATIONS, CASE EDITION

Method:

Refer to Shepard's United States Citations, Case Edition. Use bound volumes only. Cite as given in Shepard's. Answer the following questions with reference to the cases listed below.

(1) Give the parallel citation (Lawyers' Edition, Supreme Court Reporter and selected case reporters) for the same case.

(2) Give the citation(s) to the same case in lower courts and/or the United States Supreme Court.

(3) Has this case been cited by the California Supreme Court?

(4) Has the case been cited in an American Bar Association Journal article? If so, cite the most recent reference.

Questions:

1. 420 U.S. 283

2. 418 U.S. 717

3. 414 U.S. 395

4. 401 U.S. 82

5. 378 U.S. 478

6. 414 U.S. 168

7. 400 U.S. 309

8. 354 U.S. 449

9. 383 U.S. 541

10. 315 U.S 501

11. 323 U.S. 471

12. 394 U.S. 721

13. 322 U.S. 292

14. 344 U.S. 183
15. 319 U.S. 182
16. 367 U.S. 488
17. 400 U.S. 25
18. 346 U.S. 235
19. 391 U.S. 123
20. 346 U.S. 389
21. 339 U.S. 460
22. 372 U.S. 335
23. 359 U.S. 207
24. 362 U.S. 217
25. 387 U.S. 485
26. 319 U.S. 182
27. 327 U.S. 358
28. 381 U.S. 532
29. 350 U.S. 116
30. 366 U.S. 420
31. 330 U.S. 160

ASSIGNMENT 6
USE OF SHEPARD'S FEDERAL CITATIONS, FEDERAL REPORTER SECTION

Method:

Refer to Shepard's Federal Citations, Federal Reporter Section. Use bound volumes only. Answer the following with reference to the cases listed below. Each citation is followed by a Topic and Key Number from the Federal Reporter syllabus to the cited case. This identifies a specific numbered headnote in the cited case. Examine the cited case in the Federal Reporter, identify the headnote number and record it.

(1) Give the federal cases which distinguished this specific point of law of the cited case by subsequent decisions. Give only Federal Reporter and Federal Supplement citations. Cite as given in Shepard's but omit the superior numbers in your answers.

(2) List the opinions which relate to the specific headnote but have no analytical symbol preceding the citation. Give only the most recent Federal Reporter and/or Federal Supplement citations. Cite as given in Shepard's but omit the superior numbers in your answers.

Questions

1. 458 F.2d 1323.   Courts - Key #284

2. 398 F.2d 722.   Labor Relations - Key #574

3. 413 F.2d 459.   Criminal Law - Key #517.1(1)

4. 456 F.2d 112.   Civil Rights - Key #43, 44(1)

5. 453 F.2d 54.   Schools and school districts - Key #172

6. 442 F.2d 698.   Criminal Law - Key #304(1)

7. 430 F.2d 771.   Constitutional Law - Key #272, Prisons - Key #13

8. 453 F.2d 661.   Criminal Law - Key #1213

9. 450 F.2d 199.   Grand Jury - Key #36

10. 454 F.2d 696.   Civil Rights - Key #13.9

11. 449 F.2d 679.   Criminal Law - Key #394.3, Telecommunications - Key #492

12.	453 F.2d 722.	Licenses - Key #39.30
13.	461 F.2d 92.	Criminal Law - Key #641.3, 1169(1)
14.	459 F.2d 300.	Agriculture - Key #2
15.	454 F.2d 826.	Municipal Corporations - Key #121
16.	458 F.2d 649.	Constitutional Law - Key #82, 253, Elections - Key #21
17.	454 F.2d 252.	Criminal Law Key #1206(3)
18.	434 F.2d 209.	Armed Services - Key #20.8(4)
19.	429 F.2d 864.	Civil Rights - Key #13
20.	426 F. Supp. 424.	Habeas Corpus - Key #48
21.	434 F.2d 727.	Corporations - Key #202
22.	396 F.2d 601.	Administrative Law and Procedure - Key #404
23.	426 F.2d 643.	Courts - Key #508(7)
24.	425 F.2d 816.	Criminal Law - Key #1086(11)
25.	434 F.2d 1081.	Constitutional Law - Key #90 Witnesses - Key #5
26.	371 F.2d 413.	Courts - Key #101
27.	293 F.2d 609.	Poisons - Key #9
28.	306 F.2d 564.	Internal Revenue - Key #1113
29.	317 F.2d 829.	Internal Revenue - Key #284
30.	171 F. 294.	Aliens - Key #61
31.	371 F.2d 911.	Habeas Corpus - Key #59
32.	195 F. 528.	Trademarks and Tradenames - Key #10
33.	295 F.2d 531.	Criminal Law - Key #823(5)
34.	329 F.2d 789.	Labor Relations - Key #433
35.	293 F.2d 630.	Contracts - Key #155
36.	326 F.2d 968.	Labor Relations - Key #678
37.	330 F.2d 859.	Federal Civil Procedure - Key #1960

38. 306 F.2d 713.   United States - Key #78(6)
39. 333 F.2d 535.   Criminal Law - Key #275, 1026
40. 34 F.2d 328.   Internal Revenue - Key #38(2)
41. 105 F.2d 331.   Monopolies - Key #28(6)
42. 120 F.2d 121.   Bill and Notes - Key #144
43. 252 F.2d 537.   Declaratory judgment - Key #97
44. 171 F. 305.   Corporations - Key #560
45. 330 F.2d 824.   Courts - Key #528
46. 241 F.2d 289.   Insurance - Key #435.3
47. 371 F.2d 974.   Labor Relations - Key #632
48. 90 F.2d 323.   Husband and Wife - Key #49 1/2
49. 97 F.2d 691.   Evidence - Key #154
50. 333 F.2d 358.   Federal Civil Procedure - Key #1624

ASSIGNMENT 7
USE OF SHEPARD'S FEDERAL CITATIONS –
FEDERAL SUPPLEMENT, FEDERAL RULES DECISIONS,
COURT OF CLAIMS

Method:

Refer to Shepard's Federal Citations: Federal Supplement, Federal Rules Decisions, Court of Claims section. Use bound volumes only. Answer the following questions with reference to the cases listed below. Cite as given in Shepard's.

(1) Was the cited case appealed to a United States Court of Appeals? If the action of the court is indicated (e.g., affirmed, dismissed, modified, reversed) specify the action and give the latest citation to the National Reporter System.

(2) Was the cited case appealed to the Supreme Court of the United States? If the action of the Court is indicated (e.g., affirmed, dismissed, modified, reversed) specify the action and give the latest citation to the official reporter.

(3) Give the latest A.L.R., A.L.R. Federal or Lawyers' Edition annotation in which the cited case was noted. Disregard superior numbers.

Questions:

1. 3 F. Supp. 909

2. 29 F. Supp. 436

3. 38 Ct. Cl. 10

4. 96 F. Supp. 318

5. 30 F. Supp. 570

6. 30 F.R.D. 3

7. 235 F. Supp. 183

8. 59 Ct. Cl. 593

9. 156 F. Supp. 174

10. 260 F. Supp. 323

11. 2 F.R.D. 270
12. 192 F. Supp. 170
13. 87 F. Supp. 691
14. 136 Ct. Cl. 324
15. 200 F. Supp. 653
16. 63 F. Supp. 361
17. 99 Ct. Cl. 1
18. 231 F. Supp. 37
19. 37 F.R.D. 330
20. 140 F. Supp. 60
21. 236 F. Supp. 56
22. 73 F. Supp. 72
23. 21 F.R.D. 335
24. 229 F. Supp. 310
25. 198 F.Supp. 402
26. 156 F. Supp. 323
27. 347 F. Supp. 230
28. 342 F. Supp. 616
29. 191 Ct. Cl. 191
30. 43 F.R.D. 308
31. 30 F. Supp. 570
32. 21 F.R.D. 335

ASSIGNMENT 8
USE OF SHEPARD'S UNITED STATES – STATUTES AT LARGE

Method:

Refer to Shepard's United States Citations, Statute Edition, United States Statutes at Large, 1778-1981 (not included in the United States Code) Section. Use bound volumes only. Answer the following questions with reference to the sections of the Statutes at Large which are not included in the United States Code listed below. Cite as given in Shepard's.

   (1) Cite any act of Congress noted as affecting this statute and briefly give the effect (e.g., amended, repealed, etc.) of such act.

   (2) Give the latest citing of the statute by the Supreme Court of the United States. Give the official reporter citation only.

Questions:

1. 1789, July 4, ch. 2, § 1, 1 Stat. 24

2. 1799, March 2, ch. 22, § 50, 1 Stat. 627

3. 1809, March 1, ch. 24, 2 Stat. 528

4. 1817, March 1, ch. 31, § 3, 3 Stat. 351

5. 1827, July 4, 8 Stat. 346

6. 1832, July 14, ch. 227, § 13, 4 Stat. 583

7. 1863, March 3, ch. 76, § 1, 12 Stat. 737

8. 1866, July 18, ch. 201, § 3, 14 Stat. 178

9. 1870, May 31, ch. 114, § 4, 16 Stat. 140

10. 1875, Feb. 8, ch. 36, § 18, 18 Stat. 307

11. 1899, March 3, ch. 428, § 463, 30 Stat. 1250

12. 1902, May 27, ch. 888, 32 Stat. 245

13. 1905, Feb. 8, ch. 556, § 7, 33 Stat. 708

14. 1906, June 28, ch. 3572, § 9, 24 Stat. 539

15. 1921, May 19, ch. 8, 42 Stat. 5
16. 1927, Jan. 21, ch. 47, § 1, 44 Stat. 1010
17. 1935, Aug. 30, ch. 829, § 105, 49 Stat. 1014
18. 1940, July 2, ch. 508, § 1, 54 Stat. 712
19. 1944, Feb. 25, ch. 63, § 302, Subd. a, 58 Stat. 21
20. 1945, April 16, 60 Stat. 1377
21. 1947, July 16, ch. 258, Title 10, § 1, 61 Stat. 328
22. 1948, April 3, ch. 169, § 101, 62 Stat. 137
23. 1949, April 4, 63 Stat. 2241
24. 1952, July 9, ch. 608, § 245, 66 Stat. 481
25. 1958, July 7, P.L. 85-508, § 4, 72 Stat. 339
26. 1789, July 4, ch. 2, 1 Stat. 24
27. 1970, Aug. 10, ch. 39, 1 Stat. 180
28. 1801, Feb. 27, ch. 15, 2 Stat. 103
29. 1836, April 20, ch. 54, 5 Stat. 10
30. 1865, March 3, ch. 78, § 6, 13 Stat. 469
31. 1870, May 31, ch. 114, § 3, 16 Stat. 140
32. 1874, April 7, ch. 80, § 2, 18 Stat. 27
33. 1889, Jan. 14, ch. 24, 25 Stat. 642
34. 1890, Sept. 19, ch. 907, § 1, 26 Stat. 426
35. 1897, June 7, ch. 3, § 1, 30 Stat. 62
36. 1901, March 3, ch. 854, § 823, 31 Stat. 1189
37. 1906, June 20, ch. 3446, § 2, 34 Stat. 316
38. 1959, Sept. 14, P.L. 86-272, § 201, 73 Stat. 555
39. 1960, Sept. 15, P.L. 86-794, 74 Stat. 1031
40. 1964, Aug. 10, P.L. 88-408, 78 Stat. 384

41. 1789, Sept. 24, ch. 20, § 32, 1 Stat. 73
42. 1798, June 13, ch. 53, 1 Stat. 565
43. 1801, Feb. 27, ch. 15, 2 Stat. 103
44. 1836, April 20, ch. 54, 5 Stat. 10
45. 1865, March 3, ch. 78, § 6, 13 Stat. 469.
46. 1870, May 31, ch. 114, § 3, 16 Stat. 140
47. 1874, April 7, ch. 80, § 2, 18 Stat. 27
48. 1889, Jan 14, ch. 24, 25 Stat. 642
49. 1890, Sept. 19, ch. 907, § 1, 26 Stat. 426
50. 1897, June 7, ch. 3, § 1, 30 Stat. 62
51. 1901, March 3, ch. 854, § 823, 31 Stat. 1189
52. 1906, June 20, ch. 3446, § 2, 34 Stat. 316
53. 1909, Jan. 11, 36 Stat. 2448
54. 1917, March 3, ch. 162, § 5, 39 Stat. 1058
55. 1919, Oct. 28, ch. 85, 41 Stat. 305
56. 1928, May 10, ch. 517, 45 Stat. 495
57. 1929, Feb. 13, ch. 182, 46 Stat. 1166
58. 1933, March 6, 48 Stat. 1689
59. 1934, May 10, ch. 277, § 701, 48 Stat. 680
60. 1938, April 5, ch. 72, § 2, 52 Stat. 198
61. 1940, Oct. 8, ch. 757, § 201, 54 Stat. 974
62. 1953, Aug. 15, ch. 505, § 7, 67 Stat. 588
63. 1959, Sept. 14, P.L. 86-272, § 201, 73 Stat. 555
64. 1960, Sept. 15, P.L. 86-794, 74 Stat. 1031
65. 1964, Aug. 10, P.L. 88-408, 78 Stat. 384

ASSIGNMENT 9
USE OF SHEPARD'S REGIONAL REPORTER CITATIONS

Method:

Refer to Shepard's Regional Reporter Citations. Use bound volumes only. Answer the following questions with reference to the cases listed below. Cite as given in Shepard's.

(1) Give the official citation of the case.

(2) Has the cited case been appealed to the Supreme Court of the United States? If appealed, give the official reporter citation.

(3) Do any of Shepard's symbols indicate that the cited case has been criticized, followed, overruled, etc., by subsequent decisions? If so indicated, designate the headnote number of the citing case. Disregard dissenting opinions.

(4) List all other states and the District of Columbia which have cited this opinion.

Questions:

1. 201 A.2d 715

2. 201 A.2d 540

3. 182 A.2d 535

4. 182 A.2d 596

5. 182 A.2d 634

6. 150 A.2d 112

7. 66 N.E.2d 755

8. 66 N.E.2d 888

9. 68 N.W.2d 705

10. 89 N.W.2d 386

11. 95 N.W.2d 273

12. 95 N.W.2d 365

13. 10 P.2d 597
14. 61 P.2d 293
15. 106 P.2d 751
16. 106 P.2d 755
17. 142 P.2d 824
18. 235 S.W. 31
19. 237 S.W. 786
20. 244 S.W. 549
21. 78 S.E.2d 462
22. 86 S.E.2d 114
23. 86 S.E.2d 141
24. 130 So. 2d 170
25. 155 So. 2d 586
26. 241 A.2d 691
27. 252 A.2d 580
28. 198 N.E.2d 590
29. 34 N.W. 1
30. 192 N.W.2d 466
31. 106 N.W.2d 286
32. 69 P. 564
33. 446 P.2d 521
34. 124 S.E.2d 653
35. 108 S.E.2d 328
36. 334 S.W.2d 119
37. 393 S.W.2d 739
38. 93 So.2d 769

39. 154 So.2d 289
40. 218 So.2d 580
41. 271 A.2d 481
42. 260 A.2d 68
43. 241 A.2d 691
44. 252 A.2d 580
45. 198 N.E.2d 590
46. 221 N.E.2d 543
47. 183 N.E.2d 579
48. 78 N.W.2d 509
49. 192 N.W.2d 466
50. 138 N.W.2d 185
51. 106 N.W.2d 286
52. 464 P.2d 64
53. 450 P.2d 775
54. 446 P.2d 521
55. 416 P.2d 67
56. 124 S.E.2d 653
57. 108 S.E.2d 388
58. 108 S.E.2d 328
59. 243 S.W.2d 683
60. 523 S.W.2d 377
61. 393 S.W.2d 739
62. 399 S.W.2d 658
63. 93 So.2d 769
64. 154 So.2d 289
65. 218 So.2d 580

ASSIGNMENT 10
USE OF SHEPARD'S ACTS AND CASES BY POPULAR NAMES

Methods:

Refer to <u>Shepard's Acts and Cases by Popular Names</u>. Use 1979 bound volume. Answer the following questions. Cite as given in <u>Shepard's</u>.

Questions:

1. (a) Give the citation for the Golden Nematode Act.
   (b) When was it enacted?

2. (a) Has California passed an act to provide incentive for the employment of Vietnam Veterans?
   (b) Provide the citation to the act.

3. How many states have enacted Sunshine Laws?

4. What is the U.S. Supreme Court citation for the Busing case?

5. Give the citation to the Watergate Tapes Case.

6. Where can the Fugitive Slave Law case be found?

7. Give citations to the Abortion cases.

8. Give citations to the Aircraft Hi-Jacking Act.

9. Give citations to the Negligent Attorney case.

10. Cite Oklahoma's Law Library Act?

11. What government administrative agency ruled on the Station Facilities case? Cite the agency report of the case.

12. Give the citations to the latest U.S. Supreme Court reports on the Girard College Cases.

13. How many states have No-Knock Acts? Give citations to these acts.

14. Give the citation to the Colorado Narcotic Drug Act.

15. Give the complete citation to the National Commission on Libraries and Information Science Act.

16. (a) Give the citation for the Citizens Abroad Act.
    (b) When was it enacted?

17. (a) Was the Spike Milk case heard before the U.S. Supreme Court?
    (b) If so, give the official U.S. Supreme Court citation.

18. Give the citation to the Theatrical Productions Case.

19. (a) Give the citation for the Oil Pollution Act, 1961.
    (b) Give its Public Law number.
    (c) Give the date of enactment.

20. How many states have adopted a Sick Leave Act?

21. Give the citation to the earliest enactment of the Removal of Causes Acts.

22. Give the citation to the Municipal Railway Election case.

23. How many "Mutt and Jeff' cases have been reported?

24. Give the citations to the Milk, Cream and Butterfat case.

25. Give the citations to the Moldy Tomato Paste case.

26. Give the citation to the latest Mutual Security Act.

27. Give the citation to the New Jersey Narcotic and Drug Abuse Control Act.

28. Has Nebraska enacted an Air-Raid Precautions Act?

29. Give the citation to the official report of the U.S. Supreme Court in the Federal Maternity Act case.

30. Give the citation to the Fowler Hotel case.

31. (a) What governmental administrative agency ruled on the Station Facilities case?
    (b) Cite the agency report of the case.

32. (a) How many states have adopted a Pharmacy Act?
    (b) Give the citation(s) to the state(s) which have both a civil and criminal Pharmacy Act.

33. Give the citation to the Maine Election Act (Primary).

34. Give the citations to the Bob-Tail case.

35. How many Group Discrimination cases have been reported?

36. Give the citations to the Cutler case.

37. Give the citations to the Rat case.

38. (a) Was the Betty Boop case heard before the U.S. Supreme Court?
    (b) Give the citation to the first reported opinion in the Betty Boop case.

39. Give the citation to the Mystic River Dam Loan Act.

40. Give the citation for the Electric Companies Act.

41. Give the citation to the official report of the U.S. Supreme Court in the Federal Maternity Act case.

42. Give the latest citation to the Forty-Three Gallons of Cognac Brandy case.

43. (a) What governmental administrative agency ruled on the Geritol case?
    (b) Give the citation to the agency report of the case.

44. How many states have adopted a Commercial Feed Act?

45. Does New Hampshire have an Elevator Act?

46. Cite the latest Coca-Cola case.

47. Give the citation(s) to the Public Education Act.

48. How many states have enacted Real Estate License Acts?

49. Give the latest U.S. Reports citation to the Trilogy cases.

50. (a) Has Hawaii changed or re-enacted its Vocational Rehabilitation Act?
    (b) Cite the latest Vermont enactment of a Vocational Rehabilitation Act.

51. (a) How many Good Humor cases are reported in the Northwestern Reporter?
    (b) Give the latest Northeastern Reporter citation.

ASSIGNMENT 11
THEME PROBLEMS

Theme Problem I:

A. Find the place that the Brown decision (347 U.S. 483) first appears in Shepard's, and using that volume, answer the following:

1. Give the parallel citations.

2. What Missouri cases cite Brown?

3. Where in 373 U.S. is Brown cited in dissent?

4. What is the first U.S. Court of Appeals decision to distinguish the Brown case?

B. Find the second volume that lists Brown. Using that volume, answer the following:

1. What Alabama case cites Brown?

2. Where was Brown cited in 401 U.S.?

3. Where in volume 59 of the A.B.A. Journal will the case be mentioned?

C. Using all other U.S. Shepard's - Cases, volumes and pamphlets, listings of Brown, answer the following:

1. Has it been overruled?

2. What Florida case in 342 So. 2d cites it?

3. Where in 433 U.S. is it followed?

4. Where is it cited in 64 A.B.A. Journal?

5. Where in volume 26 of the Stanford Law Review could you find mention of Brown?

Theme Problem II:

A. Locate the first appearance of Roe v. Wade, 410 U.S. 113, in U.S. Shepard's - Cases, and using that volume answer the following questions:

1. Give the parallel citations.

2. Where is the denial of a rehearing reported?

3. What South Dakota case cites it?

4. What Federal District Court opinion "harmonizes" it?

B. Using all other available U.S. Shepard's - Cases, volumes and pamphlets, answer the following questions:

1. Has it been overruled?

2. Where in 63 A.B.A. Journal is it cited?

3. Where is it cited in volume 91 of the Harvard Law Review?

4. Where in 431 U.S. is it distinguished?

Theme Problem III:

A. Find the first appearance of Gideon v. Wainwright, 372 U.S. 335, in U.S. Shepard's - Cases, and, using that volume, answer the following questions:

1. Give the parallel citations.

2. What is the first time it is cited in dissent?

3. What is the first Idaho decision cited?

4. What is the first A.B.A. Journal citation listed?

5. Where in volume 36 of Federal Rules Decisions is it cited?

B. Find the second appearance of Gideon in U.S. Shepard's - Cases and answer the following questions:

1. What years are covered in this volume?

2. Has it been overruled or reversed?

3. Where is the first time the decision is "explained"?

4. What is the first Arkansas decision cited?

5. Where in volume 58 of the A.B.A. Journal is it mentioned?

C. Using all other U.S. Shepard's - Cases, volumes and pamphlets, answer the following questions:

1. Has Gideon been overruled or reversed?

2. Where is it cited in 433 U.S.?

3. Where is it cited in 265 N.W.2d?

4. Where is it cited in volume 55 of the Texas Law Review?

ASSIGNMENT 12
DRILL PROBLEMS

Drill Problems I:

A. Using only bound volumes of U.S. Shepard's - Cases, answer the following questions for each citation listed below::

   (1) What is the first case listed that cited the decision in dissent?

   (2) List the first citation to the A.B.A. Journal, if any.

   (3) Give the parallel citations.

   (4) Has the case been reversed or overruled?

   1. 397 U.S. 254

   2. 406 U.S. 441

   3. 93 S.Ct. 2405

B. Using only bound volumes of Federal Shepard's - Cases, answer the following questions for each citation listed below:

   (1) List the first case cited from the 1st Circuit, if any.

   (2) List the first case listed that followed the decision.

   (3) Has it been reversed or overruled?

   (4) If there is an A.L.R. citation, list it.

   1. 469 F.2d 1377

   2. 496 F.2d 1303

   3. 220 F. 545

C. Using only bound volumes of the Regional Shepard's, answer the following questions for each citation listed below:

   (1) List the first case that cites the decision in dissent.

   (2) Cite the first regional reporter case listed.

(3) Give the parallel citation.

(4) Has the decision been reversed?

1. 71 P. 453

2. 208 S.E.2d 459

3. 131 N.W.2d 293

D. Using only bound volumes of state Shepard's, answer the following questions for each citation listed below:

(1) Give the parallel citation.

(2) If any law review articles are cited, list the first one.

(3) Has the case been overruled or reversed?

1. 148 W.Va. 82

2. 230 Fla. 486

E. Using the 1968-1974 Supplement to U.S. Federal Shepard's - Statutes, answer the following questions for each citation listed below:

(1) Give the first U.S. Supreme Court citation listed, if any.

(2) Has its constitutionally been adjudicated? If yes, list the first citation.

(3) Give the first A.L.R. Federal citation listed.

1. 42 U.S.C. § 3613

2. 10 U.S.C. § 1552

3. 11 U.S.C. § 599

F. Using the U.S. Shepard's - Federal Constitution 1968 volumes, answer the following questions for each citation listed below:

(1) Give first citation to a U.S. Supreme Court case, if any.

(2) Give first citation to A.L.R., if any.

(3) Any special action (i.e., amended) noted? If so, provide the first citation.

1. Art. III, § 1

2. Art. II, § 1

G. Using only bound volumes of the state <u>Shepard's - Statutes and Constitutions</u>, answer the following questions for each citation listed below:

(1) Give the first court decision listed, if any.

(2) Has it been amended, repealed or declared constitutional or unconstitutional? If so, give the first citation.

1. <u>Code of Va.</u>, § 3-207 (1950)

2. <u>Minnesota Statutes Annoted</u>, § 291.34 (1971)

3. <u>Colorado Constitution of 1876</u>, Art. I, § 7

H. Using only bound volumes of <u>Shepard's U.S. Administrative Citations</u>, answer the following questions for each citations listed below:

(1) Give the parallel citation, if any.

(2) Enter the last citation listed.

1. Treasury Decision 25428

2. 51 F.T.C. 583

3. 37 Decisions of Deparment of Interior, Public Lands 410

Drill Problem II:

A. Case Citations. For each of the following citations, answer these four questions, using only bound volumes of <u>U.S. Supreme Court Shepard's</u>.

(1) What is the first case listed that cited the decision in dissent?

(2) List the first citation to the <u>A.B.A. Journal</u>, if any

(3) Give the parallel citations.

(4) Has the case been reversed or overruled?

1. 360 U.S. 264

2. 403 U.S. 388

3. 36 L.Ed.2d 366

B. Using bound volumes of U.S. Federal Shepard's Cases, answer the following questions for each citation listed below:

(1) List the first case cited from the 1st Circuit.

(2) List the first case listed that followed the decision.

(3) Has it been reversed or overruled?

(4) If there is an A.L.R. cite, list it.

1. 415 F.2d 1185

2. 505 F.2d 977

3. 67 F.2d 585

4. 323 F. Supp. 799

C. Using the bound volume of regional Shepard's, answer the following questions for each citation listed below:

(1) List the first case that cites the decision in dissent.

(2) Cite the first regional reporter case listed.

(3) Give the parallel citation.

(4) Has the decision been reversed?

1. 34 P.2d 534

2. 1 So. 273

3. 256 N.E.2d 384

D. Using bound volumes of state Shepard's, answer the following questions for each citation listed below:

(1) Give the parallel citation.

(2) If any law review articles are cited, list the first one.

(3) Has the case been overruled or reversed?

1. 460 Pa. 630

2. 106 Ark. 22

E. Using the 1968-1976 supplement to U.S. Shepard's - Federal Statutes, answer the following questions for each citation listed below:

(1) Give the first U.S. Supreme Court citation listed, if any.

(2) Has its constitutionality been adjudged? If yes, list the first citation.

(3) Give the first A.L.R. Fed. citation listed.

1. 33 U.S.C. § 407

2. 45 U.S.C. § 153(1)(p)

F. Using the 1968 volume of U.S. Shepard's - Federal Constitution, answer the following questions for each citation listed below:

(1) Give first citation to a U.S. Supreme Court case, if any.

(2) Give first citation to A.L.R., if any.

(3) Any special action (i.e. amended) noted? If so, provide first citation.

1. Amendment IX

2. Amendment XVIII

G. Using appropriate bound volumes of the state Shepard's for Statutes and Constitutions, answer the following questions for each citation listed below:

(1) Give the first court decision listed.

325

(2) Has it been amended, repealed or has it been held constitutional or unconstitutional? If so, give the first citation.

1. Oklahoma Statute Annot., 1971 ed. tit.-59, ¶832

2. Idaho Constitution of 1889, Art. 14, § 1.

3. California Constitution of 1879, Art. 1. § 22.

H. Using only bound volumes of U.S. Shepard's - Administrative Citations, answer the following questions for each citation listed below:

(1) Give parallel citation, if any.

(2) Enter the last citation listed.

1. 59 Ct. of Customs and Pat. App. 113

2. 9 S.E.C. 680

3. Any litigation of the trademark Loopstick?

Drill Problem III:

A. Case Citations. Using only bound volumes of U.S. Supreme Court Shepard's, answer the following questions for each citation listed below:

(1) What is the first case listed that cited the decision in dissent?

(2) List the first citation (if there are any) to the A.B.A. Journal.

(3) Give the parallel citations.

(4) Has the case been reversed or overruled?

1. 346 U.S. 1

2. 397 U.S. 471

3. 256 U.S. 135

B. Using only bound bound volumes of U.S. Federal Shepard's, answer the following questions for each citation listed below:

(1) List the first case cited from the 1st Circuit.

(2) List the first case listed that followed the decision.

(3) Has it been reversed or overruled?

(4) If there is an A.L.R. citation, list it.

1. 471 F.2d 488

2. 185 F.2d 622

3. 62 F. Supp. 73

4. 340 F. Supp. 1343

C. Using the appropriate bound volume of regional Shepard's, answer the following questions for each citation listed below,:

(1) List the first case that cites the decision in dissent.

(2) Cite the first regional reporter case listed.

(3) Give the parallel citation.

(4) Has the decision been reversed?

1. 25 S.W.2d 293

2. 337 A.2d 893

3. 184 N.W.2d 189

D. Using the appropriate bound volume of state Shepard's, answer the following questions for each citation listed below:

(1) Give the parallel citation.

(2) If any law review articles are cited, list the first one.

(3) Has the case been overruled or reversed?

1. 75 Wash. 212

2. 249 Miss. 561

E. Using the 1968-1974 bound supplement to Shepard's - Federal Statute, answer the following questions for each citation listed below:

    (1) Give the first U.S. Supreme Court citation listed, if any.

    (2) Has its constitutionality been adjudged? If yes, list the first citation.

    (3) Give the first A.L.R. Fed. citation listed.

    1. 18 U.S.C. § 2520

    2. 28 U.S.C. § 2111

    3. 82 Stat. 815 § 23

F. Federal Constitution. Using the 1968 volume to Shepard's - Federal Constitution, answer the following questions for each citation listed below:

    (1) Give the first citation to a U.S. Supreme Court case, if any.

    (2) Give first citation to A.L.R., if any.

    (3) Any special action (i.e. amended) noted? If so, provide first citation.

    1. Art. 1, § 6, cl. 1

    2. Amendment 1

G. Using the bound volumes of the particular state Shepard's, answer the following questions for each citation listed below:

    (1) Give the first court decision listed.

    (2) Has it been amended, repealed, or has it been held constitutional or unconstitutional? If so, give the first citation.

    1. Oklahoma Constitution of 1907, Art. 5, § 14

    2. Arkansas Statutes, 1947 § 73-1221 (as amended).

H. Using Shepard's - Administrative Citations, answer the following questions for each citation listed below:

(1) Give parallel citations, if any.

(2) Enter the last citation listed.

1. 1 F.C.C. Reports 2d 1402

2. 16 Opinions of the Att'y Gen. 5

3. Any litigation on patent #2,272,841?

Chapter 16

LEGAL ENCYCLOPEDIAS

ASSIGNMENT 1
THE INDEX METHOD WITH AMERICAN JURISPRUDENCE 2D
AND CORPUS JURIS SECUNDUM

Method:

Analyze each of the following problems for words, expressed or implied, which should be in the general index or specific volume index of the encyclopedia abbreviated in the parenthesis following each problem. A completed answer to each problem should contain the following parts:

(1) A tentative answer to the legal problem;

(2) Word(s) in the index under which the encyclopedic text was found;

(3) Identification of index in which word was found (i.e., "volume index," or "general index");

(4) Citation to the encyclopedic text in which the tentative answer was discovered.

This citation should be expressed in the form set out in the latest edition of A Uniform System of Citation.

Example:

> QUESTION: As a general rule have gifts to fraternal orders been upheld as charitable? (Am. Jur. 2d)
> ANSWER: (1) Yes
> (2) Charities - Fraternal orders and benefit societies - generally
> (3) General Index
> (4) 15 Am. Jur. 2d Charities §68 (1976).

Questions:

1. Are advertising signs, with useful lives of more than one year, subject to depreciation under federal taxation laws? (Am. Jur. 2d).

2. In a civil proceeding aimed at removal of environmental pollution is a preponderance of the evidence sufficient to establish violation of statute? (C.J.S.).

3. May participants in a "rigged" quiz show bring action for damages against the broadcasting company? (C.J.S.).

4. Was the Korean conflict a war in the constitutional or legal sense? (Am. Jur. 2d).

5. Did the Nineteenth Amendment confer upon women the right to vote? (C.J.S.).

6. Is it possible for a law student to find the latest compilation of "Minimum requirements for Admission to Legal Practice in the United States," in American Jurisprudence 2d? (Desk Book).

7. In a criminal trial, did the court abuse its discretion in denying Jewish defendant's motion for continuance because the case came on for trial on Yom Kippur? (C.J.S.).

8. According to recent authority, in a juvenile court proceeding, are juveniles entitled to constitutional protection against twice being placed in jeopardy for the same offense? (Am. Jur. 2d).

9. Can a court take judicial notice that a sonic boom caused by a jet aircraft flying at low altitude was an explosion? (C.J.S.).

10. May federal courts exercise jurisdiction over criminal violations of Indian tribal laws where tribal courts have acted to punish such violations? (Am. Jur. 2d).

11. Is a professional baseball league a "business operated for gain or profit," within the meaning of the Workmen's Compensation Act? (Am. Jur. 2d).

12. Does a person who enters the military service lose thereby the domicile which he had before he entered the service? (Am. Jur. 2d).

13. In a trial, must the plaintiff ordinarily establish his prima facie case before cross-examination of defendant's witnesses? (C.J.S.).

14. Is a student at a state college entitled to notice and hearing before being expelled for misconduct? (Am. Jur. 2d).

15. In the absence of a statute, is a conversation between an accountant and his client a privileged communication? (Am. Jur. 2d).

16. In a hearing to determine whether person was incompetent, may insanity be presumed from epilepsy? (Am. Jur. 2d).

17. May a person, who has a right to treat an absolute deed as a mortgage, lose the right through laches, or prejudicial delay? (C.J.S.).

18. If a woman agrees to care for and nurse a man for the rest of his life in return for his promise to will her all his property, will their agreement be invalidated by their future illicit cohabitation? (C.J.S.).

19. If accused had been granted presidential amnesty, may he receive an increased punishment on a subsequent conviction? (C.J.S.).

20. Are punchboards exempted from the federal wagering taxes? (Am. Jur. 2d).

21. Is competition an essential element of the offense of "drag racing?" (C.J.S.).

22. Can the "Equal Rights for Men and Women" proposed Constitutional Amendment be located in American Jurisprudence 2d? (Desk Book).

23. Does a parent's failure to support his child by itself constitute such abandonment, desertion or neglect which would permit adoption without the parent's consent? (C.J.S.).

24. Do tires placed on an automobile become a part of the automobile through the law of accession? (Am. Jur. 2d).

25. In order to challenge a juror for cause based upon bias or prejudice may the juror be examined concerning his relationships with parties to the action, counsel, prospective witnesses, or other persons interested in the action who are not parties of record? (C.J.S.).

26. May a court disbar an attorney for defamatory criticisms of judicial acts incorporated in a brief? (Am. Jur. 2d).

27. Is a district or prosecuting attorney of a state entitled to extra compensation when he has a duty to perform services in another county in connection with a suit to which his county is a party? (C.J.S.).

28. Can a jury in its measurement of damages in a personal injury case be instructed on the matter of income tax consequences of a compensatory award for accrued loss of earnings? (Am. Jur. 2d).

29. May the family purpose doctrine be applied to impose tort liability for personal injury on a family corporation which owns the automobile in question and maintains it for general family use? (C.J.S.).

30. Does lack of business experience by itself render one incompetent to act as a representative of a decedent's estate and thus prevent the receipt of letters of administration? (Am. Jur. 2d).

31. Will a tenant at sufferance be liable to his landlord for an injury to the premises which was caused by a fire resulting from the tenant's negligence? (C.J.S.).

32. Does public policy require that a state recognize a bilateral Mexican divorce as a matter of comity? (Am. Jur. 2d).

33. Must other vessels exercise care to avoid a collision with a vessel which has obstructed a narrow channel? (C.J.S.).

34. Is an infant liable on the basis of quasi-contract for the value of necessaries furnished him? (Am. Jur. 2d).

35. Is a state barred from making payment of a poll tax a prerequisite to voting? (Am. Jur. 2d).

36. Is the concealment in a licensing proceeding of a prior arrest record a ground for the refusal of an application for a license to sell intoxicating liquors? (Am. Jur. 2d).

37. Will an inexperienced student pilot be held to have assumed the risk of downdraft which causes the crash of an airplane if he has had no training in meteorology? (C.J.S.).

38. May a material false statement made under oath in connection with an application for a marriage license constitute perjury? (Am. Jur. 2d).

39. Are federal war risk insurance statutes affecting seamen intended to provide insurance protection to dependents in case of loss of life or bodily injury to seamen? (C.J.S.).

40. Is the Postal Service authorized to prescribe regulations for the exclusion or withdrawal of nonmailable matter from the mail? (Am. Jur. 2d).

41. If a factor has made advances on consigned goods, is he bound to accept and pay a draft drawn on him by the principal before the advances are repaid? (C.J.S.).

42. Does the federal crime of seditious conspiracy require an overt act for its completion? (Am. Jur. 2d).

43. Is the manufacture of meat products from horsemeat illegal as a violation of a regulation prohibiting the manufacture for sale of adulterated food if there is no attempt to conceal the fact the product is horsemeat? (C.J.S.).

44. Is robbery committed when force is used to take property from a possessor who is without knowledge of what is being done and thus does not resist? (Am. Jur. 2d).

45. Does a builder have an obligation to perform extra work without compensation if that work is not specified in the construction plans which themselves form a part of the contract? (C.J.S.).

46. If an attached garage is not so attached to the house as to present the appearance of being an integral part of the dwelling house, is it an accessory building within the meaning of zoning ordinances which restrict the location of accessory buildings to the rear half of the lot? (Am. Jur. 2d).

47. Have courts found that the freedom of religion of Jewish persons is violated by Sunday closing laws? (Am. Jur. 2d).

48. Will a felony conviction bring about the per se termination of a father's right to the custody of his child? (Am. Jur. 2d).

49. Is the business of raising greyhounds for racing purposes regarded as an accessory farm use according to zoning principles if no actual farming operation is conducted on the property? (Am. Jur. 2d).

50. Under the Lanham Act, will the type of product for which a trademark is to be registered affect whether or not the mark is considered scandalous? (C.J.S.).

51. Does a school board, under its authority to adopt rules and regulations for the well-being of the school, have the power to prohibit membership in a secret society or fraternity which is shown to destroy good order, discipline and scholarship? (C.J.S.)

52. May farm and factory products be shipped in third-class mail? (C.J.S.).

53. Do the statutes regulating telephone companies include within their scope the operation of a two-way mobile radio system? (Am. Jur. 2d).

54. Is the breach of a condition contained in a pardon generally a criminal offense? (Am. Jur. 2d)

55. Can a material misrepresentation be implied from the exhibiting of fraudulent or misleading maps or plats? (Am. Jur. 2d).

56. Is the burden of proving suicide as a defense to an insurance claim ordinarily on the insurer? (C.J.S.).

57. Is an employer liable for injuries to an employee which occur while the employee has taken a brief rest period during working hours? (C.J.S.).

58. Is addiction to narcotics a crime under Federal law? (C.J.S.).

59. May the right-of-way of a railroad company be condemned through the use of eminent domain powers in order to construct telephone and telegraph lines? (C.J.S.).

60. May a person who says insulting, abusive or violent words to another be charged with criminal assault? (Am. Jur. 2d).

ASSIGNMENT 2
USE OF THE TOPIC METHOD WITH AMERICAN JURISPRUDENCE 2D AND CORPUS JURIS SECUNDUM

Method:

Analyze each of the problems below for words, expressed or implied, to determine the suggested topic(s). Using the encyclopedia indicated in the parenthesis following each problem, turn to the topic's "analysis" or list of major subject divisions and then to the more detailed "sub-analysis" or section outline. Your answer should contain the following information:

(1) An answer to the legal problem posed.

(2) A citation to the encyclopedic text in which the answer was found.

Follow the citation form set out in the latest edition of a A Uniform System of Citation.

Example:

QUESTION: May an offer of a reward be revoked at any time prior to its acceptance?
ANSWER: (1) Yes
           (2) 67 Am. Jur. 2d Rewards §5 (1973).

Questions:

1. Do ordinary officers and agents of a corporation have the power to borrow money on behalf of the corporation? (C.J.S.)

2. Is probable cause necessary in order for customs officers to conduct a search of vehicles allegedly bringing narcotics or dangerous drugs into the United States? (C.J.S.)

3. May a railroad company acquire title to land by adverse possession or prescription? (C.J.S.)

4. Does the assignment of the interest of a vendor or vendee in a contract for the sale of land as security for a debt create an equitable mortgage? (C.J.S.)

5. Does the mere issuance of a zoning or building permit give a vested or property right to the permittee? (C.J.S.)

6. Is the Securities and Exchange Commission authorized to subpoena witnesses and to require the production of relevant books, papers and documents? (C.J.S.)

7. Does mere inaction constitute negligence where a duty has been undertaken gratuitously? (C.J.S.)

8. Can a municipal corporation be held civilly liable for its failure to enact or enforce ordinances? (C.J.S.)

9. May the crime of forgery be committed by the signing of a fictitious or assumed name? (Am. Jur. 2d)

10. Are unavoidably unsafe products classified as unreasonably dangerous or purposes of the strict liability doctrine when they are accompanied by proper directions and warnings? (Am. Jur. 2d)

11. May a state ever take or authorize the taking of property situated in another state under its powers of eminent domain? (Am. Jur. 2d)

12. Must an overt act be of a criminal nature in order to warrant conviction for treason? (Am. Jur. 2d)

13. May a false statement on an income tax return constitute perjury? (Am. Jur. 2d)

14. Is the offense of fraudulent enlistment in the military service exclusively a military offense punishable only by court-martial? (Am. Jur. 2d)

15. May a corporation legally change or alter the name originally selected by it without recourse to formal proceedings? (Am. Jur. 2d)

16. Can a change in the law render a contract illegal which was legal when made? (C.J.S.)

17. May a writer of a personal letter enjoin its publication on grounds analogous to the right of privacy? (Am. Jur. 2d)

18. Is a bail bond the same as a recognizance? (C.J.S.)

19. In order to secure relief on the ground of fraud, must the complainant have a right to rely upon the misrepresentation? (Am. Jur. 2d)

20. Does the law impose on the bailee the duty of insuring the subject matter of the bailment? (C.J.S.)

21. Will refusal to permit challenges and watchers to be present at the polls, during the conduct of an election, invalidate the election? (C.J.S.)

22. May a positive offer be made by advertisement or general notice in a newspaper, fulfilling one of the essential requirements for a contract? (Am. Jur. 2d)

23. May the release of mutual claims by each of two persons constitute an accord and satisfaction? (C.J.S.)

24. In order to constitute an escrow must the deposit be irrevocable? (Am. Jur. 2d)

25. May a failure, without excuse, to obey a court order to pay money, constitute contempt? (C.J.S.)

26. Is a wife obliged to furnish her husband with a home, if she had one and he does not have a home? (Am. Jur. 2d)

27. May a will be revoked by oral declaration? (C.J.S.)

28. Does a state Sunday closing law violate the U.S. Constitution respecting establishment of religion, where the present purpose and effect of the statute is not to aid religion, but to set aside a day of rest and recreation? (Am. Jur. 2d)

29. May franchises be condemned under the right of eminent domain? (C.J.S.)

30. Is a state statute, prohibiting desertion, and nonsupport of unborn children, valid? (Am. Jur. 2d)

31. Is a contract for the sale of standing timber within the Statute of Frauds? (C.J.S.)

32. May a qualified expert testify from the nature of a wound as to the character of the weapon which inflicted or could have inflicted the wound? (Am. Jur. 2d)

33. Is the state regarded as a party to every divorce proceeding? (C.J.S.)

34. Will a court grant a decree of specific performance of a binding oral contract? (Am. Jur. 2d)

35. Under the Bankruptcy Act, may receivers or trustees be held liable personally or on their bonds to the United States for penalties or forfeitures incurred by the bankrupts? (Am. Jur. 2d)

36. Will jurisdiction for a declaratory judgment be entertained where another equally appropriate remedy is already available? (C.J.S.)

37. Are aliens entitled to the guaranty of the Fourteenth Amendment that no state shall "deny to any person within its jurisdiction the equal protection of the laws? (Am. Jur. 2d)

38. May a person maintain a proceeding for a variance from a zoning law, if his sole purpose is to obtain a higher valuation in condemnation proceedings? (C.J.S.)

39. Is an employer prohibited by law from executing a "yellow dog contract," in which the employee agrees that he will not become a member of a labor union? (Am. Jur. 2d)

40. May a beneficiary under a trust deed foreclose a mortgage on the trust property, when the trustee neglects to do so? (C.J.S.)

ASSIGNMENT 3
USE OF THE DEFINITION METHOD WITH AMERICAN
JURISPRUDENCE 2D AND CORPUS JURIS SECUNDUM

Method:

Find a legal definition for each of the following words, phrases and maxims in the encyclopedia abbreviated in the parenthesis. The answer to each problem consists solely of a citation to a text of the encylcopedia. Where the definition does not appear within the context of a topic, cite to the specific volume, the year thereof, and page of the designated encyclopedia. Where the definition does appear within a topic, cite to the encyclopedia according to the latest edition of A Uniform System of Citation.

> NOTE: To find some of the definitions, it is necessary to go to the Words and Phrases section of the legal encyclopedia, determine out under which topic the definition can be found, and then go to the indicated section.

Example:

QUESTION: Evident (C.J.S.)
ANSWER: 32A C.J.S. p. 845 (1964).

Questions:

1. Local Option (Am. Jur. 2d)

2. Disavow (C.J.S.)

3. Private school (Am. Jur. 2d)

4. Vicinetum (C.J.S.)

5. Gerrymandering (Am. Jur. 2d)

6. Cyrce (C.J.S.)

7. Tout (C.J.S.)

8. Equitable waste (Am. Jur. 2d)

9. Barratry (Am. Jur. 2d)

10. Estovers (C.J.S.)

11. Bogus check (C.J.S.)
12. Evergreen (C.J.S.)
13. Good will (Am. Jur. 2d)
14. Royal Fishery (C.J.S.)
15. Parole (Am. Jur. 2d)
16. Res ipsa loquitur (C.J.S.)
17. Mental anguish (C.J.S.)
18. Court of last resort (C.J.S.)
19. Spot zoning (Am. Jur. 2d)
20. Compte arrete (C.J.S.)
21. Equitable estoppel (Am. Jur. 2d)
22. Dielectric (C.J.S.)
23. Color of title (Am. Jur. 2d)
24. Condominiums (C.J.S.)
25. Abuse of Process (Am. Jur. 2d)
26. Advowtry (C.J.S.)
27. Chattel Mortgage (C.J.S.)
28. Overt Act (C.J.S.)
29. Implied Warranty (C.J.S.)
30. Juvenile Delinquent (C.J.S.)
31. Set-off (C.J.S.)
32. Traumatic Diseases (C.J.S.)
33. Fee Tail (Am. Jur. 2d)
34. Inebriation (Am. Jur. 2d)
35. Lis Pendens (Am. Jur. 2d)
36. Locatio Operis faciendi (Am. Jur. 2d)

37. Near Beer (Am. Jur. 2d)

38. Original Package Doctrine (Am. Jur. 2d)

39. Perpetuities (Am. Jur. 2d)

ASSIGNMENT 4
THEME AND DRILL PROBLEMS FOR LEGAL ENCYCLOPEDIAS

The purpose of the theme and drill problems is to acquaint one with the legal encyclopedias, Corpus Jurus Secundum (C.J.S.) and American Jurisprudence 2d (Am. Jur. 2d).

THEME PROBLEMS

Instructions:

Answer each question using the legal encyclopedia designated in the question. As appropriate, the answer should be in proper citation form according to the latest edition of A Uniform System of Citation.

Theme Problem I (Discrimination):

A. Use C.J.S. to answer questions the following questions:

1. Where in C.J.S. can one find a discussion of the prohibition of racial discrimination in public schools, including a textual discussion of Brown v. Bd. of Education?

2. Why is #1 difficult to locate?

3. How do you account for the textual discussion found in Schools and School Districts §447?

4. Where can C.J.S. Civil Rights §4 now be found?

5. Using the volume cited in #4, answer the following:
    (a) What is O.Ben an abbreviation of?
    (b) Where is there discussion of whether a swimming pool is a private club?
    (c) What Key Number does the discussion of Brown refer one to?

B. Use Am. Jur. 2d to answer the following questions:

1. Where can one find a discussion of discrimination in education?

2. Where can a section on desgregation in cases of de jure segregation be found?

3. What citations to other Am. Jur. sets can be found in the main volume under the same footnote that discusses <u>Brown v. Bd. of Education</u> in the section located in 82?

4. What law review article(s) is (are) cited as a practice aid in the pocket part update?

5. Using the same volume, answer the following:
   (a) Am. Jur. Charities §44 can now be found at?
   (b) 2 U.S.C.S. §2000(a) is cited in?
   (c) What is the citation of the first Annotation noted in Civil Rights §101?
   (d) Where could you find discussion of stamina tests as a method of predicting employment capability?

<u>Theme Problem II</u>:

A. Use C.J.S. to answer the following questions.

   1. Locate the discussion establishing that the Constitutional right of life, liberty and privacy includes the right to terminate a pregnancy. Cite the appropriate section.

   2. Why would one have to consult the pocket part of the General Index to have any chance of finding such discussion?

   3. Using the volume containing the section cited in #1 answer the following:
      (a) What is the footnote number under which <u>Roe</u> is found?
      (b) What California case establishes a woman's fundamental right to bear children?
      (c) Can a residency requirement be a condition precedent to the obtaining of a therapeutic abortion?

   4. Using the same volume of C.J.S., answer the following:
      (a) What is discussed under Constitutional Law §176?
      (b) What does the abbreviation "Dal.C.P." stand for?
      (c) What sections cover the discussion of privileges or immunities?
      (d) What Key Number would Constitutional Law §202 relate to?

B. Use Am. Jur. 2d to answer the following questions:

   1. Where in Am. Jur. 2d could one find the discussion described in #A.1 above?

2. Under this discussion, can Roe be located?

3. Where could one find a more general discussion of abortion?

4. Using the volume that contains the general discussion located in #3, answer the following:
   (a) Where in Am. Jur. 2d can one find discussion of the material that Am. Jur. contained in Adjoining Landowners §43?
   (b) Where in this volume is 5 U.S.C. §22 cited?
   (c) Where is Federal Rule of Civil Procedure Rule 53(b) cited?
   (d) To find an annotation on cases covered in Abduction and Kidnapping §19, where could one look?

5. Is there any discussion relevant to abortion in the New Topic Service?

6. Do you find Am. Jur. 2d or C.J.S. more useful in searching for information and locating cases?

Theme Problem III:

A. Use C.J.S. to answer the following questions:

1. Using the Criminal Law volumes, where can one find discussion of one's constitutional right to counsel in a criminal case?

2. What is the first heading under which Gideon appears in the pocket part?

3. How has C.J.S. met the problem caused by the new line of cases created by Gideon?

4. What are the copyright dates of the Constitutional Law volumes of C.J.S. and what problems does this create?

5. Using the Criminal Law volumes, answer the following:
   (a) What does the abbreviation "A.L.C." stand for?
   (b) Where can one find discussion of a red flag as a symbol of anarchy?
   (c) Cite a case in which the admission of owning heroin was not admissible to establish that X sold heroin.
   (d) Give the citation of a recent Louisiana case under §1914(1) footnote 92.

345

B. Use Am. Jur. 2d to answer the following questions:

1. Locate a general discussion of the accused's right to confront the witnesses against him/her for the opportunity of cross-examination?

2. What section covers the right of a person to represent him/herself?

3. Using the Criminal Law volumes, answer the following:
    (a) Am. Jur. 2d Criminal Law §405 can be found in Am. Jur. 2d (Rev. ed.) at?
    (b) In what section is 18 U.S.C. §2 discussed?
    (c) Can a person be punished by being banished from the jurisdiction? Cite the appropriate section.
    (d) Cite an Annotation on the topic in (c).

4. Is there any discussion relevant to right to counsel in the New Topic Service?

5. Do you find Am. Jur. 2d or C.J.S. more useful in searching for information and locating cases?

                          DRILL PROBLEMS

Instructions:

For each of the following questions:

(1) provide a "yes" or "no" answer;

(2) cite the volume, title and section of the encyclopedia under which the correct answer can be found.

The answer should be in proper citation form according to the latest edition of A Uniform System of Citation.

Drill Problem I:

A. Use C.J.S. to answer the following questions:

1. Are children born of parents who are subject to jurisdiction of a country considered citizens of that country even if their parents are aliens?

2. Does the fact of a brother-sister relationship imply that there should be a presumption that service rendered or work performed is gratuitous?

3. Does simple pursuit of game confer on a hunter a right of ownership?

B. Use Am. Jur. 2d to answer the following questions:

1. (Use Title Index to Descent and Distribution). When a person is sentenced to life imprisonment, can his/her property then be distributed as if death had occurred?

2. Is an owner who burns his/her house while it is in the possession of another guilty of arson?

Drill Problem II:

A. Use C.J.S. to answer the following questions:

1. Is a statement as to genealogy admissible as an exception to the hearsay rule?

2. Was the utterance of obscene words in public indictable at common law?

B. Use Am. Jur. 2d to answer the following questions:

1. Have the Courts traditionally viewed the use of threats or force to recover gambling losses as "robbery?"

2. If unruly spectators may have caused prejudice in a trial, can the verdict be appealed?

3. Can one find discussion and text of Federal Rules of Evidence? Where?

Drill Problem III:

A. Use C.J.S. to answer the following questions:

1. Under negligence theory, if someone habitually trespasses upon your land, does your knowledge of the trespass create a duty of care for the trespasser's safety?

2. Can counsel use medical texts on the cross examination of an expert witness?

B. Use Am Jur 2d to answer the following questions:

1. Could one find a discussion of "a designing woman" in an action for seduction? Where?

2. Does the act of advertising to treat patients by mail by means of "mental science" show a scheme to use the mails of the United States Post Office for fraud absent any other proof?

3. Does one need corroboration of the testimony of one of the parties to probe the crime of adultery?

Chapter 17

LEGAL PERIODICALS AND INDEXES

ASSIGNMENT 1
AUTHOR INDEX PROBLEMS IN THE INDEX TO LEGAL PERIODCALS

Method:

Using the INDEX TO LEGAL PERIODICALS, locate and cite the following:

Questions:

	Date	Author	Subject
1.	1973	R. H. Freilich	Missouri law of land use controls.
2.	1960	G. L. Williams	Diminished responsibility.
3.	1969	R. A. Jensen	Effect of federal truth in lending act.
4.	1975	L. B. Sohn	Settlement of disputes arising out of the law of the sea convention.
5.	1957	L. F. Powell, Jr.	Contributory negligence.
6.	1970	J. O. Newman	Prosecutor and defender reform.
7.	1966	J. F. Rill	Trend toward social competition under section 7 of the Clayton Act.
8.	1975	R. B. Ginsburg	Gender and the Constitution.
9.	1962	J. W. Wade	Defamation and the right of privacy.
10.	1956	A. T. Vanderbilt	Municipal courts.
11.	1974	A. P. Ordover	Use of written direct testimony.
12.	1966	E. E. Cheatham	Reach of federal action over the profession of law.

	Date	Author	Subject
13.	1952	R. W. Russell	"Good faith" and motor vehicle assigned risk plans.
14.	1961	M. G. Paulsen	Exclusionary rule and misconduct by the police.
15.	1967	P. J. Rohan	Perfecting the condominium as a housing tool
16.	1969	E. L. Folk	Civil liabilities under the Federal Securities Acts
17.	1963	T. S. Lawson	Public criticism of the courts by lawyers
18.	1972	J. P. S. McLaren	Common law nuisance actions and the environmental battle
19.	1942	W. H. Pedrick	War measures and contract liability
20.	1954	F. H. O'Neal	Resolving disputes in closely held corporations
21.	1959	C. A. Wright	Procedural reform in the states
22.	1961	W. H. Rehnquist	Subdivision trusts and the bankruptcy act
23.	1973	C. H. Fulda	Controls of entry into business and professions
24.	1943	H. D. Lasswell	Legal education and public policy
25.	1959	I. Younger	Congressional investigations and executive secrecy
26.	1966	V. Brudney	Fiduciary ideology in transactions affecting corporate control
27.	1948	B. M. Sparks	Tort action in Kentucky for the wrongful destruction of a will
28.	1968	T. Holton	Prevention of delinquency through legal counseling
29.	1955	L. M. Simes	Policy against perpetuities
30.	1973	J. T. Sneed	Charitable remainder trusts

	Date	Author	Subject
31.	1962	K. N. Llewellyn	Lecture on appellate advocacy
32.	1961	S. Mentschikoff	Commercial arbitration
33.	1948	J. B. Fordham	Home rule powers in theory and practice
34.	1965	S. S. Nagel	Testing the effect of excluding illegally seized evidence
35.	1942	G. Simons	Dangers of double domicile and double taxation
36.	1968	J. H. Watson	Chronic alcoholic court offenders
37.	1970	J. O'Connell	Public opinion on no-fault auto insurance
38.	1966	F. R. Strong	Toward an acceptable function of judicial review?
39.	1969	H. Couch	Realistic divorce law
40.	1971	S. T. Agnew	Case for revenue sharing
41.	1962	J. W. Harrison	Bible, the Constitution, and public education
42.	1971	R. M. Nixon	To improve the process of justice
43.	1952	M. B. Virtue	Public services to children
44.	1972	T. F. Eagleton	Congress and the war powers
45.	1942	R. I. Wilson	Billboards
46.	1972	J. C. Ortega	Plight of the Mexican wetback
47.	1971	R. E. Keeton	No-fault insurance: a status report
48.	1964	R. F. Kennedy	Halfway houses pay off
49.	1971	T. I. Emerson	Equal rights amendment
50.	1967	B. E. Wingerd	Feed lot--nuisance or not
51.	1961	W. E. Doyle	Teach the law student to be a lawyer

	Date	Author	Subject
52.	1970	J. Lindsay	Making law and order work
53.	1970	R. P. Patterson	Importance of the legal aid society to the legal profession
54.	1954	O. M. Stone	Valuation of a deceased bigamist

ASSIGNMENT 2
THE CASE APPROACH TO THE INDEX TO LEGAL PERIODICALS

Method:

Locate and cite the first (by date of law review issue) student comment on the following cases:

Questions:

	Year of Comment	Case
1.	1957	Abercrombie v. Davies, 36 Del. Ch. 445, 131 A.2d 822 (1957).
2.	1953	Bird v. Plunkett, 139 Conn. 491, 95 A.2d 71 (1953).
3.	1960	Baird v. Koerner, 279 F.2d 623 (9th Cir. 1960).
4.	1961	Sun Oil Co. v. FTC, 294 F.2d 465 (5th Cir. 1961).
5.	1966	Miranda v. Arizona, 384 U.S. 436 (1966).
6.	1968	In Re Permian Basin Area Rate Cases, 88 S.Ct. 1344 (1968).
7.	1965	Permian Basin Area Rate Proceeding, 34 F.P.C. 468 (1965).
8.	1972	People v. McKinnon, 7 Cal.3d 889, 500 P.2d 1097 (1972).
9.	1973	Nathan Cummings, 61 T.C. 1 (1973).
10.	1954	Lawlor v. National Screen Service Corp., 211 F.2d 934 (3d Cir. 1954).
11.	1955	Shachtman v. Dulles, 225 F.2d 938 (D.C. Cir. 1955).
12.	1961	State ex rel. Lake Drive Baptist Church v. Bayside Village Bd., 12 Wis.2d 585, 108 N.W.2d 288 (1961).
13.	1966	Office of Communication of the United Church of Christ v. FCC, 359 F.2d 994 (D.C. Cir. 1966).

	Year of Comment	Case
14.	1971	Investors Management Co., SEC Exchange Act Release no. 9267, CCH Fed.Sec. L.Rep. para. 78,163 (1971).
15.	1968	Hopkins v. Gardner, 374 F.2d 726.
16.	1965	Felgner v. Anderson, 133 N.W.2d 136.
17.	1957	Safeway Stores v. Barrack, 122 A.2d 457.
18.	1972	U.S. v. 16179 Molso Italian.22 Caliber Winlee Derringer Convertible Starter Guns, 433 F.2d 463.
19.	1973	Brasserie de Haecht v. Wilkin- Janssen Case 43¶72 (1973) C.M.L.R. 287.
20.	1958	People ex rel. Adamowski v. Chicago Land Clearance Comm., 150 N.E.2d 792.
21.	1966	State v. Sikora, 210 A.2d 193.
22.	1962	Lutz v. Boas, 171 A.2d 381.
23.	1973	Dodd v. Dodd, 499 P.2d 518.
24.	1955	Kloeckner Reederei und Kohlenhandel, G.M.B.H. v. A/S Hakedal, 210 F.2d 754.
25.	1965	Tellier v. Commissioner, 342 F.2d 690.
26.	1968	Hicks v. Hicks, 155 S.E.2d 799.
27.	1971	Davis v. Thornton, 180 N.W.2d 11.
28.	1972	DeFunis v. Odegaard, No. 741727 (Washington Superior Court for King County, Sept. 22, 1971).
29.	1969	Regina v. Ovenell, (1968) 2 W.L.R. 1545.
30.	1961	Johnstone v. Sanborn, 358 P.2d 399.
31.	1969	City of Piqua v. Hinger, 238 N.E.2d 766.
32.	1962	Noel v. United Aircraft Corp., 204 F. Supp. 929.
33.	1965	Mrs. Baird's Bakeries, Inc. v. Bobby Lewis Roberts, 360 S.W.2d 850.

	Year of Comment	Case
34.	1971	Morrison v. State Board of Education, 461 P.2d 375.
35.	1961	Farley Realty Corp. v. Commissioner, 279 F.2d 701.
36.	1957	Federal Trade Commission v. B. F. Goodrich Co., 242 F.2d 31.
37.	1972	Serrano v. Priest, 478 P.2d 1241.
38.	1971	Sierra Club v. Hickel, 433 F.2d 24.
39.	1963	Sunshine Biscuits, Inc. v. Federal Trade Commission, 306 F.2d 48.
40.	1971	In re Adoption of Baby Boy, 472 P.2d 64
41.	1970	U.S. v. Thirty-Seven Photographs, 309 F. Supp. 36.
42.	1966	Lorenz v. State, 406 P.2d 278
43.	1971	Stanley v. Georgia, 89 S.Ct. 1243
44.	1970	Marchetti v. U.S., 88 S.Ct. 697
45.	1963	Idlewild Bon Voyage Liquor Corp. v. Epstein, 82 S.Ct. 1294
46.	1971	In re Gault, 87 S.Ct. 1428
47.	1970	Minor v. U.S., 90 S.Ct. 284
48.	1958	NAACP v. Patty, 159 F.Supp. 503
49.	1972	Inmates of the Attica Correctional Facility v. Rockefeller, 453 F.2d 12
50.	1971	Procunier v. Atchley, 91 S.Ct. 485
51.	1962	Communist Party of the U.S. v. Catherwood, 81 S.Ct. 1465
52.	1949	Hialeah Race Course, Inc. v. Gulfstream Park Racing Association, Inc., 37 So. 2d 692
53.	1959	Tuscarora Indian Nation v. FPC, 265 F.2d 338

	Year of Comment	Case
54.	1954	Federal Communications Commission v. Columbia Broadcasting System, Inc., 74 S.Ct 593
55.	1957	Mooney v. Bartenders Union, 313 P.2d 857
56.	1967	Hoffa v. U.S., 87 S.Ct. 408
57.	1972	Law Students Civil Rights Research Council v. Wadmond, 91 S.Ct. 720
58.	1949	Alden-Rochelle, Inc. v. American Society of Composers, Authors and Publishers, 80 F. Supp. 888
59.	1958	Radovich v. National Football League, 77 S.Ct. 390
60.	1952	Bowman Gum, Inc. v. Topps Chewing Gum, Inc., 103 F. Supp. 944
61.	1948	Sun Shipbuilding and Drydock Co. v. Unemployment Compensation Board of Review, 56 A.2d 254
62.	1962	Colorado Anti-Discrimination Commission v. Continental Air Lines, 83 S.Ct. 1022
63.	1938	City of Mangum v. Brownlee, 75 P.2d 174
64.	1967	Award of Her Majesty Queen Elizabeth II for the Arbitration of a Controversy Between the Argentine Republic and the Republic of Chile Concerning Certain Parts of the Boundary Between Their Territories, Court of Arbitration November 24, 1966

ASSIGNMENT 3
LOCATING BOOK REVIEWS THROUGH THE INDEX TO LEGAL PERIODICALS

Method:

Locate and cite the first review of a book in the calendar year indicated.

Questions:

	Year Reviewed	Author and Title
1.	1969	Wise, Arthur E., Rich Schools, Poor Schools: The Promise of Equal Educational Opportunity.
2.	1955	Holden, James Milnes, History of Negotiable Instruments In English Law.
3.	1959	Sykes, Gresham M., Society Of Captives: A Study Of Maximum Security Prison.
4.	1962	Davis, F. James, et al., Society and the Law.
5.	1952	Guttmacher, Mansfred S., Psychiatry and the Law.
6.	1970	Mitford, Jessica, Trial of Dr. Spock.
7.	1970	Report and Recommendations On Disruption of the Judicial Process.
8.	1966	Coff, Robert, Law of Restitution.
9.	1973	Dobbs, Dan B., Handbook on the Law of Remedies.
10.	1953	Blum, Walter J., Uneasy Case For Progressive Taxation.
11.	1966	Kalven, Harry, American Jury.
12.	1957	Hamilton, Walton, Politics of Industry.
13.	1968	Keeton, Robert, After Cars Crash.
14.	1963	Mental Illness and Due Process.

	Year Reviewed	Author and Title
15.	1975	Schwartz, Bernard, Law In America: A History.
16.	1971	To Establish Justice, To Insure Domestic Tranquility: the Final Report of the National Commission on the Causes and Prevention of Violence (1970).
17.	1968	Alexander, George J., Honesty and Competition: False Advertising Law and Policy under FTC Administration (1967).
18.	1966	Marshall, James, Law and Psychology in Conflict (1966).
19.	1966	Schubert, Glendon, Judicial Policy-making (1965).
20.	1972	Rawls, John, Theory of Justice (1971).
21.	1973	Dobbs, Dan B., Handbook on the Law of Remedies (1973)
22.	1973	Hoffman, Paul, Lions in the Street: the Inside Story of the Great Wall Street Law Firms (1973).
23.	1967	Lang, John Temple, Common Market and Common Law (1966).
24.	1967	Uniform System of Citation (1967).
25.	1970	Szasz, Thomas A., Manufacture of Madness (1970).
26.	1971	Weintraub, Russell J., Commentary on the Conflict of Laws (1971).
27.	1971	Automobile Insurance ... For Whose Benefit? (1970).
28.	1966	Lewis, Walker, Without Fear or Favor: a Biography of Chief Justice Roger Brooke Taney (1965).
29.	1969	Menninger, Karl, Crime of Punishment (1968).
30.	1969	Keeton, Robert E., Venturing to Do Justice (1969).

	Year Reviewed	Author and Title
31.	1963	Kochu Thommen, Thamarappallil, Legal Status of Government Merchant Ships in International Law (1962).
32.	1970	Watson, Andrew S., Psychiatry for Lawyers (1968).
33.	1969	Vance, Stanley C., Corporate Director: a Critical Evaluation (1968).
34.	1968	Johnstone, Quintin and Hopson, Dan, Jr., Lawyers and Their Work (1967).
35.	1970	Dawson, Robert O., Sentencing: the Decision as to Type, Length, and Conditions of Sentence (1969).
36.	1966	Cavers, David F., Choice-of-Law Process (1965).
37.	1953	Cahill, Fred V., Jr., Judicial Legislation (1952).
38.	1971	Wasby, Stephen L., Impact of the United States Supreme Court: Some Perspectives (1970).
39.	1971	Gil, David G., Violence Against Children: Physical Child Abuse in the United States (1970).
40.	1972	First Report of the National Commission on Marihuana and Drug Abuse (1972).
41.	1970	Ridgeway, James, Politics of Ecology (1970).
42.	1968	Erwin, Richard E., Defense of Drunk Driving Cases (2nd ed. 1966).
43.	1964	Tiemann, William, Right to Silence, Privileged Communication and the Pastor (1964).
44.	1972	Williams, Colin and Weinberg, Martin, Homosexuals and the Military: A Study of Less Than Honorable Discharge (1971).

	Year Reviewed	Author and Title
45.	1969	Burns, Peter and O'Keefe, J.A.B., Functions and Powers of Justices of the Peace and Coroners (1968).
46.	1971	Manocchio, Anthony J. and Dunn, Jimmy, Time Game: Two Views of a Prison (1970).
47.	1964	Cavanaugh, James J., Lawyer in Society (1963).
48.	1970	Clark, Ramsey, Crime in America (1970).
49.	1972	Rheinstein, Max, Marriage Stability, Divorce, and the Law (1972).
50.	1971	Swartz, Edward, Toys that Don't Care (1971).
51.	1969	Euthanasia and the Right to Death (1969).
52.	1972	Pentagon Papers (1971).
53.	1968	Clark, Grenville and John, Louis, World Peace Through World Law: Two Alternative Plans (3rd ed. 1966).
54.	1971	Penniman, Howard and Winter, Ralph, Campaign Financing: Two Views of the Political and Constitutional Implications (1971).
55.	1972	Aerial Piracy and International Law (1971).
56.	1969	Chapman, Dennis, Sociology and the Sterotype of the Criminal (1968).
57.	1970	Clor, Harry M., Obsenity and Public Morality (1969).
58.	1965	Young, Leontine R., Wednesday's Children: A Study of Child Neglect and Abuse (1964).
59.	1972	Brown, Kent, Medical Problems and the Law (1971).

ASSIGNMENT 4
PROBLEM APPROACH TO THE INDEX TO LEGAL PERIODICALS

Questions:

1. Find a 1966 article concerned with attitudes toward the Los Angeles race riot.

2. Locate a case involving a prisoner's rights under the Federal Tort Claims Act, and a 1955 law review comment thereon.

3. Find a 1973 discussion of insuring the condominium.

4. Locate a 1954 American note concerned with receiving stolen goods.

5. What article discusses a resistance standard in 1966 rape legislation?

6. Cite a 1967 note on the attachment or garnishment of a jointly held bank account.

7. Find a 1971 article on the rule against perpetuities and the spendthrift trust in New York.

8. Locate a case finding non-liability of the United States for a negligent weather forecast under the Federal Tort Claims Act, and a 1954 periodical comment on it.

9. Cite a 1960 note on the common law liability of liquor vendors.

10. Find a 1973 article concerned with discrimination against women in the extension of credit.

11. Locate a 1967 article on blood transfusions where an adult Jehovah's Witness is involved.

12. Cite a 1946 article on the admissibility of ballistic evidence.

13. Find a 1972 note on the XYY chromosomal abnormality and how it may be misused in establishing responsibility for a crime.

14. Locate a 1953 article on the importance of public psychology in establishing rates for utilities.

15. Find a 1972 bibliography on "noise pollution."

16. Locate a 1966 article containing suggestions on the reporting of federal district court opinions.

17. Cite a 1972 article surveying the work of the U.S. Court of Appeals for the Fifth Circuit for the year 1971.

18. Find a 1960 note on whether evidence of drug addiction may be used to impeach a witness.

19. Locate a 1969 note calling for legislation to protect computer programs.

20. Cite a 1955 and 1956 article (printed two places) concerned with the fingerprinting of bar applicants.

21. Locate a 1970 symposium on governmental compensation for victims of violence.

22. Find a 1959 article on epilepsy in a legal context.

23. Cite a 1968 model movie censorship ordinance.

24. Locate a 1945 article on "concerted" wills.

25. Find a 1974 article concerned with airline "bumping" and baggage loss.

26. Locate a 1974 article on the taxation aspects of the transfer of appreciated property pursuant to divorce in Oregon.

27. Locate a 1960 case on "operative offers in circular letters" as establishing a contract and cite case and its discussion in a law review.

28. Cite a 1952 article concerned with the U.S. General Accounting Office's right to inspect government contractors' records.

29. Find a 1966 article on the malpractice of psychiatrists.

30. Locate an article discussing a (1959) case involving negligence for animals on the highway as a cause of a motor vehicle accident.

31. Find a survey of the work of the U.S. Court of Appeals for the Sixth Circuit for the year 1971-72.

32. Locate a 1955 article on the drafting of a book publishing contract.

33. Cite a 1962 article on the epileptic automobile driver in Ohio.

34. Cite a 1972 article on tort liability for hepatitis.

35. Locate a 1962 extended analysis on racially restrictive covenants criticizing the opinion in Shelley v. Kraemer and suggesting its revision.

36. Find a 1957 article concerned with the origin of credit life insurance.

37. Cite a 1971 article on computer program protection.

38. Find a 1975 article dealing with live organ transplants from minor donors in Massachusetts.

39. Cite a 1967 article discussing slumlordism as a tort.

ASSIGNMENT 5
DRILL PROBLEMS

Drill Problem I:

A. Using the Index to Legal Periodicals, Cumulation 18, answer the following:

   1. Compile bibliographies of articles written by the following:

      (a) William F. Fox, Jr.

      (b) Joseph J. Kalo.

   2. Locate an article discussing the status of the Navajo tribe.

   3. Which law review produced a survey of the work of the United States Court of Appeals for the Eighth Circuit?

   4. Where can you find a law review comment on the following?

      (a) Scruggs v. United States, 538 F.2d 214 (1976).

      (b) Fitzpatrick v. Bitzer, 519 F.2d 559 (1975).

B. Using Current Law Index, volume 1, answer the following:

   1. Locate an article discussing the Supreme Court's reaction to populism.

   2. Locate an article by Patricia A. Seitz.

   3. Locate a review of Free to Choose.

   4. Locate an article discussing identification of musical scores which are handwritten.

   5. Name the plaintiff in a suit defended by Lindberg. Where is the case discussed?

Drill Problem II:

A. Using the Index to Legal Periodicals, Cumulation 16, answer the following:

   1. Compile bibliographies of articles written by the following:

      (a) Ovid C. Lewis

      (b) Frank T. Read.

   2. What law review(s) prepared summaries of the work of the United States court of Appeals for the Fourth Circuit?

   3. Where can you find commentary on the following:

      (a) J. Ehrlich, Lost Art of Cross-Examination (1970)?

      (b) Cortright v. Resor, 325 F.Supp. 797 (1971)?

B. Using Current Law Index, volume 1, answer the following:

   1. Locate an article discussing the sale of vessels when ordered by the Court.

   2. Locate an article by Alan G. Gless.

   3. Locate an article dealing with the Florida Condominium Act.

   4. Locate a review of S. Leinberg, et al., Tools & Techniques of Estate Planning.

   5. Locate an article discussing psychopathological criminals.

   6. Name the plaintiff in a suit against Franco. What was the subject of the claim?

Drill Problem III:

A. Using the Index to Legal Periodicals, Cumulation 17, answer the following:

   1. Compile bibliographies of articles written by the following:

      (a) John C. Weistart.

      (b) Patricia H. Marschall.

2. Locate an article discussing how to prove ownership in cases of theft of property.

3. Which law review conducted annual surveys of the law of Texas?

4. Where can you find discussion of the following:

    (a) <u>Mason v. Arizona</u>, 504 F.2d 1345 (1974).

    (b) F. Giroud, <u>I Give You My Word</u> (1974).

5. Locate a discussion of Hans Kelson's philosophy as expressed in his essays.

B. Using the <u>Current Law Index</u>, volume 1, answer the following:

1. Locate an article discussing the proper function of enterprise conducted not for profit.

2. Locate an article by Mark G. Yudof.

3. Locate an article discussing the National Bank Act and Texas Law.

4. Locate a review of B. Reams and J. Ferguson, <u>Federal Consumer Protection</u>.

5. Locate an article tracing the history of the right to jury trials in civil litigation.

6. What is the subject of a case involving Flying Tiger Line, Inc.?

<u>Drill Problem IV</u>:

A. Compile bibliographies written between 1973 and 1977 of the periodical articles written by each of the following law professors. Include title and journal citation.

1. Robert Cover

2. Dolores Korman Sloviter

3. Peter L. Strauss

B. Using the <u>Index to Legal Periodicals</u>, locate and cite the following:

1. Find a 1974 article on the liability of airlines for "bumping" and baggage loss.

2. Cite a 1952 symposium article concerned with the U.S. General Accounting Office's right to inspect government contractors' records.

3. Find a survey of the work of the U.S. Court of Appeals for the Sixth Circuit for the year 1971-72.

4. Cite a 1972 article on tort liability for hepatitis.

5. Cite a 1971 article on computer program protection.

Drill Problem V:

A. Compile bibliographies written between 1973 and 1977 of the periodical articles written by each of the following law professors. Include title and journal citation.

1. Bruce Ackerman

2. Mary Louise Fellows

3. Olin Guy Wellborn

B. Using the Index to Legal Periodicals, locate and cite the following:

1. Locate a 1974 article on the taxation aspects of the transfer of appreciated property pursuant to divorce in Oregon.

2. Find a 1966 article on the malpractice of psychiatrists.

3. Locate a 1955 article on the drafting of a book publishing contract.

4. Locate a 1962 extended analysis on racially restrictive covenants criticizing the opinion in Shelley v. Kraemer and suggesting its revision.

5. Find a 1975 article dealing with live organ transplants from minor donors in Massachusetts.

Drill Problem VI:

A. Compile bibliographies written between 1973 and 1977 of the periodical articles written by each of the following law professors. Included title and journal citation.

1. Stephen J. Schulhofer

2. Charles E. Daye

3. William J. Carney

B. Using the <u>Index to Legal Periodicals</u>, locate and cite the following:

1. Locate a 1960 case on "operative offers incircular letters" as establishing a contract. Cite the case andits discussion in a law review.

2. Locate an article discussing a (1959) case involving negligence for animals onthe highway as a cause of a motor vehicle accident.

3. Cite a 1962 article on the epileptic automobile driver in Ohio.

4. Find a 1957 article concerned with the origin of credit life insurance.

5. Cite a 1967 article on slumlordism as a tort.

ASSIGNMENT 6
THEME PROBLEMS

Theme Problem I:

A. Using the Index to Legal Periodicals, answer the following:

 1. Locate a 1928 student comment on Palsgraf from the St. John's Law Review.

 2. Locate a 1937 article by William Prosser discussing Res Ipsa Loquitur.

 3. Using Cumulation 19, answer the following:

    (a) Who wrote an article on the liability of cruise ships to their passengers for negligence?

    (b) What was the title of an article by John M. Van Dyke?

    (c) Cite to the review of Guido Calabresi and Philip Bobbitt's Tragic Choices which appeared in the Suffolk Univerity Law Review.

    (d) Will you find reference in this volume to articles which appeared in the Nova Law Journal?

B. Using Current Law Index, volume 1, answer the following:

 1. Was Joseph W. Ginn III a law student when he wrote "Prima Facie Tort?"

 2. Where can you locate the text of the Louisiana Comparative Negligence Act?

 3. Locate a comment on Harris v. Grizzle, 599 P.2d 580 (Wyo. 1979).

Theme Problem II:

A. Using the Index to Legal Periodicals, answer the following:

 1. United States v. Garland, 122 F.2d 118 (5th Cir. 1941), cert. denied 314 U.S. 685 (1941), held that mutual mistake as to the existence of facts will render an insurance contract voidable. Cite to the discussion of it in the Columbia Law Review.

2. Locate Arthur L. Corbins' 1939 analysis of Cardozo's contract law decisions.

3. Using cumulation 18, answer the following:

   (a) Give the citation of an article on the law governing mistaken bids.

   (b) Give the citation of Elwin Griffith's article on rescission.

   (c) To whom should you write to subscribe to the Dalhousie Law Journal?

B. Using the Current Law Index, volume 1, answer the following:

1. Give the citation of Marianne M. Jennings' article in the Whittier Law Review. At what university does she teach?

2. Locate a discussion of U.C.C 2-209.

3. Locate a discussion of Earhart v. William Low Co., 25 Cal.3d 503, 158 Cal Rptr. 887, 600 P.2d 1344 (1979).

Theme Problem III:

A. Using the Index to Legal Periodicals, answer the following:

1. Locate a 1938 discussion of Erie v. Thompkins in the Texas Law Review.

2. Locate the text of a 1945 address wherein Karl Llewellyn discusses the methodology of appellate courts.

3. Using Cumulation 17, answer the following:

   (a) Locate an article applying the concept of primary federal jurisdiction to the Securities Exchange Act.

   (b) Cite a review of Wright & Miller's Federal Practice and Procedure.

   (c) What law school produces the Southwestern Law Journal?

B. Using Current Law Index, volume 1, answer the following:

1. Locate a discussion of Fed. R. Civ. P. 3. Who wrote it?

2. Locate an article discussing choice of law in the context of personal jurisdiction.

Theme Problem IV:

A. Find a case note on Brown v. Board of Education (1954) that appeared in the Yale Law Journal shortly after the opinion was handed down.

B. Locate that case note and answer the following:

   1. Is this piece of work signed?

   2. Which footnote discusses antitrust suits prosecuted by the government?

   3. What is the citation to the article by Borinski that is noted by the author?

C. Using the 1970-1973 (Cum. 16) Index to Legal Periodicals, answer the following:

   1. Under what headings should one search for cases or articles on desegregation of schools?

   2. Give the citation for an article by Preyer on what should be done beyond desegregation.

D. Locate the article cited in (4) and answer the following:

   1. Which footnote refers to a series of decisions on methods of school financing?

   2. Who was editor-in-chief of this volume?

   3. Is Mr. Preyer a professor?

E. Using the 1970-1973 (Cum. 16) Index to Legal Periodicals, answer the following:

   1. Cite a review of Douglas A. Kahn's Basic Corporate Taxation.

   2. Give citations for all articles written by Alan Bible.

   3. What does U.ILL.L.F. stand for?

   4. Is the Women Lawyer's Journal indexed?

Theme Problem V:

A. Give the citation for a case note on the Roe v. Wade (1973) decision that appeared in the Harvard Law Review.

B. Locate that case note and answer the following:

1. What is special about this issue?

2. Is this note student authored?

3. What is the title and citation of the article by Profs. Heymann and Barzelay mentioned in the footnotes?

C. Find the article cited in B.3 and answer the following:

1. What is the citation of the article cited in footnote 84?

2. What book is reviewed by James L. Oakes in this volume?

D. Using the Index to Legal Periodicals, answer the following:

1. Under what topic could you search under to find other articles on Roe?

2. B.M. Littlewood authored an article on this topic in March, 1975. Give its title and citation.

3. Cite two articles written by Joseph Witherspoon on the subject before September 1976.

E. Using the 1973-1976 (Cum. 17) volume of the Index to Legal Periodicals, answer the following:

1. Law.Am. is the abbreviation for what journal?

2. What was the mailing address of the Texas Law Review?

3. What is "SS" an abbreviation for?

4. Who authored a review in the Yale Law Journal of Robert Nozick's Anarchy, State and Utopia?

5. Is Learning and the Law indexed?

Theme Problem VI:

A. Give the citation to a case note on Gideon v. Wainwright (1964) that was published in the Kentucky Law Journal.

B. Locate that case note and using it, answer the following:

1. Is it student authored?

2. At the time of writing, how many states would appoint counsel in any felony case?

3. What is the citation of the article by Prof. Kamisar noted by the author?

C. Locate the article cited in question B.3 and answer the following:

1. How many footnotes are there?

2. Of what do the two appendices consist?

3. What book is reviewed in this volume by Prof. Ernest J. Brown?

D. Using the Index to Legal Periodicals, answer the following:

1. Under what Index to Legal Periodicals topics might you search to find articles on the topics covered in Gideon?

2. J.E. Norton authored an aritcle on Gideon in 1966. Give the citation.

E. Using the 1964-1967 (Cum. 14) volume of the Index to Legal Periodicals, answer the following:

1. Give the citation of a review of Patterson's Law in a Scientific Age.

2. Give the citations of all articles by Warren G. Sullivan.

3. Give the address of the Rutgers Law Review.

4. What does F. L. Rev mean?

5. Is the Journal of the American Trial Lawyers Assoc. indexed?

Chapter 18

TREATISES, RESTATEMENTS, MODEL CODES, AND UNIFORM LAWS

ASSIGNMENT 1
USE OF TORTS TREATISES

Method:

(1) Answer each problem with either a "Yes" or "No" according to the majority view.

(2) Using the source indicated in parentheses find the answers to the following questions. Properly cite the applicable section number and page. For example:

F. Harper & F. James, Jr., The Law of Torts sec. ___, at ___ (1956).

Prosser and Keeton on the Law of Torts sec. ___, at ___ (5th ed. 1984).

(3) Properly cite the cases or other materials as requested.

Questions:

1. Can loud noises constitute an actionable private nuisance? Cite a law review article on point cited in a footnote. (Prosser and Keeton)

2. May a woman bring an action in battery for being kissed without her consent? Cite a Missouri case on point. (Harper & James)

3. Does a person have a right to dynamite a house if this is necessary to stop the spread of a conflagration that threatens a town? Cite a California case on point. (Prosser and Keeton)

4. May a child maintain an action for the consequences of prenatal injuries? Cite a 1951 New York case on point. (Harper & James)

5. Is it necessary for a person to be physically restrained in order to bring an action for false imprisonment? Cite a 1924 Maryland case on point. (Prosser and Keeton)

6. If, without negligence, a person cuts down a tree on his own land and it falls on adjoining land, does the adjoining landowner have a cause of action? Cite an 1841 North Carolina case on point. (Prosser and Keeton)

7. May words which would be defamatory to an individual be likewise defamatory when directed against a partnership? Cite a Connecticut case on point. (Harper & James)

8. Does an experienced baseball spectator have a cause of action if he is injured by a batted ball while attending a baseball game? Cite a Washington case on point. (Harper & James)

9. Is "hostile intent" the gist of an action of battery? (Prosser and Keeton)

10. May damages be awarded for mental distress suffered at the hands of a practical joker? Cite an English case on point. (Harper & James)

11. May an insane person be held liable for wrongful death? Cite a 1887 case on point. (Prosser and Keeton)

12. May a father be held liable for the damage caused by his son's negligent driving of the family car? Cite a 1915 Georgia case on point. (Harper & James)

13. May a funeral parlor located in a residential community be considered a private nuisance? Cite a Michigan case holding that a nuisance exists. (Prosser and Keeton)

14. Can a defendant who engages in blasting activities within city limits be held strictly liable for concussion damages? Cite a 1963 Indiana case on point. (Prosser and Keeton)

15. Should a minor engaged in driving an automobile be held to the same standard of care as an adult? Cite a 1981 Minnesota case on point. (Prosser and Keeton).

16. Does the erroneous dissemination of a credit rating by a credit rating bureau, falsely alleging an account was overdue, constitute defamation? Cite a 1918 Florida case on point. (Harper & James)

17. Are police and firemen deemed invitees rather than licensees when summoned to a public place in the line of duty? Cite a 1974 Nebraska case on point relating to police. (Prosser and Keeton)

18. Is an insane person held to the same standard of conduct as that required of a sane person? Cite a 1905 law review article on point. (Prosser and Keeton)

19. Does a municipality enjoy the same sovereign immunity as the state? Cite the original 1788 case on point. (Harper & James)

20. Is an ordinary man free to act in reliance upon the opinion of an expert jeweler as to the value of a diamond? Cite a 1862 Michigan case on point. (Prosser and Keeton)

21. Will a court enjoin a church from ringing its church bell because a sick person in the area considers the noise a nuisance? Cite a Massachusetts case on point. (Harper & James)

22. Does the physician's standard of conduct differ from that of the reasonable man in general? Cite a 1959 law review article. (Prosser and Keeton)

23. In a civil action for damages against more than one person, are all of the defendants who acted in concert equally liable? Cite a 1920 Minnesota case on point. (Prosser and Keeton)

24. Is owner of a known vicious watchdog liable for damages if the dog attacks a trespasser who has not been warned of the dog's presence? Cite a 1837 New York case on point. (Harper & James)

25. Is a credit agency, such as a mutual credit organization, liable for defamation of character of a person as a bad credit risk if made in good faith? Cite a 1959 California case on point. (Prosser and Keeton)

26. Has there been a false arrest where a woman's purse was taken from her as security so that she would not leave a store? Cite a 1946 Kentucky case on point. (Prosser and Keeton)

27. Is the owner of a leopard responsible for injury it may cause? Cite a 1919 California case on point. (Harper & James)

28. Is it considered trespass to mine under adjoining land? Cite a 1863 California case on point. (Harper & James)

29. Does an automobile manufacturer give an implied warranty as to the safety of his product? Cite the leading 1960 case and the classic periodical article which traced subsequent development of the principle. (Prosser and Keeton)

30. Is snatching a newspaper out of another person's hand sufficient to satisfy the elements of battery? Cite an Illinois case on point. (Harper & James)

31. If the driver of an automobile has a heart attack while driving, is he liable for injury inflicted in an ensuing accident? Cite a 1963 law review article on point. (Prosser and Keeton)

32. Is a person in charge of a restaurant privileged to retain for thirty minutes a customer he suspects may not have paid his bill? Cite an 1873 Massachusetts case on point. (Harper & James)

33. Is a child liable for torts such as slander or defamation of another? Cite a 1898 Missouri case on point. (Harper & James)

ASSIGNMENT 2
USE OF CONTRACTS TREATISES

Method:

   (1) Answer each problem with either a "Yes" or "No" according to the majority view.

   (2) Using the source indicated in the parentheses, find the answers to the following questions. Properly cite the applicable section number and page. For example:

      Corbin on Contracts sec. ___, at ___ (1950).

      S. Williston, A Treatise on the Law of Contracts sec. ___, at ___ (3d ed. 1957).

   (3) Properly cite the cases or other materials as requested in the problems.

Questions:

1. May the winner of a bet judicially recover money from a wager which was won where the money was not paid? Cite a Louisiana case on point. (Corbin or Williston)

2. May a department store advertise well-known brands of radios at reduced prices without being held to have made an offer? Cite a New York case on point. (Corbin)

3. May a person claim a reward for the return of lost property if he had no prior knowledge of the existence of such reward? Cite a District of Columbia case on point. (Corbin or Williston)

4. Does a marriage constitute sufficient consideration to support a contractual promise? Cite an Ohio case on point. (Corbin)

5. Does failure of an instalment purchaser to pay for an instalment excuse the seller from delivering later instalments? Cite a 1925 federal case on point. (Corbin)

6. Must a memorandum in writing be written in ink to satisfy the statute? Cite a New York case on point. (Corbin)

7. Does a statement on the face on an instrument that it has been executed in pursuance of a specified contract satisfy the Negotiable Instruments Law? Cite a North Carolina case on point. (Corbin)

8. May one make a gift of money by giving another his savings account passbook? Cite a Michigan case on point. (Williston)

9. Is a barred action for a tort revived by a new promise to pay? Cite a Washington case on point. (Corbin)

10. Is a credit card holder responsible for purchases made by a thief who uses such credit card? Cite an Oregon case on point. (Williston)

11. If a farmer buys a specific type of seed warranted to grow a certain crop, and the seed grows another crop, is that farmer entitled to the full value of the warranted crop? Cite a leading New York case. (Corbin)

12. Will the courts enforce the promise of a widow to pay the debts of her deceased husband? Cite a North Carolina case on point. (Corbin)

13. May a contract be accepted by the act of dropping a letter of acceptance into a mail box? Cite an Iowa case on point. (Corbin)

14. Does the fall of the hammer at an auction constitute the acceptance of a contract? Cite an Illinois case on point. (Williston)

15. If a document has been properly sealed and delivered, will it also require a signature in order to be valid? Cite an Arkansas case on point. (Williston)

16. May the renting of the upper story apartment unit to a college fraternity be sufficient reason for the tenant below to claim constructive eviction? Cite a 1926 Wisconsin case on point. (Corbin)

17. Can the estate of a mural painter be sued for damages because the painter died and could not fulfill the contract himself? Cite a 1930 New York case on point. (Corbin)

18. Will a court enforce an indefinite contract which provided one party a division of the profits "upon a very liberal basis?" Cite a 1907 Pennsylvania case on point. (Corbin)

19. Can an auction seller contract with a "puffer" to make false bids on items in order to drive up the price? Cite a 1926 Kentucky case on point. (Corbin)

20. Must the subject of a portrait pay an artist for painting a portrait whereby payment was to occur only if the painting satisfied the artistic taste and personal fancy of the subject? Cite a 1878 Michigan case on point. (Corbin)

21. Can an airline or other common carrier bargain to render service for a price and at the same time provide for exemption from liability for its negligence? Cite a 1944 federal case on point. (Corbin)

22. Does dishonesty (e.g., accepting gifts from seller for buying from him) on the part of an employee terminate a contract of employment at the option of the employer? Cite a Missouri case on point. (Corbin)

23. Has "Bank Night" at a movie theatre ever been held to be an illegal lottery? Cite a Georgia case on point. (Corbin)

24. Is a real estate broker entitled to receive his sales commission if he locates a buyer at the agreed price and the owner then refuses to make a conveyance upon the agreed terms? Cite an Alabama case on point. (Corbin)

25. Can the offer of a sizable reward by display of a poster be revoked by simply removing the poster? Cite an Iowa case on point. (Corbin)

26. Can a company refuse to honor a "contract" made by one of its salesmen when every salesman's order pad has printed on it: "All contracts and orders are subject to the approval of the home office," though this statement has not been specifically called to the attention of the buyer? Cite a 1915 New York case on point.a school board contract with a teacher to employ her for a specified limited period of time on condition that she shall remain unmarried during such period? Cite an Ohio case on point. (Corbin)

28. Can a murderer recover on an insurance policy if he is named as the beneficiary? Cite a Supreme Court case on point. (Williston)

29. Is a drunkard's contract voidable? Cite a North Dakota case on point. (Williston)

30. Can a minor who has by bond or contract agreed to support his bastard child avoid his transaction? Cite an Indiana case on point. (Williston)

ASSIGNMENT 3
USE OF A.L.I. RESTATEMENTS

Method:

    (1) Answer each problem with either a "Yes" or "No".

    (2) Referring to either <u>Restatement (Second) of Contracts</u> (1979) or <u>Restatement (Second) of Torts</u> (first 2 vols.) (1964), give the applicable section number of the Restatement volume where the answer was found.

    (3) Cite cases on point under applicable section headings in the following volumes:

        <u>Restatement in the Courts</u>, 1970-71 Supplement, 1972-73 Supplement, or 1984-85 Supplement.

        <u>Restatement (Second) of Torts</u> (Appendix 1964).

Questions:

1. Must a donee beneficiary be identified at the time a contract promise is made in order to have rights under that contract? Cite a 1983 case on point.

2. If one of the remedies for breach of contract is not available to the plaintiff and he in good faith has sought that remedy, will this be a bar to a suit for a different remedy? Cite a 1982 case on point.

3. In a breach of contract action, may damages be awarded for mental suffering in the absence of wanton or reckless action which did not cause bodily harm? Cite a 1982 New York case on point.

4. Is an agreement entered into under coercion voidable? Cite a 1982 case on point.

5. Does a reply to an offer which purports to accept it but adds qualifications constitute an acceptance? Cite a 1982 Nebraska case on point.

6. Is an antenuptial agreement which does not unreasonably encourage divorce void as against public policy? Cite a 1981 Massachusetts case on point.

7. Is a former employee entitled to receive punitive damages from his former employer for breach of an employment contract? Cite a 1983 Virginia case on point.

8. Does bad faith behavior amount to a repudiation of a contract if it does not constitute a failure to provide the other party with goods or services called for in the contract? Cite a 1982 case on point.

9. Will contributory negligence bar recovery in a suit based upon an intentionally inflicted tort? Cite a 1963 Alaska case on point.

10. Can a threat made merely in words constitute an assault? Cite a 1960 Pennsylvania case on point.

11. Is a soldier liable civilly for injury to another which results from following the orders of a superior officer? Cite a 1941 Massachusetts case on point.

12. Will the courts recognize a citizen arrest without a warrant where the citizen-passerby is a witness to the crime which has been committed? Cite a Pennsylvania caseon point.

13. Does the granting of permission by a home owner to a canvasser to enter a home make such canvasser an invitee as opposed to a licensee? Cite a 1919 Washington case on point.

14. Does the so-called "reasonable man" standard apply equally to children? Cite a 1934 Connecticut case on point.

15. Is an actor liable for negligent conduct which results in emotional disturbance alone, without bodily harm or other compensable damage? Cite the first A.L.R. annotation listed under this section as a cross reference.

16. May one use the same means of self-defense to protect himself against confinement as he may use to protect himself against bodily harm? Cite the Digest System Key Number under this section.

17. Is a common carrier or other public utility liable for gross insults to patrons by its employees? Cite a 1970 California case on point.

18. Was the employer of a contractor who began excavation for construction of a building on a vacant lot responsible for cracks appearing in the wall of a building already on an adjacent lot by virtue of the withdrawal of "lateral support" for such an older building? Cite a 1971 Iowa case on point.

19. Is a person or business liable for "conversion" of a chattel if he alters its physical condition or changes its identity? Cite a 1969 New Hampshire case on point.

20. Does the negligence of a husband or wife bar the other from recovery for his or her physical harm? Cite a 1972 New Hampshire case on point.

21. Does the parking of an automobile illegally and too close to another parked auto permit the owner of the second car to "abate the private nuisance" of the first by repeatedly bumping into the offending auto? Cite a 1951 D.C. case on point.

22. Is a person civilly liable who, by his extreme and outrageous conduct, causes severe emotional distress, as by hiding and burying a pedestrian's body after hitting him with an automobile? Cite a 1970 Pennsylvania case on point.

23. Unless a contrary intention is manifested, do bids at an auction embody the terms made known by advertisements or other publications of which bidders are or should be aware? Cite a 1981 Illinois case on point.

24. Is a person liable to another for battery if his contact is not intended to cause an offensive contact? Cite a 1972 Missouri case on point.

25. Is a person who instigates the unlawful confinement of another liable to him for false imprisonment? Cite a 1969 case on point.

ASSIGNMENT 4
DRILL PROBLEMS

Drill Problem I:

A. Using J. White & R. Summers, Handbook of the Law Under the Uniform Commercial Code (2d ed. 1980), answer the following, properly citing the supporting section and/or case where applicable.

   1. Once liability is established, what kinds of damages may plaintiff recover from a warehouseman for damaged goods?

   2. Where is the case of Segall v. Finlay discussed?

B. Using J. Calamari & J. Perillo, The Law of Contracts (2d ed. 1977), answer the following, citing the supporting section and/or case where applicable.

   1. Does a sealed contract require consideration?

   2. Where can one find a discussion of Patton v. Arney?

C. Using Prosser and Keeton on The Law of Torts (5th ed. 1984), answer the following, citing a supporting section or page where appropriate.

   1. Can a child recover for damages due to an injury caused to the mother when pregnant?

   2. Have lunatics generally been held liable for their torts?

Drill Problem II:

A. Using J. White & R. Summers, Handbook of the Law Under the Uniform Commercial Code (2d ed. 1980), answer the following, citing the supporting section and/or case where applicable.

   1. What state was the first to enact the U.C.C. and when did it do it?

   2. Where can one find a definition of the term "trade usage"?

B. Using J. Calamari & J. Perillo, The Law of Contracts (2d ed. 1977), answer the following, citing the supporting section and/or case where applicable:

   1. What is the modern definition of duress?

2. Cite a case where an unlicensed milk dealer was allowed to recover despite the fact the services rendered were illegal.

C. Using Prosser and Keeton on The Law of Torts (5th ed. 1984), answer the following, citing a supporting section or page where appropriate.

1. Does an action lie against a dealer who describes what turns out to be a lemon as a "dandy," a "bearcat" and a "sweet job"? Cite a 1932 Texas case.

2. Where can one find discussion of Clary v. Hale?

3. Does the consent of the plaintiff constitute an absolute privilege to speak without fear of being sued for defamation?

Drill Problem III:

A. Using J. White & R. Summers, Handbook of the Law Under the Uniform Commercial Code (2d ed. 1980), answer the following, citing the supporting section and/or case where applicable.

1. On what page will you find discussion of U.C.C. 2-206(1)?

2. Where can one find a definition of the term "floating lien"?

B. Using J. Calamari & J. Perillo, The Law of Contracts (2d ed. 1977), answer the following, citing the supporting section and/or case where applicable:

1. Will a plaintiff be granted equitable relief if he comes to court with "unclean" hands?

2. Where can one find mention of Continental Illinois Bank & Trust Co. v. Clement?

C. Using Prosser and Keeton on The Law of Torts (5th ed. 1984), answer the following, citing a supporting section or page where appropriate.

1. At common law could the wife sue for interference with domestic relations?

2. When did the special rule as to injuries to children who are hurt while trespassing first appear in the United States?

3. Does revenge qualify as a defense to intentional assault?

Drill Problem IV:

A. Using the Restatement (Second) of Agency (1957), answer the following.

1. Can an agent authorized to make a contract also be a servant?

2. Locate an article in the Yale Law Journal discussing the concept embodied in sec. 194. Properly cite the article.

3. Cite a 1975 case discussing section 35 of the Restatement of Agency.

B. Using the Model Code of Evidence, answer the following. Put your answer in proper cite form.

1. Can a parishioner prevent her priest from testifying to facts she told him in the confessional? Cite the rule.

2. Where can you find a discussion by Mason Ladd of the Model Code of Evidence?

3. Properly cite a case approving the practice of taking fingerprints.

C. Using Uniform Laws Annotated, locate the Uniform Arbitration Act. Use the latter to answer the following questions. Put your answers in proper cite form.

1. As of December 31, 1978, the date of publication of the bound volume, how many jurisdictions had adopted the Act?

2. Do arbitrators have the power to require the attendance of witnesses?

3. Cite a 1973 Massachusetts case discussing the authority of an arbitrator to award counsel fees absent any provision for it in the agreement or enabling statute.

Drill Problem V:

A. Using the Restatement (Second) of Trusts (1957), answer the following. Put your answers in proper cite form.

1. Can a trust to pay the salary of a rabbi be deemed charitable?

2. Give citations to treatises discussing sec. 214.

3. Cite a 1966 case discussing sec. 294.

B.   Using the American Law Institute's Model Penal Code and Commentaries, Part II (3v.), answer the following. Put your answers in proper cite form.

1. Cite to the comment on the sale of a human corpse.

2. Has one committed a crime who deceived another into committing suicide?

3. What is the maximum fine in Wisconsin for fraudulently making an item seem rarer than it is? Cite the section of the Model Penal Code in which you locate the answer.

C.   Using Uniform Laws Annotated, locate the Uniform Residential Landlord and Tenant Act. The jurisdiction chart appears before the act itself.

1. As of 1978, how many jurisdictions had adopted the Act?

2. Can a landlord file a suit seeking distraint for rent as a remedy against a tenant?

3. Cite a 1976 case discussing interest on security deposits.

Drill Problem VI

A.   Using the Restatement (Second) of Conflict of Laws (1969), answer the following, giving citations when needed.

1. What state's law will usually govern whether a particular act is the cause of an injury?

2. Cite an article by Currie discussing sec. 358.

3. Cite a 1970 case discussing sec. 37.

B.   Using the Model Business Corporations Act Annotated (2d ed. 1971), answer the following, giving citations when needed.

1. Cite a case holding that the vice president of a corporation has authority to settle a lawsuit.

2. Cite an article by Weis discussing sec. 15.

3. Cite a 1974 Virginia case discussing sec. 36.

C. Using the Uniform Anatomical Gift Act, answer the following, giving citations when needed.

1. When did your jurisdiction adopt the Act (if at all)?

2. May an unaccredited medical school be an organ donee under the Act?

3. Where is there a recommended form for a gift under the Act?

ASSIGNMENT 5
THEME PROBLEMS

Theme Problem I:

A.   Brown v. Bd. of Educ. touched many areas of the law. The school desegregation plans that were one of its products spawned a great deal of administrative law. One scholar, K. Davis, has dominated the administrative law field, publishing both a multi-volume treatise and a one volume student treatise.

   Using K. Davis, Administrative Law (6th ed. 1977) answer the following. Using the latest edition of A Uniform System of Citation, put your answers in Blue Book form.

   1.   In what section can one find discussion of a New York decision that a city is not liable to an assault victim for its failure to supply police protection on request?

   2.   Where can one find a discussion of discretionary justice?

   3.   Where can one find the text of the Administrative Procedure Act?

B.   Is there a Restatement of Administrative Law?

Theme Problem II:

A.   Roe v. Wade dealt with constitutional issues of privacy. Using L. Tribe, American Constitutional Law (1978), answer the following. Put your answers in Blue Book form.

   1.   List the first three places that Roe v. Wade is discussed.

   2.   When was executive privilege first asserted?

   3.   On what date was the Equal Rights Amendment passed by Congress? Where does the text of the amendment appear?

B.   Using J. Nowak, R. Rotunda & J. Young, Constitutional Law (2d ed. 1983), answer the folllowing, putting your answer in Blue Book form.

   1.   Give the first three places that Roe v. Wade is discussed.

   2.   May a state eliminate the teaching of certain ideas because they conflict with certain religious beliefs?

3. Is a partnership interest tangible or intangible property for the purpose of state taxation?

4. What Edmund Wilson novel was adjudged obscene?

C. Is there a Restatement on Constitutional Law?

D. How could one find other texts on Constitutional Law?

Theme Problem III:

A. The <u>Gideon</u> case dealt with constitutional rights to representation in a criminal trial. The criminal area has always had a varied literature. Answer the following in proper Blue Book form.

1. Give the full citation of the 1978 edition of <u>Wharton's Criminal</u> Law.

2. Give the full citation for the Perkins & Boyce hornbook on criminal law.

3. Give the full citation for LaFave & Scott.

B. Using LaFave & Scott, answer the following and cite a relevant section if applicable:

1. When is one justified in using deadly force in self-defense?

2. How was the common law crime of suicide punished in England?

3. How did Blackstone define "Mayhem"?

4. Where is the case of <u>Letner v. State</u> discussed?

C. Using Perkins & Boyce, answer the following and give the citation of the page:

1. Does the fact that a burglar was drunk at the time of entering negate his/her intent?

2. Was bigamy a common law crime in England?

3. On what page is <u>Stover v. State</u> discussed?

D. What is the <u>Model Penal Code</u> (1962) sec. 223.3 concerned with?

Theme Problem IV:

A. Use of a treatise: F. Harper & F. James, Jr., <u>The Law of Torts</u> (1956).

   1. Locate the primary discussion of <u>Palsgraf</u> in this treatise.

   2. Locate and properly cite a case in the same section holding it was not negligent to give a paddle to a 13-year-old boy who threw it at a companion.

   3. What 1921 English case do the authors cite as establishing the British test of foreseeability?

   4. Was this case later disapproved, according to the authors?

B. Use of the Restatements:

   1. What section of the <u>Restatement (Second) of Torts</u> (1969) states who bears the burden of proving legal cause?

   2. Using this section, if a person successively stores an object in three warehouses and then notices the object is damaged, who has the burden of proving who damaged the item?

   3. What 1940 California case forms the basis for your answer in B.2?

   4. Locate a 1968 Ohio case referring to the section located in B.1.

Theme Problem V:

A. Use of a treatise: S. Williston, <u>A Treatise on the Law of Contracts</u> (3d ed. 1957).

   1. Locate the first reference to <u>Sherwood v. Walker</u>.

   2. In a later reference to <u>Sherwood</u>, the author mentions a case approving it. Give the proper citatation of the second case.

   3. Where can you find a form for an allegation in a complaint seeking rescission based on mutual mistake? Looking at the form, where can you find a related discussion?

   4. Can one party ratify a contract based on mututal mistake of material fact?

B. Use of the Restatements.

   1. What section of the Restatement (Second) of Contracts (1979) reflects Sherwood?

   2. If both the buyer and seller of land believe valuable timber still exists on the land, but the timber has been destroyed by fire, can the buyer avoid the contract? Cite to where you find the answer.

   3. On what section of the first Restatement of Contracts is the section you located in B.1 based?

   4. Locate a 1961 Oregon case referring to the section you located in B.3. Properly cite it.

Theme Problem VI:

A. Use of a treatise: J. Moore, Moore's Federal Practice (2d ed. 1948).

   1. Locate the discussion of Erie's overruling of Swift v. Tyson.

   2. Using this section, give the citation of a 1940 article in the Missouri Law Review discussing Erie.

   3. Does the author of the treatise believe Erie requires conformity by federal courts to state law in matters of forum non conveniens?

   4. Locate a case from the Southern District of New York discussing the applicability of Erie to the doctrine of forum non conveniens.

B. Use of the Restatements: Restatement (Second) of Conflict of Laws (1969).

   1. Does a court have the power to issue an injunction against performing an activity in another state? Cite to the section number.

   2. On which sections of the original restatement is this based?

   3. Using the sections located in B.2, locate an Arizona case holding an Arizona court had no jurisdiction over a Mexican executor in a suit for specific performance to convey a lead mine.

4. Using the section located in B.1, locate allied sections of another Restatement.

5. Section 37 of the Second Restatement deals with a subject similar to that discussed in B.1. Locate a 1975 Hawaii case discussing it.

Chapter 20

RESEARCH IN INTERNATIONAL LAW

ASSIGNMENT 1A
PRE-1950 UNITED STATES TREATIES AND
INTERNATIONAL AGREEMENTS

Sources: Treaties in Force, 1984;

Treaties and Other International Agreements of the United States of America, 1776-1949, by Charles E. Bevans;

United State Treaties and Other International Agreements Cumulative Index, 1776-1949, compiled by Igor I. Kavass and Mark A. Michael; and

Shepard's United States Citations, Statute Edition, for part (e) of each question.

Method:

Give the following for each treaty or international agreement listed below:

(1) Its citation in Statutes at Large and concurrent citation in Bevans' Treaties (if any), for example, 43 Stat. 1621, 6 Bevans 1033;

(2) Its date or dates of signature, opening for signature, exchange of notes, etc. (but not the dates of ratification, proclamation, or entry into force), for example, Nov. 10, 1922; and

(3) Its E.A.S., T.S., or T.I.A.S. number, for example, T.S. No. 668.

(4) Is it in force? If so, give the date of its entry into force. Also give year and page reference to the 1983 edition of Treaties in Force containing this information, for example, April 27, 1923, 1984 T.I.F. 36.

(5) Its subsequent judicial, legislative, or diplomatic developments (if any), as shown in <u>Shepard's United States Citations, Statute Edition 1968, 1968-74, 1974-79, 1979-83</u>. Copy as appearing in Shepard's, for example, 290US294, 78LE324, 54SC105.

The easiest way to determine the answer to questions a,b, c, and d is to first check <u>Treaties in Force</u>. If you do not find the answer in <u>Treaties in Force</u>, check the index to the Bevans' work or the Kavass, Michael Index.

<u>Treaties in Force</u>, though not the best index ever produced, is easy to use. It has two main divisions: Part 1 for bilateral treaties and agreements between the United States and other countries or political entities and Part 2 for multilateral treaties and agreements. Part 1 is arranged alphabetically by country, with subject entries under each country. Territories of a country are placed at the end of that country. Part 2 is arranged alphabetically by subject.

The weakness of <u>Treaties in Force</u> is the choice and number of subject headings and the inadequate use of cross references. However, once you determine if the treaty or agreement is bilateral or multilateral, you can usually find the answer. If bilateral and you know the country, you can quickly scan the appropriate or related subject headings under the country in Part 1 and determine whether the treaty or agreement is in force. If the treaty or agreement is multilateral, you can determine whether it is in force by scanning the appropriate correlated subject headings in part 2.

If the treaty or agreement is not listed in <u>Treaties in Force</u>, the quickest way to find it is to search the index volume to Bevans' work. This will lead you directly to the answer. You can also search the Kavass, Michael Cumulative Index. The advantage of the former is that it leads you directly to the text in the appropriate Bevans' volume.

You can answer question (e) by Shepardizing the citation in <u>Shepard's United States Citations--Statute Edition 1968, 1968-74, 1974-79, 1979-83</u>.

Questions:

1. Commerce and Navigation treaty with Turkey

2. Extradition Treaty with Canada, 1925 (Narcotic Violations)

3. Treaty of Arbitration with Estonia, 1930

4. Convention with Mexico for rectification of the Rio Grande, 1933

5. Air transport agreement with Austria, 1947

6. Agreement with Canada to raise the level of Lake St. Francis

7. Extradition Treaty with Bavaria, 1853

8. Parcel post agreement with Bahamas, 1936

9. Convention with Great Britian defining rights of nationals in Togoland

10. Treaty establishing friendly relations with Hungary, 1921

11. Multilateral treaty for Inter-American arbitration with fifteen Latin American countries

12. Agreement with Norway relating to customs treatment of importations for consular offices

13. Agreement with Sweden for exemption of pleasure yachts from navigation dues

14. Provisional agreement about commerce with Egypt

15. Arrangement with Brazil for exemption of shipping profits from double income taxation

16. Treaty of arbitration with Sweden

17. Treaty of amity and commerce with Japan, 1858

18. Treaty of amity, commerce, and navigation with Congo, 1891

19. Treaty about traveling salesmen with Venezuela

20. Extradition treaty with Costa Rica

21. Treaty for prevention of smuggling of intoxicating liquors with Denmark

22. Treaty of commerce with Ethiopia, 1914

23. Fuel and vegetable oil agreement with Argentina

24. Relief assistance to Austria, 1947

25. Exchange of official publications with Brazil

26. Agreement relative to postal money orders in Postal Union of the Americas and Spain, 1936

27. Air transport services agreement with Brazil, 1946
28. Cooperative education program with Dominican Republic
29. Agricultural experiment station agreement with Ecuador, 1942
30. Military obligations agreement with Finland
31. Customs privileges for institutions in Syria and Lebanon with France
32. Treaty establishing friendly relations with Germany
33. Agreement for "Haitinization" with Haiti
34. Educational exchange program with Iran
35. Rights of U.S. in Iraq
36. Proclamation of copyright extension with Australia, 1949
37. Agreement for maritime claims and litigation with France
38. Ferrous scrap disposition agreement with Great Britain, 1948
39. Agreement with Great Britain concerning rights and preservation of fur seal fisheries in Bering Sea, 1891
40. Reciprocal military service agreement with Italy, 1918
41. Erection of American battle monuments in Belgium, 1929
42. Treaty of peace, friendship, commerce, and navigation with Bolivia
43. Motion picture films agreement with Czechoslovakia, 1938
44. Memorandum of understanding regarding claims with Luxemburg
45. Jurisdiction over prizes with New Zealand
46. Protocol with respect to rights to hold real estate in Ottoman Empire
47. Treaty of immigration with China, 1880

ASSIGNMENT 1B
PRE-1950 UNITED STATES TREATIES AND
INTERNATIONAL AGREEMENTS

Source: Treaties in Force, 1984; and

Treaties and Other International Agreements of the United States of America, 1776-1949, by Charles E. Bevans.

Method:

Give the following for each treaty or international agreement listed below:

(1) Its citation in Statutes at Large and concurrent citation in Bevans' Treaties (if any) for example, 43 Stat. 1621, 6 Bevans 1033;

(2) Its date or dates of signature, opening for signature, exchange of notes, etc. (but not the dates of ratification, proclamation, or entry into force), for example, Nov. 10, 1922.

(3) Is it in force? If so, give the date or its entry into force. Also give year and page reference to the 1983 edition of Treaties in Force containing this information, for example, April 27, 1923. 1984 T.I.F. 36.

(4) Its E.A.S., T.S., or T.I.A.S. number, for example, T.S. No. 668.

The easiest way to determine the answers to these questions is to first check Treaties in Force. If you do not find the answer in Treaties in Force, check the index to the Bevans' work.

Treaties in Force, though not the best index ever produced, is easy to use. It has two main divisions: Part 1 for bilateral treaties and agreements between the United States and other countries or political entities and Part 2 for multilateral treaties and agreements. Part 1 is arranged alphabetically by country, with subject entries under each country. Territories of a country are placed at the end of that country. Part 2 is arranged alphabetically by subject.

The weakness of Treaties in Force is the choice and number of subject headings and the inadequate use of cross references. However, once you determine if the treaty or agreement is bilateral or multilateral you can usually find the answer. If bilateral and you know the country, you can quickly scan the appropriate or related subject headings under the country in Part 1 and determine whether the treaty or agreement is in force. If the treaty or agreement is multilateral, you can determine whether it is in force by scanning the appropriate or related subject headings in Part 2.

If the treaty or agreement is not listed in <u>Treaties in Force</u>, the quickest way to find it is to search the index volume to Bevans' work. This will lead you directly to the answer.

Questions:

1. Exchange of notes concerning tariff treatment of Norwegian sardines

2. Treaty of amity and commerce with Muscat

3. Protocol relating to military obligations of persons with dual citizenship

4. Rights in Togoland under French Mandate

5. Convention relating to liquor traffic in Africa

6. Multilateral agreement on courts in the International Settlement of Shanghai, 1930

7. Treaty providing for the renunciation of war

8. The Pan American Sanitary Code

9. Agreement with Mexico regarding plantation rubber investigations

10. Extradition treaty with Ceylon (Sri Lanka)

11. Declaration with the Russian Empire governing sizes of ships

12. Polish debt funding agreement

13. Treaty of friendship with Austria

14. Convention concerning requirements for professional capacities for ship masters

15. Extradition treaty with Guyana

ASSIGNMENT 2A
POST-1950 UNITED STATES TREATIES AND INTERNATIONAL AGREEMENTS.

Sources: Treaties in Force, 1984;

Cumulative Index to United States Treaties and Other International Agreements, 1950-1970, compiled by Igor I. Kavass and Adolf Sprudzs; and

Shepard's United States Citations, Statute Edition, for part (e) of each question.

Method:

Give the following for each treaty or international agreement listed below:

(1) Its citation in United States Treaties and Other International Agreements, for example, 12 U.S.T. 908;

(2) Its date or dates of signature, opening for signature, exchange of notes, etc. (but not the dates of ratifiction, proclamation, or entry into force), for example, Oct. 1, 1951; and

(3) Its T.I.A.S. number, for example, T.I.A.S. No. 4797.

(4) Is it in force? If so, the date of its entry into force. Also give year and page references to the 1983 edition of Treaties in Force containing this information, for example, July 30, 1961, 1984 T.I.F. 40.

(5) Its subsequent judicial, legislative, or diplomatic developments (if any), as shown in Shepard's United States Citations, Statute Edition 1968, 1968-74, 1974-79, 1979-83. Copy as appearing in Shepard's, for example, 297FS349.

The easiest way to determine the answer to questions (a), (b), (c), and (d) is to first check Treaties in Force. (See the explanation for the use of Treaties in Force under Assignment 1.) If you do not find the answer in Treaties in Force, check the appropriate volume of the Kavass and Sprudzs work. Volumes 3, Country, and 4, Subject, will, in most cases, supply the answer if Treaties in Force does not.

You can answer question (e) by Shepardizing the citation in Shepard's United States Citations--Statute Edition 1968, 1968-74, 1974-79, 1979-83.

Questions:

1. Economic cooperation agreement with France, 1950 amendment

2. Economic cooperation agreement with Italy, 1950 amendment

3. U.S. Educational Commission agreement with Korea, 1950

4. Multilateral agreement regulating the production and marketing of sugar, 1952

5. Technical cooperation agreement with Bolivia, 1951

6. Telecommunications agreement with Ceylon, 1951 (Radio Ceylon)

7. Multilateral agreement concerning the prewar external debt of the German Reich

8. Agreement with United Kingdom concerning civil airport facilities in Bermuda, 1951

9. Agreement concerning administration of income tax in Canada of U.S. Government employees in Canada

10. Multilateral General Agreement on Tariffs and Trade--third protocol of rectifications to the general agreement

11. Agreement with Korea concerning U.S. military advisory group

12. Agreement with Korea concerning mutual security assurances

13. Agreement with Thailand concerning the U.S. Educational Foundation, 1953

14. Agreement with Brazil for a military advisory mission, 1952

15. Two agreements with Mexico concerning Mexican agricultural workers, 1954

16. Agreement with Turkey for the exchange of commodities and sale of grain, 1955

17. Multilateral agreement concerning amendments to the Constitution of the United Nations Educational, Scientific, and Cultural Organization, 1954

18. Agreement with Japan concerning agricultural commodities, 1956

19. Multilateral international wheat agreement of 1956

20. Agreement with Italy concerning surplus agricultural commodities, March, 1957

21. Multilateral General Agreement on Tariffs and Trade- eighth protocol of supplementary concessions, 1957

22. Agreement with Korea concerning atomic energy cooperation for civil uses, 1958 amendment

23. Agreement with Canada governing tolls on the Saint Lawrence Seaway, 1959

24. Agreement with Italy concerning loan of vessel, 1959

25. International telecommunication convention, Malaga-Torremolinos, 1973

26. Multilateral convention of 1960 concerning postal unions of the Americas and Spain

27. Guarantee of private investments agreement with Afghanistan, 1957

28. Cultural relations agreement with Afghanistan, 1958

29. Peace Corps in Afghanistan

30. Agency for the Safety of Air Navigation in Africa and Madagascar

31. Double taxation agreement with Argentina concerning the operation of ships and aircraft

32. Agreement with Australia for cooperation concerning civil uses of atomic energy, 1956

33. Agreement concerning participation of Belgian Armed Forces in United Nations Operations in Korea

34. Mutual Defense Assistance agreement with Belgium of October 27 and December 1, 1959

35. Treaty of friendship, establishment, and navigation with Belgium, 1963

36. Peace Corps agreement with Bolivia, 1962

37. Agreement relating to oil shale study in Brazil, 1951

38. Convention for the exchange of postal money orders with the colony of British Virgin Islands

39. Convention with Canada for the preservation of the halibut fishery of the Northern Pacific Ocean, 1953

40. Agreement with Canada relating to the organization and operations of the North American Air Defense Command, 1958

41. Agreement to rescue and return astronauts, 1968

42. Agreement with the U.S.S.R. about embassy sites, 1969

43. Space coooperation with Japan, 1969

44. Consular Convention with Korea

45. Statute of the Hague Conference on Private International Law, 1951

46. Convention on the high seas

47. International convention for the safety of life at sea, 1960

48. Geneva convention relating to treatment of prisoners of war, 1949

49. The Pacific Charter, 1954

50. Convention relating to the reorganization of international courts in Tangier, 1952

ASSIGNMENT 2B
POST-1950 UNITED STATES TREATIES AND INTERNATIONAL AGREEMENTS

Sources: Treaties in Force, 1984.

Cumulative Index to United States Treaties and Other International Agreements, 1950-1980, compiled by Igor I. Ravass and Adolf Sprudzs; and

Cumulative Index to United States Treaties and Other International Agreements, 1971-1975, compiled by Igor I. Kavass and Adolf Sprudzs.

Method:

Give the following for each treaty or international agreement listed below:

(1) Its citation in United States Treaties and Other International Agreements, for example, 12 U.S.T. 908;

(2) Its date or dates of signature, opening for signature, exchange of notes, etc. (but not the dates of ratification, proclamation, or entry into force), for example, Oct. 1, 1951.

(3) Is it in force? If so, give the date of its entry into force. Also give year and page reference to the 1983 edition of Treaties in Force containing this information; for example, July 30, 1961, 1984 T.I.F. 40.

(4) Its T.I.A.S. number, for example, T.I.A.S. No. 4797.

The easiest way to determine the answer to these questions is to first check Treaties in Force. (See the explanation for the use of Treaties in Force under Assignment 1.) If you do not find the answer in Treaties in Force, check the appropriate volume of the Kavass and Sprudzs work. Volumes 3, Country, and 4, Subject, will, in most cases, supply the answer if Treaties in Force does not.

Questions:

1. Convention terminating the Nicaraguan canal route treaty of 1914

2. Agreement regarding construction of telephone lines in Malagasay Republic

3. Extradition convention with Sweden

4. Agreement regarding elementary school education for Palestinian refugees in the Middle East

5. Is Lebanon required to deposit any amount for military assistance? Give cites.

6. Agreement with Japan concerning salmon fishing

7. Is the U.S. an adherent to the "Supplementary convention on the abolition of slavery, slave trade (etc.)" Geneva, 1956? Would this specifically cover American Samoa?

8. Understanding with Saudi Arabia concerning National Guard modernization

9. Educational exchange program financing agreement with Iceland

10. Articles of agreement establishing the Asian Development Bank

11. Extradition treaty with Spain

12. U.S. technical cooperation agreement for Surinam

13. Two multilateral conventions dealing with terrorism on airplanes (Hijacking and Sabotage)

14. Australia, New Zealand, U.S. Security Treaty

15. Agreement for U.S. assistance in clearing mines from the Suez Canal

ASSIGNMENT 3A
UNITED NATIONS TREATY SERIES
(CHRONOLOGICAL INDEX)

Source: United Nations Treaty Series Cumulative Index, Nos.1-9 (covering volumes 1-650 of United Nations Treaty Series).

Method:

By using the Chronological Index, give the following for each of the treaties listed below:

(1) The U.N.T.S. number, e.g. I:7999; and

(2) The U.N.T.S. volume and page number where the text of the treaty may be found, e.g. 549 U.N.T.S. 173.

The answers to these problems are relatively easy to find. You have only to locate the date of the treaty concerned in the Chronological Index of the appropriate Cumulative Index volumes. You may have to look in several different volumes, however, to find the date of the treaty or agreement in question.

Questions:

1. Charter of the Organization of American States, April 30, 1948

2. Agreement between Italy and the Netherlands about free assistance before the courts for indigents and waiver of security costs, January 9, 1884

3. An exchange of notes between Luxemburg and the Netherlands on freedom of the air for regular international air services, April 14, 1948

4. Agreement between Hungary and Soviet Union on mutual legal assistance in matters relating to the temporary presence of Soviet forces on Hungarian territory, April 24, 1958

5. Multipartite agreement for research on the effects of radioactivity in the sea, March 8/10, 1961

6. Agreement between Austria and Soviet Union concerning settlement of the technical and commercial questions relating to navigation of the Danube, June 14, 1957

7. Loan to Norway by Canada of three frigates, December 20, 1955

8. Exchange of notes between Colombia and the United States on the service of nationals of one country in the armed forces of the other, January 27/February 12, 1944

9. Multipartite agreement of armistice with Bulgaria, October 28, 1944

10. General agreement of technical cooperation between Egypt and the United States, May 5, 1951

11. Trade agreement between India and Burma, September 29, 1951

12. Agreement for health projects in Korea, September 19, 1951

13. Commercial agreement between France and Greece, December 23, 1952

14. Air transport agreement between Luxemburg and Iceland, October 23, 1952

15. The Brussels Treaty for collaboration in economic, social, and cultural matters, March 17, 1948

16. Manila accord, July 31, 1963

17. Agreement between Canada and France on films and film production, October 11, 1963

18. Nordic mutual emergency assistance agreement, October 17, 1963

19. Agreement between Netherlands and Nigeria for the development of the Faculty of Engineering at the University of Nigeria, Nsukku, December 4, 1964

20. Trade agreement between Australia and Philippines, June 16, 1965

21. Consular convention between Finland and Soviet Union, January 24, 1966

22. Exchange of notes on the use of seamen's books as travel documents, June 15/20, 1967

23. Exchange of notes on abolition of visas between Austria and Dominican Republic, February 21, 1968

24. Treaty of friendship between Gabon and Israel, May 15, 1962

25. Monetary agreement between Switzerland and the United Kingdom, March 12, 1946

ASSIGNMENT 3B
UNITED NATIONS TREATY SERIES
(ALPHABETICAL INDEX)

Source: United Nations Treaty Series Cumulative Index, Nos.1-9
(covering volumes 1-650 of United Nations Treaty Series).

Method:

By using the Alphabetical Index, give the following for each treaty described below:

(1) The U.N.T.S. number, e.g. I:7741; and

(2) The U.N.T.S. volume and page number where the text of the treaty may be found, e.g. 533 U.N.T.S. 157.

As in the preceding set of questions, the answers to these are relatively easy to find. You have only to locate the correct heading in the Alphabetical Index of the appropriate Cumulative Index volume. The Alphabetical Index has four types of major headings: (1) Countries and Organizations, (2) Subjects, (3) General International Agreements (entered under this heading), and (4) Multipartite Instruments (entered under this heading). All four types are listed in the Alphabetical Index. Most of the answers can be found under the names of the countries in question, but you may have to search in several volumes before finding the answer.

Questions:

1. Agreement to avoid double taxation and to prevent fiscal evasion between Finland and Israel, January 21, 1965

2. Agreement to exchange information on mental patients between the Netherlands and West Germany, July 13 and 18, 1961

3. An agreement of cultural cooperation between Poland and Mongolia, December 23, 1958

4. Agreement to permit Faroese fishermen to engage in hand line fishing off the coast of Iceland and Denmark, August 1, 1961

5. A multipartite agreement to issue to war-disabled veterans an international book of vouchers for repair of prosthetic and orthopaedic appliances, December 17, 1962

6. Transfer to the USSR of part of Finland, February 3, 1947

7. War damage claims agreement between Italy and United States, March 29, 1957

8. India and Pakistan agreement about the recovery of abducted persons, May 8, 1954

9. Agreement between Italy and Australia about the graves of Italian soldiers buried in Australia, August 27, 1953

10. Agreement to protect frontier forests against fire between Argentina and Chile, December 29, 1961

11. United States-Canadian settlement by arbitration of claims relating to Gut Dam, March 25, 1965

12. Swedish-Danish agreement about Swedish fish landings in Denmark, December 5, 1967

13. Czechoslovakia Mongolian cooperation on quarantine of plants and their protection against pests, diseases, and weeds, December 9, 1966

14. Agreement between the United Kingdom and Cameroon for interest free loan towards modernizing Cameroon's telecommunication system, June 16, 1967

15. Agreement between Canada and Bolivia on exchange of messages for third parties by amateur radio stations, May 31, 1963

16. Agreement between Canada and Italy on sale of waste materials and scrap belonging to Royal Canadian Air Force, December 18, 1961

17. Supplement of September 18, 1963 to the agreement between Canada and Italy about the sale of waste materials and scrap belonging to Royal Canadian Air Force, September 18, 1963

18. Netherlands-Germany settlement of frontier questions, April 8, 1960

19. Agreement between Romania and Yugoslavia on compensation for damages caused by the construction of the Iron Gates water power and navigation system on the Danube, November 30, 1963

20. Agreement between Netherlands and Ecuador on establishment of a dairy farming training center and modernization of technique of slaughtering cattle for consumption in Ecuador, January 14, 1965

21. Agreement between the United States and Vietnam on television broadcasting in Vietnam, January 3, 1966

22. Agreement between the United Kingdom and Greece for restoration of land on which Anglo-French Crimean War Cemetery at New Phaleron is situated, December 17, 1965-January 12, 1966

23. Service of national contingent provided by Finland with United Nations Peace-Keeping Force in Cyprus, February 21, 1966

24. Agreement between the United States and Ireland for the use of counterpart of special account for a scholarship exchange program, March 16, 1957

25. Agreement between Hungary and Iraq on cooperation in radio, television, cinema, theater, and news, October 11, 1961

ASSIGNMENT 3C
GENERAL TREATIES

Sources: <u>Cumulative Index</u>. <u>United Nations Treaty Series</u>

<u>General Index</u>. <u>League of Nations Treaty Series</u>

Parry, C., <u>Consolidated Treaty Series</u>, 1969, and

Parry, C., <u>Index Guide to Treaties</u>, based on the Consolidated Treaty Series, General Chronological List 1648-1809.

Method:

By using the above indexes and, when called for, consulting the treaty itself, answer the questions below. When a cite is called for, give either the <u>United Nations</u> or <u>League of Nations Treaty Series</u> volume and page number or the volume and page of treaty given in the <u>Consolidated Treaty Series</u>, for example, 364 U.N.T.S. 3, 25 L.N.T.S. 12, 1 C.T.S. 271.

Please note that the U.N.T.S. and the L.N.T.S. indexes are divided into chronological and alphabetical sections.

Questions:

1. Where can a copy of the Capitulation of Yorktown, 1781 (Generals Washington and Cornwallis) be found?

2. Is Upper Volta a signatory to the African Migratory Locust Convention of 1962? Is Zaire?

3. Where can a copy of the Locarno Pact of 1925 (treaty of mutual guarantee final protocol) be found?

4. Is the agreement establishing the Asian Coconut Community (1968) in force? Has the Philippines ratified it?

5. Where can a copy of the Treaty of Amity, Conciliation, and Arbitration between Italy and Ethiopia (Abyssinia), 1928 be found?

6. During 1963 what nations ratified the European Convention on Academic Recognition of University Qualifications, Dec. 14, 1959?

7. Where can a copy of the agreement between the Free City of Danzig with Germany, Great Britain, Denmark, Poland, and Sweden, 1929, on the regulation of plaice and flounder fishing in the Baltic Sea be found?

8. Where can a copy of the Peace of Westphalia, 1648 (two parts) be found?

9. Cite best source for a list of the denunciations made in 1952 of the Convention for the Safety of Life at Sea, May 31, 1929.

10. Where can a copy of the Tokyo Agreement of February 19, 1954 on status of U.N. forces in Japan be found?

11. Where can a copy of the Polish/Democratic Republic of Korea Cultural Cooperation Treaty of 1956 be found?

12. Where can a copy of the Mutual Assistance Treaty, Poland-Great Britain, 1939, be found?

13. Where can a copy of the Agreement Abolishing Visas, Israel-Austria, 1968, be found?

14. Where can a copy of the Treaty Between the U.S. and the Sioux Indians, 1851, be found?

15. Where can a copy of the Buraimi Oasis Arbitration Agreement of 1954 be found?

ASSIGNMENT 4
RESTATEMENT OF THE LAW

Source: American Law Institute. *Restatement (Second) of Foreign Relations Law of the United States* (1965).

Method:
   Give reference to the relevant section(s) dealing with the topics listed below, for example, Limitation on Jurisdiction of Coastal States Over Vessel Entering in Distress--answer: Sec. 48(2). These questions may be answered rather easily by quickly scanning the Table of Contents or by checking the Index.

Questions:

1. Hot pursuit

2. Continental Shelf

3. Arrest and detention of an alien as denial of procedural justice

4. Nationality of vessels

5. United States practice on taxation of diplomatic personnel

6. Thalweg Doctrine

7. Statement about the date when a treaty becomes effective in the United States

8. Definition of right of innocent passage

ASSIGNMENT 5
WHITEMAN'S DIGEST OF INTERNATIONAL LAW

Source: Whiteman, Marjorie M., Digest of International Law (1963-1973)

Method:

Use the index to Whiteman to cite the volume and page references to the topics listed below.

Sample answer: 10:577.

Questions:

1. Withdrawal of Cuba from International Monetary Fund

2. Dangerous or humiliating labor for prisoners of war

3. Proof of nationality

4. The right to blockade Suez Canal

5. The legal bases of Arctic (sector principle)

6. Epicontinental sea distinguished from continental shelf: superjacent waters

7. Demilitarization of Aegean Sea islands.

8. European Commission of Human Rights

9. Diplomatic status of governments-in-exile

10. Estrada Doctrine

11. The legality of submarine use in war

12. Exclusion of Nazis or Facists from employment in United Nations Secretariat

13. Military air service to Berlin

14. Use of foreign flags by insurgent vessels

15. Seizure of fishing vessels in waters of contested jurisdiction off the coast of Mexico

16. List of treaties and agreements concerning refugees

17. The use of embargo as a means of reprisal

18. The passage of belligerent warships through the Turkish Straits

19. Repatriation of diplomatic officers in time of war

20. The difference between pillage and booty

21. Harvard draft convention on piracy, 1932

22. Exclusion of Cuba from OAS

23. Legal status of Enderbury Island

24. The use of Shatt-al-Arab River between Iran and Iraq by commercial vessels of all nations

25. The definition of "Hostile Propaganda"

ASSIGNMENT 6
MULTINATIONAL TREATIES

Sources: American Society of International Law, <u>International Legal Materials</u>, 1962;

United Nations. Office of Legal Affairs. <u>Multilateral Treaties Deposited with the Secretary-General</u>, Status as at 31 December, 1982; and

Whiteman, M., <u>Digest of International Law</u> (1963-1975).

Method:

By consulting the above, answer questions below and cite the source in which the answer is found, for example, 14 Int'l. Leg. Mat. 43, 1982 Multilateral Treaties 449, 10 Whiteman 66.
There is an overall index to Whiteman and a <u>Cumulative Index to Volumes I-Viii of International Legal Materials</u>. Another Cumulative Index has been announced but is not available as of this writing. Consult the Table of Contents when using <u>Multilateral Treaties Deposited with the Secretary- General</u>.

Questions:

1. Where can a copy of the agreement establishing the Arab Emirates Federation be found?

2. Have any of the peoples' republics of Eastern Europe ratified the International Coffee Agreement of 1968? Which one(s)?

3. Has the U.S. taken an official position regarding the implementation of the International Genocide Convention as far as extraditing a criminal under this conviction?

4. Where can a copy of the English text of the European Patent Convention (Convention on the Grant of European Patents, Munich, 1973) be found?

5. Is the special protocol concerning statelessness, The Hague, April 12, 1930, in force?

6. Where can a substantial exposition of the U.S. position on measures of redress available against a government oppressive of human rights be found? Use the former country, Southern Rhodesia, as an example.

7. What are the organs of the OPEC as stated in its statute, effective May 1, 1965?

8. Has the U.S. ratified the Vienna Convention on the Law of Treaties? Has the United Kingdom?

9. Is it correct to state that the U.S. position on the Calvo Clause is that the alien, in asserting a claim or property right, need not observe the rule requiring exhaustion of local remedies before his government may intervene?

10. Where can a copy of the Joint Declaration of the Presidents of Columbia, Costa Rica, Venezuela, and Panama on the Panama Canal, 1975 be found?

11. Has the United States of America ratified the 1948 Convention on the Prevention and Punishment of the Crime of Genocide?

12. Locate a reference which discusses the scope of the Warsaw Convention of Private Air Law.

13. In the early 1960's NASA and the Academy of Sciences of the U.S.S.R. explored the possibilities of cooperation in outer space research. Give the citation to the First Memorandum of Understanding.

14. Where can a discussion and explanation of presidential power to make executive agreements be found?

15. Where can a copy of the English text of the Act Implementing the Ceasefire in the Dominican Republic (1965) be found?

Chapter 21

ENGLISH AND CANADIAN LEGAL RESEARCH

ASSIGNMENT 1
ENGLISH REPORTS, FULL REPRINT

Method:

Using the Index of Cases volumes, provide the English Reports Full Reprint citation for each of the cases cited.

Questions:

1. In re Pugh, 17 Beav. 336.
2. Robinson v. Stone, 2 Strange 1260. Rep. 1168.
3. Smith v. Dixon, 2 Curt. 264.
4. Wagstaffe v. Bedford, 1 Vern. 95.
5. White's Case, 6 Mod. 18.
6. R. v. Coke, 5 B. & C. 797.
7. Leach v. Morris, 1 Mod. 36.
8. Lumbury v. Tailor, 1 Sid. 269.
9. Megot v. Davy, 4 Leonard 60.
10. Norton's Vail, 1 M. & W. 632.
11. Price v. Harris, 10 Bing. 331, 557.
12. R. v. Nixon, 1 Strange 185.
13. Smarte v. Edsum, 1 Lev. 30.
14. Gibbon v. Budd, 2 H. & C. 92.
15. Dean v. Abel, Dick. 287.

16. Henry v. Adey, 4 Esp. 228.
17. Hill v. Dobie, 8 Taunt. 325.
18. Ashton v. Dalton, 2 Coll. 565.
19. Duke v. Andrews, 2 Ex. 290.
20. Knight v. Young, 2 V. & B. 184.
21. Knox v. Brown, 1 Eq. Rep. 126.
22. Drew v. Coles, 2 C. & J. 505.
23. Buttler v. Mathews, 19 Beav. 549.
24. Aarons v. Williams, 2 Bing. 304.
25. Carter v. Hall, 2 Stark 361.
26. Burrel v. Peacock, 1 Keble 467.
27. Worts v. Clyston, Cro. Jac. 350.
28. Cator v. Butler, Dick. 438.
29. Lecome v. Shiers, 1 Eq. Rep. 260.
30. Greasly v. Codling, 2 Bing. 263.
31. Locke v. Colman, 1 My. & Cr. 423.
32. Jenney v. Brook, 6 Q.B. 323.
33. Lampley v. Blower, 3 Atk. 396.
34. In re The Comet, 5 C. Rob. 285.
35. Wilson v. Millar, 2 Stark. 1
36. Farrell v. Gleeson, 11 Cl. & Fin. 702.
37. Udall v. Nelson, 3 Ad. & E. 215.
38. Bateman's Case, 1 Mod. 76
39. Sweetapple v. Bindon, 2 Vern. 536.
40. Horn v. Horn, 1 Eq. Rep. 75.

ASSIGNMENT 2
HALSBURY'S LAWS OF ENGLAND, THIRD EDITION, CASE METHOD

Method:

Locate the citation for each case, using Halsbury's Laws of England (3rd ed.). Most cases can be found in the main volumes by using volume 40, Consolidate Table of Cases. However, it will be necessary to use the Cumulative Supplement and its table of cases to identify some of these citations. If more than one citation is given, cite only the first.

Questions:

1. Adley v. Whitstable.

2. Ashworth v. Browne.

3. A-G v. Prossor.

4. Bane v. Methuen.

5. Allott v. Wagon Repairs.

6. Baylee v. Quin.

7. Blackbeard v. Lindigren.

8. Bolam v. Allgood.

9. Bole v. Horton.

10. Burke v. Johnson.

11. Hudson v. Buck.

12. Guy v. Churchill.

13. Dorset (Duke) v. Crosbie.

14. The Firethorn.

15. Hearn v. Hearn.

16. Shutt v. Lewis.

17. Vane v. Fletcher.
18. Hicks v. Hicks.
19. Ship v. Crosskill.
20. Stevens v. Stevens.
21. Clarke v. Barber.
22. Coleman v. North.
23. Ekin v. Flay.
24. Price v. Hall.
25. R. v. Noe.
26. Acton v. White.
27. Armour v. Walker.
28. Bevens v. Bevens.
29. Butler v. Hunter.
30. Ashbee v. Jayne.
31. Clark v. Mumford.
32. Davis v. Rolleston.
33. The Durham City.
34. Dutch Machines Case.
35. Dickie v. Singh.
36. Gilbert v. Tomlinson.
37. Goldsmith v. Orr.
38. Gowar v. Bennett.
39. Graham v. Candy.
40. Hickman v. Walker.

ASSIGNMENT 3
HALSBURY'S LAWS OF ENGLAND, FOURTH EDITION, INDEX METHOD

Method:

Using the Index volumes to the Fourth Edition of Halsbury's Laws of England, locate statements in the text which answer each of the following questions. Indicate where this statement was found by citing to the volume and page number of the encyclopedia.

Questions:

1. Did the Highway Acts modify the common law to make it a duty of the highway authorities to light certain roads?

2. Is there a remedy for breach of contract to marry?

3. Can a husband be held criminally liable for the acts of his wife?

4. Is a promoter a trustee or agent of the company he attempts to form?

5. What is the minimum number of persons necessary to form a new company?

6. Can money lent to an illegal company be recovered?

7. May a person accept a revocable offer if it was not made to him?

8. Is a contract void if one party was intoxicated when he or she entered into the contract?

9. Is past consideration a real consideration?

10. Is taking a group picture in front of a sculpture in a museum's foyer a violation of the copyright code?

11. Is a person professing the Jewish religion disqualified from holding the position of Lord Chancellor of Great Britain?

12. May a parent be fined and even imprisoned for failure to comply with a school attendance order?

13. How many kinds of estoppel are there?

14. May a witness by asked leading questions during cross-examination in a criminal case?

15. Is it true that public statutes are judicially noticed and they need not be proved as evidence?

16. There being no special exception, may a young person be employed on Sunday?

17. May a ferry owner discriminate against certain persons as to use of his ferry?

18. Does the sale of milk containing minute particles of dirt constitute an act of adulteration violative of the food and drug laws?

19. Is there any special restriction for inventions that produce atomic energy?

20. Are prison officers exempt from jury duty?

ASSIGNMENT 4
HALSBURY'S LAWS OF ENGLAND
THIRD AND FOURTH EDITIONS, INDEX METHOD

Method:

Using the Index volumes to the Third Edition or the Temporary Index volume to the completed portion of the Fourth Edition of Halsbury's Law of England, answer the following questions. Give the full citation to a case or statute which supports your answer. Indicate the edition, volume and paragraph number of the encyclopedia where you located your citation, e.g., Smith v. Jones [1891] 1 Q.B. 406, ed. 4, vol. 2, para. 611.

Questions:

1. Jones is hunting wild game on public land, but when the game crosses onto the land of one Smythe, Jones trespasses in pursuit. Jones catches and kills the game. Smythe, as owner of the land, sues Jones for possession of the game. Who will be awarded the game?

2. Sam wishes to qualify as auctioneer. Before doing so must he meet the requirements and become a member of the Auctioneers' Institute of the United Kingdom?

3. As a general rule counsel cannot be heard in court unless they are robed. Is this rule equally true in cases where counsel appears on his own behalf?

4. A performed certain services at the request of B. B subsequently promised A to pay for those services. When B failed to pay, A sued for breach of the alleged contract. B maintains the services performed amounted to "past consideration" that will not support the contractual agreements. A argues an exception to the general rule. Will A succeed?

5. At the common law is there generally a right of contribution between adjoining owners to the expense of building or maintaining a party wall on the boundary of their property?

6. The Betting, Gaming and Lotteries Act of 1963 states "Any person ... loitering in a street or public place ... for the purpose of bookmaking, betting ... receiving or settling bets, commits an offense." Charlie, while driving through Soho Square, slowed down to receive bets and was charged with loitering. Will the Crown succeed with its charge?

7. Is the Isle of Man part of the United Kingdom?

8. As a general rule most jet aircraft operating in the United Kingdom must have "noise certificates." Will the new supersonic plane Concorde require such a certificate? [Use 4th edition only.]

9. F's dog chased sheep off F's land but then continued chasing them on the land of M even though the dog was called back by F. Is F answerable in trespass because of the unauthorized entry of his dog on M's land?

10. The branches of a large tree belonging to E overhang the land of N, adjoining. N cut off the overhanging branches on the boundary without trespassing on E's land. Was N within his rights in cutting these branches?

11. The law of bailment can be traced to early Roman authorities. Cite the leading English case wherein Holt,, C.J., divided bailments into six classes.

12. Where goods have been delivered to a carrier, and they are lost or injured, who is the proper person to seek a remedy against the carrier?

13. A was duly elected to office of the XYZ Corporation. Subsequently, however, a bylaw was approved seeking to impose a disqualification on A. Does A in the face of this bylaw have the right to assume the office for which elected?

14. With regard to the assignment of a chose in action the general rule is that a person's capacity to take an assignment is governed either by the law of his domicile or by the law of the country where the assignment takes place. But if A is capable of receiving an assignment by virtue of the law in the country of his domicile but incapable of receiving the assignment of the chose in action by virtue of the law in the country in which the assignment took place, which law will previal?

15. What is the minimum age at which a person may take part in gaming on licensed premises?

ASSIGNMENT 5
CURRENT LAW, STATUTE CITATOR

Method:

For each of the statute citations below provide the citation to the citing case, instrument, or act as listed in the Current Law Statute Citator volume.

Questions:

1. 5 Edw. 3 (1331), c. 9.

2. 23 & 24 Vict., c. 90, s. 13.

3. 28 & 29 Vict., c. 78.

4. 50 & 51 Vict., c. 35 s. 35.

5. 60 & 61 Vict., c. 6, s. 1.

6. 5 & 6 Geo. 5, c. 1, s. 1.

7. 4 & 5 Geo. 5, c. 60.

8. 10 & 11 Geo. 5, c. 63, s. 1.

9. 19 & 20 Geo. 5, c. 22.

10. 19 & 20 Geo. 5, c. 23, s. 173.

11. 26 Geo. 5 and 1 Edw. 8, c. 11.

12. 2 & 3 Geo. 6, c. 118.

13. 11 & 12 Geo. 6, c. 38, s. 401.

14. 2 & 3 Eliz. 2, c. 61, s. 19.

15. 1 Hen. 8, c. 15, 18.

16. 1 Rich. 2, c. 4.

17. 3 & 4 Ann. c. 11.

18. 5 & 6 Vict., c. 4.

19. 23 & 24 Geo. 5, c. 12, s. 21.
20. 2 & 3 Geo. 6, c. 90.
21. 10 & 11 Geo. 6, c. 48, s. 87.
22. 10 & 11 Eliz. 2, c. 51, s. 21.
23. 9 Edw. 7, c. 12, s. 1.
24. 13 & 14 Geo. 5, c. 32, s. 9 (1).
25. 19 & 20 Geo. 5, c. 22.

ASSIGNMENT 6
HALSBURY'S STATUTES, THIRD EDITION,
ALPHABETICAL LIST OF STATUTES

Method:

　　Use the Tables of Statutes and Index volume of Halsbury's Statutes (3rd ed.) to locate the text and annotations to the statute in question. Indicate, by volume and page number, where this statute can be found in this set.

Questions:

1. Act of Supremacy (1558).

2. Admirality Courts Act 1861.

3. Barristers Act 1961.

4. Caravan Sites Act 1968.

5. Children Act 1948.

6. Roosevelt Memorial Act 1946.

7. Prorogation Acts 1867.

8. Tokyo Convention Act 1967.

9. Wills Act 1968.

10. Dangerous Drugs Act 1967.

11. Statute of Westminster 1931.

12. Married Women's Property Act 1964.

13. Bill of Rights (1688).

14. Forcible Entry Act 1381.

15. Union with Ireland Act 1800.

16. Street Offenses Act 1959.

17. Tattooing of Minors Act 1969.

18. Status of Children Born Abroad (1350-1).

19. Statute of Frauds (1677).

20. Radioactive Substances Act 1960.

21. Criminal Justice Act 1965.

22. Abortion Act 1967.

23. Firearms Act 1968.

24. Town Development Act 1952.

25. Marriage with Foreigners Act 1906.

26. Act of Settlement of 1700.

27. Administration of Justice Act 1932.

28. Auctioneers' Act 1845.

29. British North American Act 1840.

30. City of London Militia Act 1662.

31. Colonial Marriages Act 1865.

32. County Courts Act 1924.

33. Cyprus Act 1960.

34. Ecclesiastical Appeals Act 1532.

35. Enemy Property Act 1953.

36. Fireworks Act 1964.

37. Immigration Appeals Act 1969.

38. John F. Kennedy Memorial Act 1964.

39. Leeds University Act 1904.

40. London Cab Act 1968.

ASSIGNMENT 7
HALSBURY'S STATUTE, THIRD EDITION, INDEX METHOD

Method:

Use the <u>Index</u> volumes of <u>Halsbury's Statutes</u> (3rd ed.) to find the statutory answers to the following questions. ANSWER the question and cite <u>Halsbury's Statutes</u> by volume and page.

Questions:

1. What is the age limit for solemnized marriage?

2. In the interpretation of a penal act does the term "person" as stated in such act include corporate bodies?

3. In non-emergency situations how many registered medical practitioners must approve before a pregnancy may be legally terminated?

4. What is the maximum prison term for assaulting a seaman?

5. Is a will witnessed and attested to by only two witnesses valid?

6. Is playing football in the street an offense punishable by fine?

7. In whom is vested the executive power of Canada?

8. Does a husband retain any curtesy right to the estate of his intestate wife?

9. Is martial law permitted?

10. In regard to awarding compensation for riot damage where shall the regulations be published?

11. Must a vehicle being towed show red lights to the side?

12. For the purpose of the law of libel and slander is the broadcasting of words by means of wireless telegraphy permanent publication?

13. For what reason may the local authorities exclude Sue, age 6, from attending the circus?

14. What is the maximum prison term for a second conviction for possession or sale of a flick knofe?

15. How many incorporators are necessary in order to form a non-private company?

16. What government official has the duty of causing dangerous fireworks to be destroyed?

17. What is the penalty for contravening the requirement that the keeping of stallions is subject to license or permit?

18. Colossal Condominiums's newest effort is on a disused burial ground. Will they be allowed to build on that location?

19. Does the Constitution of the Board of Architectural Education permit the Cambridge University School of Architecture to nominate one person to that Board?

20. Modern Canada was divided into provinces in 1867. Two of the provinces, Quebec and Ontario, were derived from two earlier independent provinces. Name these earlier provinces.

21. When did Burma become independent from England?

22. Can a pregnant woman be given a death sentence if she is found guilty of an offense punishable with death?

23. Although the statutes require that the indictment for an act of treason must be processed within three years, there is one treasonous act not bound by this limitation. Name that act.

24. What law guides the penalties for selling fireworks to children?

25. Determine if the Bath Corporation is an authorized undertaker for providing electricity.

26. A deserted from the Navy and later surrendered to the civilian police. Is it necessary to bring A before a court of summary jurisdiction prior to turning him over to the military?

27. Capt. Bligh is about to sail from London to Bombay with 97 persons aboard his ship. He has been told that with his many persons on board he must also carry a "qualified medical practitioner." Is this true?

28. Are powers conferred on Her Majesty, to be exercisable by Order in Council, governed by the Statutory Instruments Act in the same way as powers conferred on ministers of the crown?

29. Shall the construction of a will be altered by reason of a change in the testator's domicile after the execution of the will.

30. A pawnbroker has loaned 9 pounds on a pledge of a camera which was subsequently destroyed by fire resulting from a war time bombing. Will the broker be liable for the damage to the camera?

ASSIGNMENT 8
HALSBURY'S STATUTES, THIRD EDITION, CURRENT MATERIALS

Method:

Use the 1976 or later Cumulative Supplement to determine if the indicated statute has been affected by subsequent legislation. Name the subsequent affecting act, if any, and the volume and page number in Halsbury's where it can be located.

Questions and Answers:

1. Cockfighting Act 1952, Vol. 2, p. 257.

2. Schedule 3 of the Diseases of Animals Act 1950, Vol. 2, p. 372.

3. West Indian Prisons Act 1838, Vol. 4, p. 592.

4. Section 1 of the Administration of Justice (Miscellaneous Provisions) Act 1933, Vol. 8, p. 307.

5. Section 116 of the Education Act 1944, Vol. 11, p. 261.

6. Fireworks Act of 1964, chapter 23, Vol. 13, p. 242.

7. Section 19 Civil Evidence Act 1968, Vol. 12, p. 932.

8. Shop Clubs Act 1902, Vol. 14, p. 329.

9. Guardianship of Infants Act 1886, Vol. 17, p. 415.

10. Section 36 of the Rent Act 1965, Vol. 18, p. 628.

11. Greek Loan Act 1898, Vol. 22, p. 865.

12. Pensions (Increase) Act 1920, Vol. 24, p. 774.

13. Section 21-23 of the Public Health Act of 1936, Vol. 26, p. 218.

14. Trustee Savings Bank Act 1969, Vol. 30, p. 284.

15. Section 121 of the Town and Country Planning Act 1971, Vol. 41, p. 1726.

ASSIGNMENT 9
STATUTORY INSTRUMENTS

Method:

Use Halsbury's <u>Statutory Instruments</u> or <u>Statutory Rules and Orders</u> Index and/or Text volumes to answer the following questions. Cite to instrument date and number.

Questions:

1. Is alcuronium chloride on the list of poisons to be controlled by the Pharmacy and Poisons Act 1933?

2. Must the accidental inrush of water in a coal mine be reported to an inspector?

3. Have Japan and England entered into agreements designed to prevent double taxation of income?

4. Under the High Court adoption rules may an applicant for an adoption order keep his identity confidential?

5. Must the administrator of a children's home provide for appropriate religious instruction?

6. To whom would a claim under the Family Allowance Act be made?

7. Where are banns of marriage to be posted aboard a naval ship?

8. May the petitioner in a matrimonial cause serve the petition personally?

9. May the Registrar under the Registered Designs Act refuse an application?

10. What instrument governs the production of milk?

11. May a mental health tribunal allow a hearing to institutionalize a person to be held in public?

12. What is the probationary period for constable without any prior experience as a police officer?

13. Must an unheated factory provide for adequate thermal insulation in its roof?

14. Are scaffolds for building and engineering construction in factories regulated?

15. What instrument governs the statutory form of conditions of sale of real property?

16. What is the subject matter of Statutory Will Form Number 3?

17. Machines to weigh persons are regulated by which statutory instrument?

18. May a judicial trustee retain trust account funds in his hands longer than is necessary?

19. Driving tests requirements are set out in which statutory instrument?

20. Which government agency has the responsibility to cause an annual volume of statutory instruments to be prepared?

21. During what period is the burning of heather and grass generally proscribed?

22. Is it true that 200 lbs. is the maximum any agricultural worker is allowed to carry unaided?

23. Are the regulations concerning the importation of honey bees applicable to those imported from the Isle of Man?

24. The Anthrax Prevention Order of 1961 relates to which commodities?

25. Cite the 1973 Statutory Instrument which contained the Grenada Constitution order.

26. Cite the 1972 Statutory Instrument specifying an alien's duty to register with the police.

27. On what date in 1972 and by what Statutory Instrument were the Thermal Insulation (Industrial Building) Regulations of 1958, Statutory Instrument 1958, No. 1220, replaced?

28. With the United Kingdom's accession to the European Economic Community, rules regarding new areas of access for the fishing boats of signatories to the treaty had to be issued. Which statutory instrument describes these new rules?

29. Locate the statutory instrument which sets forth the details of the supplementary protocol between France and the United Kingdom concerning double taxation relief for taxation on income.

30. Comprehensive regulations made under Part 4 of the Agriculture Act 1970 as amended by Schedule 4E of the European Communities Act 1972 superseded the Fertilizers and Feeding Stuffs Regulation 1968. What was the date that these new regulations came into effect?

31. On October 1, 1973, substantial new regulations regarding the General Dental Services portion of the National Health Service came into effect. One of the more important elements of this regulation enables the Secretary of State to publish a statement of dental renumeration, indicating the details of treatment and the materials used in treatment. What is the citation to this regulation?

32. Cite the 1974 Statutory Instrument which sets forth the qualifications for speech therapists employed in the National Health Service (supersedes Statutory Instrument 1964, No. 941).

33. In 1970 the Whitefish Authority developed a scheme to promote the consumption of whitefish in the United Kingdom. To finance this scheme a tax was charged on various forms of whitefish. What was the tax on one stone of whole whitefish?

34. What is the maximum basic fee to a solicitor for hearing and preparing a case going to the Court of Appeal in which the solicitor has been assigned by legal aid in criminal proceedings in England on October 2, 1968?

35. Cite the 1973 Statutory Instrument which established the Severn-Trent Water Authority.

36. Cite the 1972 Statutory Instrument which places restrictions on the landing of salmon and migratory trout.

37. Were corporate taxes of the United Kingdom subject to the double taxation relief order to income taxes in Malaysia and the United Kingdom in 1973?

38. Cite the 1967 Statutory Instrument dealing with the application for and issue of postal money orders.

39. What is the citation to the regulation which extended the Genocide Act 1969 to the Isle of man?

ASSIGNMENT 10
ENGLISH AND EMPIRE DIGEST - CASE METHOD

Method:

Locate the following case names in the Table of Cases volumes (Vols. 52-54) or in the Table of Cases in the most recent Cumulative Supplement to the English and Empire Digest. Using the volume number, topic name and the page or case number which you find, locate the digest of the case in question and indicate its citation. If there is more than one citation, give only the first.

NOTE: At the time that this publication is being prepared, the English and Empire Digest Blue Band Series is being replaced by a more up to date series which is bound in a Green Band. Because of this situation, the Table of Cases volumes are citing to volumes that have already been replaced. Therefore, where a case has been reissued in a Green Band volume, it is necessary to look up the case again in the separate Table of Cases at the front of the relevant Green Band volume.

A new Consolidated Table of Cases for all the Green Band volumes will be compiled and published at the end of the Green Band edition in 1986.

Questions:

1. Barner v. Barner (Can.)

2. Bolden v. Brogden (1838).

3. Crewe v. Corbett (N.Z.).

4. Mills v. Edwards (1971)

5. Z. v. Z. (1972) (Aus.).

6. R. v. Rew (1662).

7. Wilson v. Grey (1866).

8. Sheardown v. Good (Can.).

9. Taylor v. Willoughby (1953).

10. Brown v. Nisbett (1750).

11. Gray v. Gray (1852).

12. The Kauss (1904).
    ANSWER: [1904] 20 T.L.R. 326.

13. Kearon v. Kearon (Ir.).

14. Overseas Tankship v. Morts Dock (1961).

15. R. v. Cornwell (1972) (Aus.).

ASSIGNMENT 11
ENGLISH AND EMPIRE DIGEST - INDEX METHOD

Method:

Using the <u>Index</u> and not the <u>Table of Cases</u> to the <u>English and Empire Digest</u>, answer the following questions and cite authority (case or statute) for your answers. In addition, indicate the digest volume and page number where authority for your answers was found.

Questions:

1. Must two ships actually collide in order that a damaged ship will have a cause of action over which the Court of Admiralty may assert jurisdiction?

2. Are members of the clergy exempt from bankruptcy action?

3. Is the destruction of one or two apple trees waste? An entire orchard? What is the very earliest authority?

4. A put up a sign that dogs trespassing on his land would be shot. P's dog went onto A's land and A shot and killed the dog. Was the notice posted by A sufficient as defense to P's action for the loss of his dog?

5. The highest bidder at an auction, under the usual conditions, is the purchaser. At 100 pounds B's bid was the highest, but before the fall of the hammer B retracted his bid. Who must pay--B or A, who was the second highest bidder to that moment?

6. How does an inn differ from a lodging house?

7. A bastard cannot succeed as heir-at-law to real property in England. Cite the earliest case supporting this proposition.

8. P left his to car to be sold by D. One of the terms of the Bailment stated: "Customers' cars are driven by our staff at customers' sole risk." The car was subsequently damaged while being driven by D's agent. Does the contract term quoted relieve D of liability in the hire of custody?

9. Under the principles of jurisdiction in conflict of laws, are foreign penal laws enforceable in England?

10. A entered into a contract with B while B was in a state of complete intoxication. A now tries to sue B for breach of contract. Will A succeed?

11. As a general rule it is stated that past consideration is no consideration in determining the existence of a contract. Cite one of the earliest authorities in support of that rule.

12. At common law did there seem to be any obligation to fence one's land?

13. Is a building society analogous in nature to a joint stock company or a common law partnership?

14. Will a corporation be held liable in tort for intentional acts of misfeasance by its servants, provided the acts are sufficiently connected with the scope and object of the organization's incorporation?

15. Does a friendly alien have a right to sue for infringement of copyright to which he is entitled under the Copyright Acts for the time it is in force?

ASSIGNMENT 12
CITATION PROBLEMS

Method:

Locate the citation for the following and conform the citation to A Uniform System of Citation.

Questions:

1. The leading case of strict liability for abnormally dangerous conditions and activities involved one Fletcher, a mill owner being sued by Rylands, who owned an adjoining mine. The case was heard initially by the Exchequer Court of England in 1865 and was reported by Hurlstone and Coltman in the third volume of their reports at page 737.

2. In 1961 the Privy Council ruled, at page 388 of its reports, on the celebrated "Wagonmound" case which in reality involved a conflict between Overseas Tankship (U.K.) Ltd. and Morts Dock and Engineering Co., Ltd. as to the extent of foreseeable results of the defendant's negligence.

3. In 1960, the eighth and ninth year of the reign of Queen Elizabeth II, the Parliament passed Chapter 43 of the statutes entitled The Abandonment of Animals Act. Section one of that act indicated the penalty for abandoning an animal.

4. Schedule 1, being part One of Section 167, of the Consumer Credit Act enacted in 1974, the twenty-second and twenty-third year of the reign of Queen Elizabeth II, as Chapter 39 of the statutes provides for mode of prosecution and penalties under the Act.

5. Under the authority of certain statutes, the Minister of Agriculture in 1969 promulgated amendments to certain administrative regulations for the licensing of certain animals. The regulation for boars was Statutory Instrument number 1138.

ASSIGNMENT 13
INDEX TO CANADIAN LEGAL PERIODICAL LITERATURE

A. Locate and cite the following using the Index to Canadian Legal Periodical Literature. The information given in the questions is the date of publication, author, if any, and subject of the article.

1. 1964; V. Kumar; treatment of juvenile offenders

2. 1971; F.R. Scott; bilingualism in Canada

3. 1965; article; sex discimination in employment

4. 1968; P.S. Grant; regulation of program content in Canadian television

5. 1973; P. Weiler; constitutional law in Canada

B. Locate and cite comments on the following cases using the Index to Canadian Legal Periodical Literature. Include the name of the author. The information given is the year of the comment and the case citation.

1. 1972; Lavell and A.G. of Canada Re (1971), 22 D.L.R. (3d) 188.

2. 1971; R. v. Drybones, [1970] S.C.R. 282.

3. 1964; Steinberg v. Steinberg, (1963), 45 W.W.R. 562.

4. 1973; Jarvis v. Swan Tours Ltd., (1973) All E.R. 71.

C. Locate and cite reviews of the following books using the Index to Canadian Legal Periodical Literature. The information given in the questions is the year reviewed, author, title and year published.

1. 1971; Gotlieb, Alan, ed.; Human Rights Federalism and Minorities (1970).

2. 1969; La Marsh, Judy; Bird in a Gilded Cage (1968).

3. 1972; Rawls, John; A Theory of Justice (1972).

4. 1963; Laskin, Bora; Cases and Notes on Land Law (1958).

5. You are looking for an article written by J. Jowell on landlord and tenant relations.
   (a) What two ways would you go about finding this in the <u>Index to Canadian Legal Periodical Literature</u>?
   (b) Give the full citation of the article.

6. If you wanted to find legal articles on corporal punishment in prisons, under what subject heading would you look in the <u>Index to Canadian Legal Periodical Literature</u>?

ASSIGNMENT 14
LEGAL ENCYCLOPEDIAS - C.E.D. (ONT. 3RD), INDEX METHOD

Method:

Referring to the Canadian Encyclopedic Digest (Ont. 3rd) and the supplementary pages at the head of the volumes, answer the following questions, giving the citation to the C.E.D. volume, title and section where you found your answer. Subject access to the C.E.D. is through the key which includes a key words index, a statutes key and a titles key. Use the key-words index to obtain the volume and title number, then use the subject index included at the end of each title. Match the title and section number in the supplementary pages to update. Cite the encyclopedia: C.E.D. (Ont. 3rd).

Questions:

1. Must the Court of Appeal of one province follow a decision of an appellate court of another province as a matter of law or practice?

2. Under what title do you find information about the Law Society of Upper Canada? Which principal statutes does this section cite that deal with the title that we are interested in? Give citations for the statutes.

3. Are the officers of an unincorporated society liable for an alleged libel published in the association's journal?

4. Indicate where The Corporations Information Act, 1971, has been commented upon. Use the statutes key.

5. May a wife pledge her husband's credit for necessaries if they are living separately due to the husband's misconduct?

6. Does an actionable wrong arise against an auctioneer who refuses to accept a bid from a party?

7. When is joy-riding a criminal offense?

8. List any cases which consider the difference between joy-riding and theft.

9. Does dictating a defamatory letter to a stenographer constitute publication to a third person sufficient to suppport an action?

10. A, a father called to the scene of an accident, suffered mental shock on seeing his mortally injured daughter. Can he recover damages?

11. Is a garage owner relieved of liability for negligence if a notice is posted in the garage stating that vehicles are left at the owner's risk?

12. What are the principal statutes relating to bankruptcy?

13. Where may additional cases concerning bankruptcy be located?

14. Section 50 (3) of the Bankruptcy Act concerns the application of the Act to married women. Using the statutes key, indicate where this section is commented upon.

ASSIGNMENT 15
DIGESTS - THE CANADIAN ABRIDGMENT 2ND, TOPICAL ANALYSIS METHOD

Method:

Refer to the <u>Canadian Abridgment (2nd)</u> cited (Can. Abr. 2nd) to answer the following questions. Information is updated by consulting the First Permanent and Cumulative Supplements. Indicate the volume, page and case number authority where your answer was found.

Questions:

1. When must an employer notify the insurer of an accident to have liability insurance cover the incident?

2. Can the ideas of a person be copyrighted?

3. What cases do the Can. Abr. (2nd) cite which deal with the above? Give complete citations including the history of the cases.

4. Is submission, extorted by threats or fear of bodily harm, considered as consent to sexual intercourse, and therefore the act of intercourse not considered as rape? What case does the Can. Abr. (2nd) cite which deals with this issue? Use the Table of Classification in the Criminal Law Vols.

5. <u>A. v. Law Society of B.C.</u> is a case which involves the disbarment of a memeber of the Law Society who proved himself to be unfit to be a member of the Society. Locate the case in the appropriate volume of the Can. Abr. Give the citation to the <u>Abridgment</u> where you found your answer and give the citation for the case.

6. The First Permanent Supplement of the Can. Abr. (2nd) includes a titles key. Under what title will "extradition" be found?

7. Under which title may cases relating to "lunatics" be found?

8. What case is cited concerning the failure of a passenger to look and listen before stepping from a railway coach?

9. Is a doctor liable for damages for assault for having performed an unauthorized emergency operation, if the operation is done in accordance with accepted medical practice, and is necessary to preserve the plaintiff's life? Use the topical analysis to the Medicine and Surgery subject title.

10. Van Dorn v. Felger is a case in which a husband was held entitled to ask his wife to accompany him when both had entered into a contract of hire, and the employer required the wife to stay to fulfill her contract when the husband justifiably left. Locate the case in the appropriate volume of the Can. Abr. Give the citation to the Abridgment where you found your answer, and give the citation for the case.

ASSIGNMENT 16
CASE CITATORS – THE CANADIAN ABRIDGMENT 2ND
CASES JUDICIALLY CONSIDERED

Method

Note up cases from the time they were decided to the end of 1980 by referring to the Cases Judicially Considered volumes of the Canadian Abridgment (2nd) and the Cases Judicially Considered First and Second Permanent Supplements. If more than one citation is given for the case, or more than one subsequent case is noted, report only the first entry.

Questions:

1. Hurst v. Mersea

2. Clairol International Corporation v. Thomas Supply & Equipment Co.

3. Bernardin v. North Dufferin

4. Shields-Snow Ltd. v. M.N.R.

5. North Lancaster Exchange v. Bell Telephone Co.

6. Dalton v. Doran

7. Laurin v. Ginn

8. Morgentaler v. Fauteux

9. R. v. Grondkowski

10. McDonald v. Shewchuk

11. Bank of Liverpool, Re

12. Schaeffer v. Tubby, Smith & Co.

13. Vanvalkenburg v. Nor. Navigation Co.

14. Farwell v. Jameson

15. Marginson v. Blackburn Borough Council

ASSIGNMENT 17
STATUTES - LOCATING FEDERAL STATUTES BY SUBJECT WITH THE USE OF THE INDEX

Method:

Refer to the <u>Revised Statutes of Canada 1970</u> to answer the following question. Do not answer the questions with a simple "Yes" or "No"; include a citation to the appropriate statute in each case. (For example, <u>Canada Pension Plan Act</u>, R.S.C. 1970, c.C-5, s.43 (1).)

Questions:

1. What does an "adult eligible for a training allowance" refer to in the federal act which sets up a Government Retraining scheme for adults?

2. Is the inability to consummate a marriage, due to illness or disability, grounds for divorce?

3. Cite the act which deals with the interpretation of statutes.

4. Can a child, who is being detained pending hearing for a delinquency he has committed, be held in an adult prison?

5. Can an Indian woman who marries an Indian man belonging to another band, still remain a member of her own band?

6. Can an epileptic person be admitted to Canada as an immigrant?

7. Under the Criminal Code can a woman be imprisoned for an attempt to abort herself?

8. The <u>Canadian Bill of Rights</u> is located in the Appendix volume of R.S.C. 1970. Is freedom of the press one of the fundamental liberties of the Act?

9. To whom may drugs be distributed as samples?

10. Is "Dominion Day" a legal holiday in Canada?

11. Is it a criminal offense to advertise the sale of foreign lottery tickets in Canada?

12. Where may the text of the oath of office of a judge of the Supreme Court of Canada be located?

13. What is the time limitation period for a claim for redemption of an unused passenger ticket?

14. What is the difference between "year" and "calendar year" in the interpretation of statutes?

ASSIGNMENT 18
UPDATING STATUTES

Method:

Refer to the most recent Table of Public Statutes in the Canada Gazette Part III and note up the following statutes.

Questions:

1. Have there been any amendments to the Prisons and Reformatories Act s.2 since the Revision in 1970?

2. Have there been any amendments in the Act dealing with the interpretation of statutes? List the amended sections, together with the amendments, as they appear in the Table.

3. Have there been any amendments to the Narcotic Control Act? Give the full citations to them.

4. Have any sections of the act which deals with the Supreme Court of Canada been repealed? Give the full citations to them.

5. Trace the changes that have occurred to s.24 of the Old Age Security Act since the 1970 Revision.

6. Is the version of the Income Tax Act which appears in R.S.C. 1970 operative?

7. Give the citation for the amendment to s.22 of the Explosives Act, R.S.C. 1970, c.E-15 and state the amount of the fine for which a person is liable on summary conviction for a first offense.

8. Give the citation for the Saltfish Act. Cite any amendments made to the Act.

9. Is there a Youth Allowances Act still operative in Canada? If not, cite the repealing Act.

10. What is the present title of the Animal Contagious Diseases Act, R.S.C. 1970, c.A-13?

ASSIGNMENT 19
STATUTE CITATORS -
FINDING CASES WHICH GIVE JUDICIAL CONSIDERATION
TO SECTIONS OF STATUTES

Method:

Refer to the Canada Statute Citator, R.S.C. 1970 edition. The citator includes cases interpreting sections of the statutes arranged under the title of the statute, citations to the cases, and usually a short summary of the case.

Questions:

1. Cite any cases interpreting s.12(1)(b) of the Indian Act, R.S.C. 1970, c.I-6.

2. Cite any 1973 cases interpreting section 7(b) of the Trade Marks Act, R.S.C. 1970, c.T-10.

3. Cite any cases interpreting the words "any person," found in s.33(1) of the Juvenile Delinquents Act, R.S.C. 1970, c.J-3.

ASSIGNMENT 19
STATUTE CITATORS - FINDING CASES WHICH GIVE
JUDICIAL CONSIDERATION TO SECTIONS OF STATUTES

Method:

Refer to the <u>Canada Statute Citator</u>, R.S.C. 1970 edition. The citator includes cases interpreting sections of the statutes arranged under the title of the statute, citations to the cases, and usually a short summary of the case.

Questions

1. Cite any cases interpreting s.12(1)(b) of the <u>Indian Act</u>, R.S.C. 1970, c.1-6.

2. Cite any 1973 cases interpreting section 7(b) of the <u>Trade Marks Act</u>, R.S.C. 1970, c.T-10.

3. Cite any cases interpreting the words "any person" found in s.33(1) of the <u>Juvenile Delinquents Act</u>, R.S.C. 1970, c.J-3.

4. Cite a 1982 case which interprets s.44(3) of the <u>Combines Investigation Act</u>, R.S.C. 1970, c.C-23.

5. Cite a 1981 case interpreting s.5 of the <u>Canada Evidence Act</u>, R.S.C. 1970, c.E-10, which abolished the common law privilege against self-incrimination.

6. Cite any cases interpreting s.13 of the <u>Olympic (1976) Act</u>, S.C. 1973, c.31.

7. Were there any cases reported in 1974 interpreting s.70(1)(d) of the <u>Supreme Court Act</u>, R.S.C. 1970, c.S-19? Give complete citations of cases.

8. Cite a 1973 case which interprets s.11(3) of the <u>Immigration Appeal Board Act</u>, R.S.C. 1970, c.1-3.

9. Were there any cases reported in 1973 interpreting the terms "operating a commercial air service" under the <u>Aeronautics Act</u>, R.S.C. 1970, c.A-3? Give complete citations of cases.

10. Were there any cases reported in 1972 interpreting s.22 of the <u>Penitentiary Act</u>, R.S.C. 1970, c.P-6? Give complete citations.

11. Give complete citations for any cases determining whether regulations made under the <u>Migratory Birds Convention Act</u>, R.S.C. 1970, c.M-12, making the possession of migratory birds an offence, are intra vires.

12. Give complete citations for any cases determining whether persons not covered by a contract of service can be subject to regulations made under s.26(1)(d) of the <u>Unemployment Insurance Act</u>, 1971, S.C. 1970-71-72, c.48.

ASSIGNMENT 20
STATUTORY INSTRUMENTS - CONSOLIDATED INDEX

Method:

Referring to the latest quarterly cumulative <u>Consolidated Index of Statutory Instruments, Canada Gazette Part II</u>, locate and cite the following regulations.

Questions:

1. Where may the <u>Copyright Rules</u> be located?

2. Give the citation for the <u>Canada Student Loans Regulations</u>.

3. Which regulations respecting the Royal Canadian Mounted Police have been published?

4. Does the Clean Air Act include leaded gasoline regulations?

5. Where are the lead-free gasoline regulations promulgated because of the Clean Air Act located?

6. With what countries was the Treaties of Peace Act of 1948 made?

7. The Hazardous Products Act has regulated what items used by children?

8. Where are the Canadian Wheat Board Regulations published?

Notes